BOTH SIDES OF
THE CHESSBOARD

An Analysis of the Fischer / Spassky Chess Match

Grandmaster Robert Byrne
and Master Ivo Nei

Introduction by Grandmaster Max Euwe

Quadrangle/The New York Times Book Co.

Library of Congress Catalog Card Number: 73-79908
International Standard Book Number: 0-8129-0379-X

Design by Jerry Lieberman
Production by Planned Production

CONTENTS

INTRODUCTION

Many books about the "match of the century" have already been published. Some were published immediately after the match; others months later, after consideration of the many comments made in earlier books and various contributors to chess periodicals.

An "outsider"—a non-chess player—may think that after so many hours spent by so many experts, the absolute truth about the nearly one thousand moves played in the twenty-one games between Robert Fischer and Boris Spassky should have been discovered. Chess, however, is not that simple. It cannot be overpowered and solved even by an army of experts. Chess comprises an almost infinite number of possibilities and—apart from positions containing forced continuations—there are only relatively few situations in chess in which the correct move for either side can be established with complete certainty.

What does a good chess player do when analyzing a game or trying to make a judgment about a certain position? He looks for moves and variations in order either to form a judgment or to confirm a judgment he has already made. For that purpose, he makes use of his knowledge of what happened in similar previous positions, he has at his disposal various general principles and rules of thumb. But the validity of all these guidelines is not absolute; there are almost as many exceptions to the rules as confirmations. Chess is not mathematics. It has often happened in chess history that long and deep analyses of important positions have been rejected or refuted only for later examination to show the incorrectness of the refutations, which has led to a kind of rehabilitation of the original points of view.

In the entire theory of openings, only a few of the variations played with regularity fifty or a hundred years ago by the leading masters of that time— comparable in strength to the greatest masters of our own day—are still considered correct or satisfactory today. This process will surely continue. In the sciences, and certainly in mathematics and other exact fields, we can be certain that each change is an improvement. But this is not the case in chess. It sometimes seems as though we are moving in a circle, as old truths collapse only to be revived later.

So what is the use of a new book about the Fischer–Spassky match? Some previous analysis may be corrected, some positions will be more correctly judged and the variations more accurately worked out and it will be possible to better evaluate the performances of the players in the various stages of the match. Is all this worthwhile? It certainly is—not only because this book was written by two strong players who were present during the entire match—but also because of the special position held by each of them.

One of the authors, Ivo Nei, belonged to the Soviet team that accompanied and assisted Spassky in his great and difficult struggle. This means that Nei was privy to inside information, both technical and psychological. The technical aspects are of particular interest in the adjourned games. The players and their helpers produce, in general, much better analysis of an adjourned position than experts who were not involved at the time. Nei, as one of Spassky's closest assistants, played a great role in the tracing of the hidden secrets of adjourned positions, most likely an even greater role than Spassky himself. It is a well-known fact that in many cases the player is only indirectly involved in the analysis. Exhausted by the hard struggle, he retires for a long rest in order to appear the next morning fresh and able to examine the position objectively, having learned the result of the work done during the night by his seconds.

The other author, Robert Byrne, was not in the same position toward Fischer as Nei was toward Spassky. He could not be. Fischer usually prefers to play without seconds, relying on his own abilities, although in this match he did have the assistance of William Lombardy. Still, Robert Byrne is a friend and countryman of Fischer's. As one of the very few American grandmasters present during the whole match, he could become aware of many details not available to anyone else. Moreover, one of the duties which fell to Robert Byrne during the match meant an extra stimulation for him to find the truth about the games as nearly as possible. At the start of the match, he was contacted by the Dutch television network and asked to participate with two

Dutch grandmasters in discussions of the moves played and the chances for each side.

Therefore, since both Nei and Byrne occupied privileged positions, this umpteenth book on the match had to be—and is!—unique in more than one respect.

Ivo Nei was born in 1931 in Estonia. He won the championship of his republic for the first time in 1951 and on a number of occasions since. He won the Baltic Championship in 1956. His greatest success came in the Hoogoven Tournament in Holland in 1964, when he tied with Keres for first place with 11½ (out of 15!), followed by Portisch 11, Ivkov 10, Parma, Larsen, Lengyel 9½, Filip 8½, Darga 7½, Bobotsov, Donner, Zuidema 6½, van Scheltinga 5, van den Berg 3½, Dunkelblum 2, de Rooi 1½.

The number of points needed for a grandmaster result in that tournament was 9½. Even though Nei far exceeded this norm—and despite the fact that the international rules specified that only one grandmaster result was needed for the title—Nei did not become a grandmaster. The reason was the illogical rule then in effect that a player could not "skip" a title; that is, to become an international grandmaster he first had to be an international master, which Nei was not due to his infrequent appearances in international play. Consequently, at that tournament he received the title of international master, not international grandmaster, the latter being the title he fully deserved. Nei has remained a grandmaster in strength, although without official recognition as such.

Robert Byrne, born in 1928, became an international master in 1952 and a grandmaster in 1964. He has been a regular representative of the United States in world team tournaments. He won the open championship of his country several times but his best result was attained in the 1972 United States Championship, where he came in first place with Reshevsky and Kavalek. In the playoff he succeeded in scoring 1½–½ against each of his rivals, thus breaking the tie in his favor. Although the playoff did not take place until 1973, Byrne's victory puts him in the record books as the 1972 United States Champion. That tournament was also a qualification event for Zone 5 of the FIDE. By winning it, Byrne has qualified for the Interzonal to be held in Leningrad in the summer of 1973. The Interzonal is a preliminary test for the Candidates' Matches. Should he succeed in attaining one of the first three places, Byrne would qualify for the Candidates' Matches and could become the next challenger for World Champion Fischer! But many obstacles will have to be overcome first.

The match itself was very spectacular and was followed eagerly both by chess players and nonplayers all over the world. Spassky, the loser, was criticized very much for his bad play, especially in his own country. The criticism was threefold: he was reproached for shortcomings in the technical, theoretical and psychological fields. These reproaches were only partially justified and they do not fully explain Spassky's failure.

Spassky's preparations in the openings were certainly not excessive. He did not come up with innovations and if one should mention his fine and convincing opening play in the eleventh game, it should be noted that his surprising retreat 14 N-N1 was not the fruit of prematch industry but rather a result of Spassky's experiences during the match. We must realize that the same variation was used in the seventh game, in which Spassky did not show a refutation of Black's 8 ... QxNP, a move he could have expected since Fischer had played it many times before the match. Spassky must have found the crucial 14 N-N1 either between the seventh and eleventh games or during the eleventh game itself (he spent half an hour before playing it).

In most of the games Fischer showed a greater knowledge of the openings, although he did not come up with world-shaking innovations either. Spassky's preparations were not primarily concerned with the openings; for some reason he considered psychological factors the most important ones, perhaps even decisive. Shortly before the match I spoke with Spassky and he confirmed this. In my opinion, Spassky did not fail seriously in a psychological sense. He did not break down after the very disappointing results of the sixth, tenth and thirteenth games. Even the bad blunder in the eighth game did not have a serious psychological effect.

Spassky's shortcomings in his preparations can only partly explain his loss of the title by a margin of four points. The main point is that Spassky's technical power was no greater during this match than during his 1969 match against Petrosian, when Spassky won the world title. It is a most remarkable fact that most world champions slow down after reaching the highest honor. Botvinnik, who won every tournament (in at least ten very strong contests!) before he became World Champion, did not maintain this pattern during his reign as champion. Even the great Capablanca failed, in a relative sense, by coming first only twice in four first-class tournaments during the period of his championship. Tigran Petrosian, champion from 1963 to 1969, complained repeatedly that as World Champion he had much less practice than his direct rivals, who played in Zonals, Interzonals and Candidates' Tournaments or matches to qualify. Petrosian, during his tenure, participated in only a small number of tournaments and seldom finished first. The same was the case with Spassky between 1969 and 1972: he did not not play much and even when he did play his results were not as convincing as those before 1969.

Considering all this, and in view of Fischer's overwhelming victories in the interzonal tournament and in the Candidates' Matches, one could have expected an easy win for Fischer. All the more, then, must one appreciate the marvelous fight Spassky offered, especially in the second half of the match. Fischer's preponderance became clear mainly in the third and fifth games, in which he showed unbelievably great skill in handling certain middle-game positions which were not known as favorable for either side. Fischer, however, showed with iron logic in those games that it was only Black who could obtain winning chances. It was a little sad to see how helplessly the former world champion floundered for hours in the face of unavoidable disaster.

It is usual to divide a match into phases, each bearing its special characteristics. In my view, we have to distinguish between the following phases:
Phase one, games 1–4, an unusual start: chess or poker?
Phase two, games 5–9, Fischer crushes his opponent
Phase three, games 10–13, Spassky fights back
Phase four, games 14–21, Spassky at his best, but Fischer survives

PHASE ONE

An Unusual Start: Chess or Poker?

Spassky two wins, Fischer one win, one draw.

Neither player seemed fully alive to the earnestness, the importance of the match. In the first game, in a drawish position Fischer made a risky move, which offered no future prospects and only opened possibilities to lose. No one knows what Fischer expected with this strategy. Did he intend to confuse his opponent by showing that he could draw at any time, even with only two pawns for a piece? It is possible, but he only jeopardized his chances in the match by this risk, especially with the saying in mind that "he who wins the first game wins the match." This could have been suicidal. However, everything turned out well for Fischer in the long run; although he missed more than one chance to draw the first game, he did win the match.

The second game was even stranger than the first—Fischer did not appear and lost by forfeit. We will not go into the reasons here for Fischer's non-appearance. It was certainly not, as suggested by non-chess players, a psychological masterstroke. Still, Spassky was a little confused by his lead of two points without having performed very much; so he began the third game hesitating between a life-and-death struggle and giving the point back. After the match, Botvinnik expressed the opinion that Spassky should have countered Fischer's "sacrifice" of the second game by not appearing for the third. Maybe this would have been the right response, psychologically. But it would not have contributed to match standards and would certainly not have been received with enthusiasm by the spectators. In any case, Spassky's uncertain attitude was definitely wrong. One should never play with extraneous thoughts in the back of one's mind: either one does his best or one does not play at all. There is no middle course. Personally, I must admit, I could see no signs of Spassky's hesitation in this game. I can only state that, from the beginning, Fischer kept a firm grip on the position and eventually forced his opponent to make all kinds of concessions. Spassky sealed his move unusually rapidly, which could be explained as his wish to give the point back. Analysis showed that a better move would have given him some small drawing chances.

For Spassky, the match began only with the fourth game. He treated it very aggressively and larded it with unexpected turns; in short, it was the "old" Spassky who played this game. Fischer showed a capacity he had seldom showed in the past: the ability to limit the damage and narrowly escape with a draw.

PHASE TWO

Fischer Crushes his Opponent

Spassky no wins, Fischer three wins, two draws.

A clear and overwhelming preponderance for the challenger, not only in points but also in the quality of the games. The fifth and sixth games are beautiful examples of Fischer's rectilinear style. Spassky was completely surprised and got no counterchances whatsoever. He should have lost the seventh game as well but a small inaccuracy by his opponent saved him.

The eighth game was played by Spassky with unmotivated optimism—the only time Spassky really failed in a psychological sense—and he was severely punished for this wrong attitude. An elementary blunder concluded the mess. I would like to add that bad blunders have always occurred in matches for the world championship. Abundant examples can be found in the Botvinnik–Smyslov, Botvinnik–Petrosian and Petrosian–Spassky matches. Therefore, I do not share the often-heard opinion that it was this blunder which made it clear that Spassky was not at his best.

The blunder had one good effect: it woke up Spassky with a start. He realized that he was in deadly peril and he made what has been generally recognized as a wise decision: not to try to strike back immediately but first to ease the tension and then to start a new struggle. So Phase two ended with a quiet, unemotional draw.

PHASE THREE

Spassky Fights Back

Spassky one win, Fischer two wins, one draw.

I consider this phase the most valuable of the match. The players were in good condition and determined to do their utmost. The tenth and thirteenth games are particularly fine examples of the fighting spirit exhibited continually by both Spassky and Fischer. Under such conditions, only rarely are common-place games produced. Each player took some punishment but recovered and fought back. Chess is too difficult to be played faultlessly; so in these games analysis shows that both players missed the best continuations from time to time. The fact that in the end Fischer won both of these games may prove that he has the greater endurance and that he really is the better player.

PHASE FOUR

Spassky at his Best, but Fischer Survives

Spassky no wins, Fischer one win, seven draws.

After the thirteenth game the score was: Fischer six wins, Spassky three wins, with four draws. Fischer had already attained the six wins which were required, for example, in the famous Alekhine–Capablanca match and which will probably constitute the basis of new regulations to be used in the world championship match of 1975.

It was perhaps this circumstance that led Fischer to remain passive, having as his only goal to maintain his lead and coast quietly to the finish. It is a fact that almost all the games in this phase were in Spassky's favor. In the four-teenth and fifteenth games he had a sound extra pawn but he spoiled both games, the fourteenth by a blunder, the fifteenth by a poorly considered advance which even brought Spassky to the brink of the precipice.

In the sixteenth and seventeenth games Spassky won material but not enough to gain full points. In the eighteenth and nineteenth games Spassky excelled by his inventiveness and enterprise but again without success. In the eighteenth game he chose a wrong continuation in a complicated position and in the nineteenth game his superhuman efforts led only to a draw. It must be stated that in all three of these games, Fischer showed (as he had in the fourth game) a wonderful skill to discover just that one way in complicated positions to bring him safely to port.

After idle attempts to win a rather dull ending in the twentieth game, Spassky made an all-or-nothing effort in the twenty-first. "Nothing" is what it became and so ended the match.

The best man has won, but Spassky's style in the second half of the match is an indication that his role in top competition is not yet played out. Spassky will come back!

MAX EUWE
President, International Chess Federation (FIDE)
World Chess Champion, 1935–1937

Chapter I

FISCHER VS. TAIMANOV

Bobby Fischer, who has accustomed us all to his extraordinary exploits—winning tournaments by three points, his clean sweep of the United States Championship by 11–0—has done it again! Who would have imagined that any challengers' match would ever have been decided by a perfect score, when the participants are all to be ranked among the strongest players in the world? If one attempts to explain his fantastic achievement by pointing out that he terrifies his opponents, the explanation falls on its face, since their fear arises from his wonderful playing strength. So we merely return to the fact with which we began.

We can restate what has already been said of him: that his play is remarkably mistake-free, incisive, and devolves from extraordinarily simple, classical themes, such as his exploitation of the superiority of bishop over knight where pawns are distributed on both sides of the board. But it should be taken into account that what really lies behind his astonishing success with pure classical themes is his unusual capacity for creating the positions in which such themes are operative. And that is a secret known, if at all, only to himself.

In this match, his opening preparation, as it so often is, was quite superior to that of his opponent. Taimanov was undoubtedly surprised by the gambit in game two and was bested in the argument concerning the King's Indian variation of games one and three. The only openings that were not clearly to Taimanov's disadvantage were the Gruenfeld of game five and the Sicilian of game six. But by that time he was so punch-drunk that nothing mattered—witness the horrible blunder (after adjournment!) in game five.

As Bobby prepared himself for the sterner test coming up with Larsen, he could look back with considerable satisfaction on his first-round play, although such a perfectionist as Fischer was bound to be kicking himself for messing up the endgame of game two and looking hard to find a forced advantage in game five.

GAME 1
King's Indian Defense

MARK TAIMANOV	ROBERT FISCHER
1 P-Q4	N-KB3
2 P-QB4	P-KN3
3 N-QB3	B-N2
4 P-K4	P-Q3
5 N-B3	...

How did each prepare for the other regarding choice of openings? Taimanov loves P-Q4 as much as Fischer loves P-K4, so a surprise on the first move was almost unthinkable. After that, Fischer's defensive choice could run anywhere from the Nimzo–Indian to the Semi-classical to the King's Indian or a Gruenfeld. In deciding on the King's Indian, Fischer could be fairly certain of facing the classical system initiated by Taimanov's last move, for the Russian grandmaster is one of the presiding geniuses of the variation. So, Bobby had surely decided that Black cannot be subjected to anything worse than the normal White initiative.

5 ...	O-O
6 B-K2	P-K4
7 O-O	N-B3
8 P-Q5	N-K2
9 B-Q2	...

This comparatively new move aims, just as the well-tried N-K1 or N-Q2, at preparing to attack along the QB file, the important difference being that, by keeping his king's knight where it is, White hopes to exploit the hole created at K6 with N-KN5,

after Black launches his essential counter P-KB4.

| 9 ... | N-K1 |

Differing circumstances determine whether the knight should clear for the KBP at K1 or Q2. Here, against the idea outlined in the previous note, it is necessary for the QB to remain unimpeded in observing the K3 square. As will be seen at Black's 14th move, it is also very important that the knight defend the QBP.

| 10 R-B1 | ... |

In the third match game between Korchnoi and Geller, which took place in Moscow at the same time, Korchnoi tried 10 P-QN4, which may be better. There is so little experience with these lines that it is very hard to make any kind of definitive judgments regarding them.

| 10 ... | P-KB4 |
| 11 PxP | ... |

When this opening was repeated in the third game, Taimanov improved with Q-N3.

| 11 ... | PxP |

11 ... NxP is worse because it gives White too good a knight outpost at K4.

| 12 N-KN5? | ... |

There was still a chance to transpose into the preferable line of the third game with Q-N3 or to try Korchnoi's idea, P-QN4, but Taimanov is intent on a positional gambit of a type with which he has had considerable success in the past. Unfortunately for him, Fischer refutes it at once.

12	...	P-KR3
13	N-K6	BxN
14	PxB	Q-B1
15	Q-N3	...

Because Black's king knight guards the QBP, the move usually so strong in this sort of position, N-Q5, now would have no effect at all. What this means, of course, is that the KP goes down the drain without exchanging itself for any counterplay to speak of. One can only wonder which of Fischer's simple, logical moves was overlooked by Taimanov in his pre-match analysis.

| 15 | ... | P-B3 |

Threatening R-N1 or P-N3 followed by QxP.

16	B-R5	QxP
17	QxP	N-B3
18	B-K2	KR-N1
19	Q-R6	RxP
20	KR-Q1	P-K5

Quite unlike most other grand-masters, Fischer sharply courts complications even when he has a solid winning material advantage, as he has here.

21	Q-R3	R-N2
22	B-B4	P-Q4
23	PxP	PxP
24	N-N5	N-N3

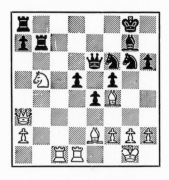

Sacrificing the Exchange, but Taimanov, possibly wrongly, refuses to accept. It is true that 25 N-B7 Q-B2, 26 NxR NxB, 27 B-R6 R-K2, 28 B-B1 N-N5 gives Black strong kingside attacking chances, while the knight is pretty much out of things at R8, but at least White is no longer behind in material, and, if his defense holds, he would have winning possibilities of his own. Instead, he adopts blockading strategy in the center, hoping to uncover weaknesses in his opponent's position.

| 25 | N-Q4? | ... |

But this is inaccurate, allowing Black to diminish the pressure on his game. Q-KN3! would have set far harder problems for Fischer to solve.

25	...	Q-Q2
26	Q-K3	K-R2
27	P-KR3	R-KB1
28	B-R6	R-N3
29	R-B7	...

A last futile bid to stir up complications, since passive play would allow Black to win routinely.

29	...	Q-R5
30	RxBch	KxR
31	BxPch	K-B2
32	B-K2	R/1-QN1

Paring down the rooks will drastically reduce White's powers of resistance.

33	NxP	R-N8
34	RxR	RxRch
35	K-R2	Q-Q2
36	N-Q4	Q-Q3ch
37	P-N3	Q-N5

An excellent move which turns what could be a difficult winning task into an easy one. The threat is 38 ... Q-K8 and mate, so the exchange of queens cannot be avoided.

38	N-B6	Q-N3

38 ... Q-K8? would have allowed a draw: 39 QxPch K-K1, 40 Q-R8ch K-Q2, 41 Q-Q8ch KxN, 42 QxNch, and the Black king has no refuge.

39	NxP	QxQ
40	BxQ	R-K8!

Black could have recovered a pawn by R-QR8, but that would have permitted strong resistance after N-B6-Q4, while the text move doesn't give White a prayer. 41 B-QN5 N-K4, 42 P-KR4 N/3-N5ch, 43 K-R3 NxB, 44 PxN RxP lets the Black pawns queen, while the White ones sit around looking pretty. Here 42 P-N4 would be even worse: 42 ... P-Q5!, 43 B-B4 N-B6ch, 44 K-N3 R-N8 mate. And 43 B-KR6 N-B6ch, 44 K-N3, K-N3, 45 B-B8 N-Q4, 46 P-KR4 R-N8ch, 47 K-R3 N-B5 mate is even prettier.

41	B-N4	...

White resigned. There is still nothing to be done about 41 ... N-K4.

GAME 2
Sicilian Defense

ROBERT FISCHER   MARK TAIMANOV

1	P-K4	P-QB4
2	N-KB3	N-QB3
3	P-Q4	PxP
4	NxP	P-K3
5	N-N5	P-Q3
6	B-KB4	...

The first surprise, because Bobby has not tried this since his game with Najdorf at the Piatigorsky Cup Tournament, 1966, relying instead on 6 P-QB4, as in his encounter with Taimanov in the last Interzonal. The move is supposed to be time-wasting, but whether it is or not is the question the present test reopens. It forces a hole at Q5, for 6 ... N-K4 is met by 7 N/1-R3 P-QR3, 8 BxN PxB, 9 QxQch KxQ, 10 O-O-Och B-Q2, 11 N-B4, with advantage to White.

6	...	P-K4
7	B-K3	N-B3
8	B-N5	Q-R4ch
9	Q-Q2	...

Only by this gambit is it possible to justify White's opening, since 9 B-Q2 is answered by 9 ... Q-Q1, when there is nothing better than repeating moves—10 B-N5 Q-R4ch, etc.

9	...	NxP
10	QxQ	NxQ
11	B-K3	K-Q2
12	QN-B3	...

It was evident as early as the eleventh move that White can recover the gambit pawn, but it is equally evident that he cannot be in a hurry about it without forfeiting all chance for advantage. Thus, 12 BxP? P-Q4 and Black has a beautiful position. So, White must proceed with his freer development, counting on the awkward placement of the enemy king and pressure on the queen file to give him something tangible.

12	...	NxN
13	NxN	K-Q1?

In my opinion, Taimanov puts too much stock in the idea of getting the QB to K3, but he took forty-six minutes to decide on it. Correct was 13 ... P-QN3, after which the burden is squarely on White to show how he can get the advantage, or even make up for the pawn.

14	N-N5	B-K3
15	O-O-O	P-QN3
16	P-KB4!	...

Both 16 NxQP BxN, 17 RxBch K-K2, 18 R-Q1, and 16 NxRP K-B2, 17 N-N5ch K-B3 only develop Black, but the text puts new pressure on him. He cannot reply 16 ... P-B3, because 17 PxP PxP, 18 NxQP BxN, 19 RxBch K-K2, 20 R-Q1 would give him an exposed king, an isolated KP, and some difficulty getting his rooks into the game.

16	...	PxP
17	BxP	N-N2
18	B-K2	...

25	P-QN4	P-QR4
26	B-Q5	K-N1
27	P-QR3	KR-Q1

Was there any way to hang onto the gambit pawn? 27 ... B-B6 loses at once to 28 R-K7!, while 27 ... R-B2 fails against 28 BxN! Black is virtually in Zugzwang, but abandoning his material advantage, although granting some simplification, does not enable him to equalize positionally.

It's still too early to recover the gambit pawn, for 18 NxQP NxN, 19 BxN BxB, 20 RxBch K-B2, 21 R-Q1 QR-Q1 is a dead draw. Now White threatens 19 B-B3, while Black dare not force his hand by 18 ... P-QR3 which loses after 19 NxP NxN, 20 BxN BxB, 21 RxBch K-B2, 22 KR-Q1 P-QN4, 23 B-B3 R-R2, 24 R-B6ch K-N1, 25 R/1-Q6 B-B1, 26 R-N6ch K-B2, 27 R/Q-B6ch K-Q1, 28 R-N8 R-B2, 29 RxRP.

28	BxP	B-B6
29	B-Q2	P-Q4

The pawn must advance to give the knight some air, even though it becomes more vulnerable.

18	...	B-Q2
19	R-Q2	B-K2
20	KR-Q1	BxN

At last the knight had to be eliminated, for once the rooks are doubled White threatened to win by taking the QP.

30	R-Q1	P-Q5
31	BxB	RxB
32	K-N2	P-Q6

By giving up the pawn right away, Black assures himself of further simplification and a chance to get his knight into play, fearing that otherwise he will lose the pawn under far worse circumstances. He may be right, but his game is clearly lost now.

21	BxB	K-B2
22	R-K2	B-B3
23	R/1-K1	...

The horrendous threat is 24 R-K7ch!, winning.

33	KxR	PxR
34	R-K1	N-Q3
35	B-R5	N-N4ch
36	K-N2	PxP
37	PxP	R-Q5
38	P-B3	R-R5

23	...	QR-QB1
24	B-B4	KR-B1

If, with 4½ minutes left on his clock, he had counted on 38 ... R-Q7ch, 39 K-N3 R-Q6?, he now sees 40 K-B4.

39	BxP	N-Q3
40	R-Q1	K-B2
41	P-R3	R-KB5
42	R-KB1	R-K5
43	B-Q3	R-K4
44	R-B2	. . .

The liquidation 44 BxP R-K7ch, 45 K-N3 RxP only helps Black.

44	. . .	P-R4
45	P-B4	. . .

Maybe better was 45 B-K2, with the idea, B-B3, K-B2-Q3 and R-R2-R7ch.

45	. . .	K-Q2
46	K-B3	R-KN4
47	R-R2	K-B1
48	K-Q4	K-B2
49	R-R7ch	K-Q1
50	P-B5?	. . .

This advance only results in great technical difficulties for White, who should have freed his rook first in the manner suggested in the last note.

50	. . .	PxPch
51	PxP	N-K1
52	R-R2	N-B2
53	B-B4	K-Q2
54	R-QN2	K-B3
55	B-N3	. . .

55 R-N6ch would not have accomplished anything, since, after 55 . . . K-Q2, the rook would have had to return at once to the defense of the KNP.

55	. . .	N-N4ch
56	K-K3	KxP
57	K-B4	R-N3
58	B-Q1	P-R5
59	K-B5	R-KR3

60	K-N5	N-Q3
61	B-B2	N-B2ch
62	K-N4	N-K4ch
63	K-B4	K-Q5
64	R-N4ch	K-B6
65	R-N5	N-B2
66	R-B5ch	K-Q5
67	R-KB5	P-N4ch
68	K-N4	N-K4ch
69	KxP	R-N3ch
70	KxP	RxP

White is once again a pawn ahead, but it is the only one left and the bishop is the wrong one for the queening square, so his winning chances are just about nil.

71	B-Q1	R-N1
72	B-N4	K-K5
73	K-N3	R-N2
74	R-B4ch	K-Q4
75	R-R4	N-N3
76	R-R6	N-K4
77	K-B4	N-N3ch
78	K-N5	N-K4ch
79	K-B5	R-B2ch
80	R-B6	RxRch
81	KxR	K-K5???

After lucking into a draw as a result of one of Fischer's very rare bouts of sloppy technique, Taimanov throws it away with one move. 81 . . . K-Q3 was the move because if the bishop then moves along the Q1-R5 diagonal, . . . N-Q2ch will ensure that the Black king reaches the kingside in time to cooperate with the knight in stopping the pawn, while if the bishop moves along the B8-R3 diagonal, Black simply plays N-B6-R5 and stands there to be taken while the king runs straight for KR1.

82	B-B8	K-B5	86	P-R6	N-N4
83	P-R4	N-B6	87	K-N6	N-B6
84	P-R5	N-N4	88	P-R7	N-R5ch
85	B-B5	N-B6	89	K-B6	Resigns

GAME 3
King's Indian Defense

MARK TAIMANOV   ROBERT FISCHER

1	P-Q4	N-KB3
2	P-QB4	P-KN3
3	N-QB3	B-N2
4	P-K4	P-Q3
5	N-B3	O-O
6	B-K2	P-K4
7	O-O	N-B3
8	P-Q5	N-K2
9	B-Q2	N-K1
10	R-B1	P-KB4
11	Q-N3	...

This new try is obviously superior to the premature N-KN5 of game one, since it hampers the enemy queen bishop by bearing down on the QNP, while preparing a delayed, stronger N-KN5 and threatening an immediate P-B5!

11	...	P-N3
12	PxP	PxP
13	N-KN5	N-KB3

13 ... P-KR3 could have led to difficult complications: 14 N-K6 BxN, 15 PxB Q-B1, 16 P-B5 NPxP, 17 B-R5 K-R1, 18 B-B7, and White has a bind for the pawn plus threats on the kingside, such as Q-R4-KR4, etc.

14	P-B4	P-KR3 ·
15	PxP?!	...

15 N-K6 came strongly into consideration, because 15 ... BxN, 16 PxB P-B3 (not Q-B1, 17 N-Q5), 17 Q-R3 exerts enough pressure on Black's center to prevent him from removing the thorn at K3.

15	...	PxP
16	P-B5?!	...

Impressive looking, but the sequel shows that it was played intuitively, with no idea of a concrete follow-up. He had nothing better than 16 N-B3, which is, however, not lacking in chances.

16	...	N/3xP
17	NxN	NxN
18	PxP	RPxP
19	R-B6	...

Threatening 20 B-QB4 when ... P-B3 is not available.

19	...	K-R1
20	N-B3?	...

In backing off he concedes the game. It was necessary to risk 20 N-K6 BxN, 21 RxB Q-Q2, 22 RxPch BxR, 23 BxB, or 20 R-KB3, or 20 Q-KR3 R-B3, 21 B-QB4 P-B5, 22 RxR BxQ, 23 N-B7ch K-R2, 24 RxPch BxR, 25 NxQ RxN, 26 PxB B-B1, but Black should win. In this line, if 22 Q-R4 or Q-R5, then 22 ... B-N2 wins.

20	...	B-N2
21	R-N6	N-B5!

Puts an end to White's demonstrations for good.

22	BxN	PxB
23	R-Q1	Q-K2
24	R-K6	Q-B4ch
25	K-B1	KR-Q1
26	RxRch	RxR
27	Q-R4	Q-B8ch
28	K-B2	B-KB1
29	P-QN4	B-K5
30	R-K8	...

In a position as awful as Taimanov's, losing the queen for rook and bishop cannot be classed as a blunder, but he might have considered resigning.

30	...	B-B3
31	QxB	QxQ
32	RxR	Q-B3
33	R-B8	Q-K2
34	K-B1	K-R2
35	N-Q4	B-N2
36	N-N5	B-K4
37	P-QR3	Q-Q2
38	R-QR8	P-B6
39	PxP	BxP
40	K-N2	Q-N2ch
41	KxB	Q-K4ch
	Resigns	

GAME 4
Sicilian Defense

ROBERT FISCHER   MARK TAIMANOV

1	P-K4	P-QB4
2	N-KB3	N-QB3
3	P-Q4	PxP
4	NxP	Q-B2

Taimanov deviates from his 4 ...
P-K3 of game two, presumably because he has not figured out a way to handle the gambit which Fischer threw at him there. Against the present move White can also play N-N5 followed by P-QB4, but the Black queen would not be badly placed at QN1, from which square it can later support the freeing P-QN4.

5	N-QB3	P-K3
6	P-KN3	P-QR3
7	B-N2	N-B3
8	O-O	NxN
9	QxN	B-B4

Bringing the bishop out aggressively in this manner has lately achieved considerable popularity, although care must be taken to ensure that its absence will not be felt on the kingside. After White's next move Black cannot go in for an exchange of queens, since he would then have difficulty developing his queen bishop and defending his Q3 square in the resulting endgame.

10	B-B4	P-Q3
11	Q-Q2	P-R3

It is important to prevent 13 B-N5 after 12 QR-Q1 P-K4.

12	QR-Q1	P-K4
13	B-K3	B-KN5
14	BxB	PxB

Of course, Black need no longer worry about the backward pawn, but his inability to control his Q4 will continue to plague him.

15	P-B3	B-K3
16	P-B4	R-Q1
17	N-Q5	BxN
18	PxB	P-K5

What other defense was there? White threatened 19 P-Q6 powerfully, even in answer to 18 ... PxP, but now it seems that Black has found a way to evade all difficulties.

19	KR-K1!	RxP
20	RxPch	K-Q1

Black is doing the best he can after White's strong nineteenth, as one can observe by comparison with 20 ... K-B1?, 21 R-K8ch KxR, 22 BxR, wherein the defense is spoiled by the awkwardness of the king.

21	Q-K2	RxRch
22	QxRch	Q-Q2
23	QxQch	KxQ
24	R-K5	...

Once again Bobby has gleaned the superior endgame of bishop versus knight where the pawns are spread out on both sides of the board and now proceeds to give a fine demonstration of how to press such an advantage.

24	...	P-QN3
25	B-B1	P-QR4

26	B-B4	R-KB1
27	K-N2	...

Having created weak squares on the queenside, through which the king can later threaten to enter, and having stuck the enemy rook in a defensive backwater, it is time for White to get the king into the action.

27	...	K-Q3

Only by getting his knight to Q3 could Black hold this ending, but 27 ... N-K1, 28 B-N5ch K-Q1, 29 R-Q5ch K-B1, 30 R-Q7 demonstrates that he cannot attempt to carry out the plan without wrecking his position.

28	K-B3	N-Q2
29	R-K3	N-N1
30	R-Q3ch	K-B2
31	P-B3	...

Showing that the knight will achieve nothing by arriving at QB3.

31	...	N-B3
32	R-K3	K-Q3
33	P-QR4	N-K2
34	P-R3	N-B3
35	P-R4	P-R4

It is unpleasant to put another pawn on the same color as the bishop, but there is a danger that White may either open kingside lines or force still more weaknesses by P-KN4-5.

36	R-Q3ch	K-B2
37	R-Q5	P-B4

On 37 ... P-N3, 38 B-N5 would set

up the threat to expose the king's wing further by P-B5.

38	R-Q2	R-B3
39	R-K2	K-Q2
40	R-K3	P-N3
41	B-N5	R-Q3
42	K-K2	K-Q1
43	R-Q3	K-B2
44	RxR	KxR
45	K-Q3	...

White threatens to win the king and pawn ending after BxN and K-B4.

45	...	N-K2
46	B-K8	K-Q4
47	B-B7ch	K-Q3
48	K-B4	K-B3
49	B-K8ch	K-N2
50	K-N5	N-B1
51	B-B6ch	K-B2
52	B-Q5	N-K2
53	B-B7	K-N2
54	B-N3	K-R2
55	B-Q1	K-N2
56	B-B3ch	K-B2
57	K-R6	N-N1
58	B-Q5	N-K2
59	B-B4	K-B3
60	B-B7	K-B2
61	B-K8	K-Q1
62	BxP!	...

The bishop sacrifice is the culmination of White's infiltration strategy, which left Black no other option at the last move than to allow it. Now the knight will be no match for the pawns.

62	...	NxB
63	KxP	K-Q2
64	KxBP	N-K2
65	P-QN4	PxP
66	PxP	N-B1
67	P-R5	N-Q3
68	P-N5	N-K5ch
69	K-N6	K-B1
70	K-B6	K-N1
71	P-N6	Resigns

GAME 5
Gruenfeld Defense

MARK TAIMANOV   ROBERT FISCHER

1	P-Q4	N-KB3
2	P-QB4	P-KN3
3	N-QB3	P-Q4

Bobby chose this defense because he either feared that Taimanov might have learned how to improve on his play in their last King's Indian or he wanted to introduce some variety into the match openings.

4	B-N5	N-K5
5	B-R4	. . .

White's fourth is an old continuation which got a bad reputation primarily because it was always followed by 5 NxN instead of the far stronger text move, an original idea of Taimanov's aiming to keep the KP under surveillance, and thus to restrict Black's freedom of choice.

5	. . .	NxN
6	PxN	PxP

No surprise to Taimanov was this predilection of Fischer's, which involves a quite serious attempt to hang onto the gambit pawn. In this game White recovers it well enough, but without achieving anything special otherwise.

7	P-K3	. . .

7 P-K4 would have permitted 7 . . . P-QN4 (now answered by 8 Q-B3),

while 7 Q-R4ch would have not only wasted time, but also would have put the queen into an awkward, exposed position.

7	. . .	B-K3
8	R-N1	P-N3
9	B-K2	B-R3

This unusual move is designed to prevent N-B3-N5, which otherwise could ruin the Black position.

10	N-B3	P-QB3
11	N-K5	B-N2
12	P-B4	B-Q4
13	O-O	N-Q2

Black decides to give the pawn back, since 13 . . . P-QN4, 14 P-R4 P-QR3, 15 B-B3 O-O, 16 P-K4 gives White a tremendous position.

14	NxP/4	O-O
15	P-R4	P-QB4
16	N-K5	NxN
17	QPxN	P-B3
18	R-N2	B-K3
19	R-Q2	Q-B2
20	B-N4	Q-B1
21	B-B3	. . .

White would have gotten nowhere after 21 BxB QxB, 22 R-Q7 R-B2.

21	. . .	R-N1
22	Q-K2	R-Q1
23	KR-Q1	RxR
24	QxR	Q-K1
25	PxP	PxP
26	Q-Q6	R-B1

White's initiative on the queen file is balanced by Black's better pawn formation, so the position is quite level. The last move was necessary to stop both B-B6 and Q-B7.

27	P-R5	B-B1
28	Q-Q2	B-K2
29	B-Q5	Q-B2
30	BxB	QxB
31	Q-Q7	K-B2
32	QxP	PxP

Now matters are not so clear, because White cannot capture the dangerous RP without losing two of his own, nor can he play 33 B-B2 Q-N6!, 34 R-R1 QxP, 35 QxRP QxQ, 36 RxQ P-B4 without conceding Black the endgame advantage. He should have aimed at a draw on the last move by 32 PxP.

33	P-K4	Q-B3!
34	R-Q7	QxP
35	P-R3	P-R5
36	B-B2	K-B1
37	P-B4	P-R6
38	QxRP	R-R1?

Was it time pressure that led him to play this nothing of a move instead of 38 ... QxKBP?

39 Q-N2!   . . .

Preventing the queen from taking either of the loose pawns, for 40 RxB! would win a piece.

39	. . .	K-K1
40	Q-N5	K-B1
41	R-Q1	QxKBP
42	BxP	BxB
43	QxBch	K-N2

What is there to stop either player from offering a draw hereabouts?

44	R-KB1	Q-K5
45	Q-B7ch	K-R3

46	RxP??	Q-Q5ch
	Resigns	

Such a blunder as White's forty-fifth is unbelievable after the time control had been passed and the game adjourned. He must have seen only 47 R-B2 R-R7?, while forgetting about 47 ... R-R8ch.

GAME 6

Sicilian Defense

ROBERT FISCHER   MARK TAIMANOV

1	P-K4	P-QB4
2	N-KB3	N-QB3
3	P-Q4	PxP
4	NxP	P-K3
5	N-N5	P-Q3
6	B-KB4	P-K4
7	B-K3	N-B3
8	B-N5	B-K3

Taimanov is still unwilling to try out the gambit of game two again, but the move he adopts this time also has a good reputation.

9	QN-B3	P-QR3
10	BxN	PxB
11	N-R3	N-Q5

11 ... P-N4 leaves the queenside shaky after 12 N-Q5, followed by 13 P-QB4.

12	N-B4	P-B4
13	PxP	NxP
14	B-Q3	R-B1
15	BxN	RxN

A Reuben Fine would have jumped at the chance for 15 ... BxB and dared Fischer to make something out of his much coveted hole at Q5, but Taimanov is content to exchange a pair of bishops, if it means getting a pawn to control his Q4.

16	BxB	PxB
17	Q-K2	R-Q5

At this point, two other choices came strongly into consideration: 17 ... Q-B2, 18 R-Q1 B-N2, 19 Q-R5ch K-K2, with an unclear position (but not 19 RxP? RxN, 20 RxPch K-Q2!, 21 Q-N4 Q-B5, 22 QxBch KxR, 23 QxR Q-K5ch, 24 K-B1 RxP, and wins), or 17 ... R-B3, 18 P-B4!? B-N2, 19 P-B5, which is also unclear.

18	O-O	Q-N4

Perhaps better was 18 ... B-N2.

19	QR-Q1	Q-B4

Why not 19 ... RxR, 20 RxR P-Q4? Does 21 P-KR4 Q-B3, 22 NxP!? PxN, 23 RxP B-Q3, 24 P-KB4 hold some terrors?

20	RxR!	PxR
21	N-K4	...

Now White's lead in development becomes a decisive factor, while the Black center pawns are very weak.

21	...	B-K2
22	R-Q1!	...

Bobby is all ready to cash in some of his time lead for a little material. The defense 22 ... P-K4 is met smashingly by 23 RxP!, and 22 ... P-Q4 is useless against 23 N-N3 Q-B3, 24 N-R5.

| 22 | ... | Q-K4 |
| 23 | Q-Q3 | R-B1 |

Nor would 23 ... P-Q4, 24 N-N3 B-B4, 25 N-K2 save the pawn.

24	QxQP	QxQ
25	RxQ	P-Q4
26	N-B3	B-B4
27	R-Q2	R-B5
28	P-KN3	R-B5
29	N-K2	...

From here on to his sixth straight point and the match, the road is merely one of technique, and Bobby has plenty of it.

29	...	R-QR5
30	P-QR3	K-Q2
31	K-N2	P-N4
32	P-QB3	P-QR4
33	N-Q4	P-N5
34	N-N3	B-N3
35	RPxP	PxP
36	P-QB4	K-B3
37	P-B5	B-B2
38	N-Q4ch	K-Q2
39	P-B4	P-K4
40	P-B6ch	K-B1
41	N-N5	R-R7
42	P-B5	B-Q1
43	RxP	Resigns

Chapter II

FISCHER VS. LARSEN

Having used up all my superlatives for the Fischer–Taimanov match, now I have no way to do justice to Bobby's even more astounding triumph. To a certain extent I could grasp the Taimanov match as a kind of curiosity—almost a freak, a strange chess occurrence that would never occur again.

But now I am at a loss for anything whatever to say. I cannot help thinking about the forthcoming battle between Bobby and Petrosian and wondering, "Will he do it again?" As I remind myself of the glorious careers of both Petrosian and Korchnoi, embellished with so many brilliant and beautiful games, I cannot but hold it unthinkable. But, then, I would have scoffed had anyone suggested the possibility before the Taimanov encounters, and doubly so had anyone broached it before the incredible series with Larsen.

So, it is out of the question for me to explain how Bobby, how anyone, could win six games in a row from such a genius of the game as Bent Larsen. Does anyone realize that if he were to win a close match with Spassky for the World Championship, he might **lose** rating points?

As for the games themselves, they are extraordinary in that the Fischer play is at once creative and virtually free from errors. Scarcely less impressive is the consistent success he has had with his openings repertoire. He seems to avoid any real trouble as Black and almost always has something going for him with White.

But the match could have taken a somewhat different course had Larsen not set himself up for such a bad beating. What I mean is: had he not been so stubborn about playing to win the dead level position of the second game, he would have had a half point right there, and surely would not have been so demoralized as to blunder as early as the eleventh move of the next game. Once again in the fifth game he could have chosen a colorless draw, but once again refused, at the expense of his humiliation. For the sake of practicality, he simply had to curb his romanticism.

GAME 1
French Defense

ROBERT FISCHER   BENT LARSEN

1 P-K4   P-K3

In general, I believe this is an excellent choice of defense against Fischer, since he does not handle the close game with quite the same peak of brilliance that he gives to wide open games. On the other hand, Larsen has not employed the French for years and could hardly acquire a perfect feel for it, even considering the intensive months of analysis he must have spent preparing for the match.

2 P-Q4   P-Q4
3 N-QB3   B-N5

In match play, as opposed to tournament play, such sharp, aggressive defenses as the Winawer Variation are considered too adventurous. The prevailing advice favors tame, defensive defenses which aim cautiously at the draw, saving all winning attempts for the White pieces. But Larsen does not like passivity and, thus far, I am in agreement with him. It is only later that he goes too far out on a limb.

4 P-K5   . . .

Fischer has tried 4 P-QR3 intermitently, but only with intermittent success. The move of the text is probably best, leading to the acute opposition of White's space advantage plus bishop pair to Black's sounder pawn position and play against the doubled pawns.

4 . . .   N-K2
5 P-QR3   BxNch
6 PxB   P-QB4
7 P-QR4   . . .

Bobby told me a long time ago that he felt 7 Q-N4 was only giving Black what he wanted, the chance for a dangerous counter gambit by sacrificing the KNP. Originally I disagreed with him, but I came around to his point of view after my game with Uhlmann at Monaco a few years ago which, though I won, demonstrated some of the brilliant possibilities for Black.

The sounder move chosen here prepares for the development of the QB at QR3 and prevents any queenside bind by . . . Q-R4-R5.

7 . . .   QN-B3
8 N-B3   B-Q2
9 B-Q3   . . .

It has been argued that this only invites a lost tempo when Black plays the cramping advance . . . P-B5 later, but on the tame 9 B-K2, Black can safely castle.

9 . . .   Q-B2
10 O-O   P-B5
11 B-K2   P-B3

Attacking the enemy center and defending against an awkward N-KN5 later.

12 R-K1   N-N3

This is the beginning of a seductive but wrong plan to win the KP. There is nothing better than 12 ... O-O-O with the usual double-edged battle, probably slightly favoring White. Just what persuaded Larsen, in his pre-match analysis, to try the idea, is, of course, something he alone can clear up for us.

13   B-R3!   ...

13 P-N3 could have been played, giving White a slight advantage, but the sacrifice in Fischer's continuation is infinitely more powerful, too powerful to accept, but—

13	...	PxP
14	PxP	QNxP
15	NxN	NxN
16	Q-Q4!	N-N3

After 16 ... N-B3, 17 B-R5ch, Black can pack them up and go home.

17   B-R5   ...

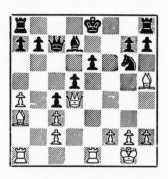

This is much stronger than 17 QxNP, which was easily answered by 17 ... O-O-O. But, if now 17 ... O-O-O,

then 18 QxRP P-N3 (forcing the exchange of queens, without which the king cannot survive), 19 Q-R8ch Q-N1, 20 QxQch KxQ, 21 P-R5! P-N4, 22 B-B5, and White has a terrifically strong endgame. In this line, 21 ... PxP would expose the king fatally, for 22 B-Q6ch K-N2, 23 RxRP R-R1, 24 R-B5 KR-QB1, 25 R-N1ch K-R3, 26 B-B7 B-N4, 27 R/5xB RxB, 28 R/5-N2 R-B4, 29 R-R2ch R-R4, 30 RxRch KxR, 31 R-R1ch nets White a rook. Another pretty sub-variation would be 23 ... K-B3, 24 B-R3 R-R1, 25 R-B5ch K-Q3, 26 RxQPch! KxR, 27 B-B3 mate.

| 17 | ... | K-B2 |
| 18 | P-B4! | ... |

Now Black cannot prevent the breakup of his center, so he must put up with his king riskily exposed in the middle of the board. 18 ... K-N1, 19 P-B5 N-B5, 20 B-B3 R-K1, 21 R-K5 would be completely hopeless.

18	...	KR-K1
19	P-B5!	PxP
20	QxQPch	K-B3

One sharp point of Fischer's attack is that 20 ... B-K3? loses a piece to 21 RxB! RxR, 22 QxPch R-B3, 23 Q-Q5ch R-K3, 24 R-B1ch.

21   B-B3   ...

Far stronger than the superficial 21 B-B5, which gets White nowhere after 21 ... K-N4, 22 B-B3 N-K4.

| 21 | ... | N-K4? |

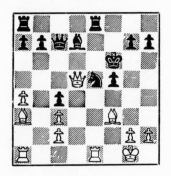

Was this a desperate attempt to complicate things, or was it based on some optimistic miscalculation, perhaps failing to perceive Bobby's answer to his twenty-sixth move? Anyhow a, good defense is hard to come by, for 21 ... B-K3, 22 QxNP QxQ, 23 BxQ QR-N1, 24 QR-N1 gives Black a very difficult endgame primarily because the QRP is vulnerable to attack by the bishops. Also 21 ... QR-Q1, 22 B-Q6 Q-B1, 23 QR-Q1 leaves Black stifled, while 21 ... RxRch, 22 RxR R-K1, 23 Q-Q4ch K-B2, 24 R-N1! P-N3, 25 P-R5! does not slow down White's attack at all.

22 Q-Q4! . . .

The pin wins material by force, but in order to succeed it was necessary for Fischer to have everything correctly calculated through Black's twenty-ninth move!

22 . . . K-N3

This must be considered the next step in the plan initiated by his previous

move, but in any event it was impossible to play 22 ... QR-Q1, 23 B-Q6 Q-R4, 24 B-Q5, curtains.

23	RxN	QxR
24	QxB	QR-Q1

In giving two pieces for a rook, Larsen is relying on White's back rank weakness and what looks like a good chance to get a rook to the seventh rank. If 24 ... QxP?, 25 Q-Q6ch K-N4, 26 P-R4ch KxP, 27 Q-B4 mate.

25	QxP	Q-K6ch
26	K-B1	R-Q7

Of course White is dangerously threatened by mate and mayhem, but he has the answers to everything.

27	Q-B6ch	R-K3
28	B-B5!	. . .

This terrible shot rips the Black demonstration to shreds, as Fischer had precisely foreseen. However, Larsen must continue onward, since 28 ... Q-K4 would be wrecked by 29 B-Q4!

28	. . .	R-B7ch
29	K-N1	RxNPch

The result of this is that he must take on a rook and two bishops with only a lone queen, but there was no decent disovered check!

30	KxR	Q-Q7ch
31	K-R1	RxQ
32	BxR	QxP/6
33	R-N1ch	K-B3
34	BxP	. . .

There are no technical problems because the bishops will inexorably shepherd the pawn in, while Black does not have even a single check.

34	...	P-N4
35	B-N6	QxP
36	P-R5	Q-N7
37	B-Q8ch	K-K3
38	P-R6	Q-R6
39	B-N7	Q-B4
40	R-N1	P-B6
41	B-N6	Resigns

English Opening

BENT LARSEN   ROBERT FISCHER

1 P-QB4   P-QB4

More unbalanced positions arise from
1 ... P-K4, either here or in a few
moves, but Bobby almost never de-
parts from the logical aim with the
Black pieces—equalize first and only
then play for a win.

2 N-KB3   P-KN3
3 P-Q4   PxP
4 NxP   N-QB3
5 P-K4   N-B3
6 N-QB3   P-Q3

It is a minor surprise to observe that
Bobby has no qualms about letting
his opponent achieve the Maroczy
Bind (KP and QBP holding Black's
QP to the third rank), when he has
employed it so successfully himself
on many occasions. Perhaps his
willingness to contest the game on
such terms may be explained by the
fact that, while the Maroczy formation enables White to obtain greater
control of space and thus to retain a
slight initiative, it also crimps the
chances for the strategically flexible
type of play in which Larsen shows
to greatest advantage.

7 B-K2   NxN

Since Black is virtually confined to
three ranks, the exchange of a minor
piece is a precaution against getting
too cramped.

8 QxN   B-N2
9 B-N5   P-KR3

This results in a slight weakening of
the KN3 square but, on the other
hand, Q-Q2 followed by B-R6 is prevented and any indirect pressure
against the KP is eliminated.

10 B-K3   O-O
11 Q-Q2   K-R2
12 O-O   B-K3
13 P-B4   . . .

There are two ways by which the
Maroczy Bind can be utilized. Either
White can quietly bolster his strong
center pawns to prevent any freeing
moves by the defense, or he can rush
his attack, risking weaknesses in his
own position if it does not succeed.
Temperamentally, Larsen was a sure
thing to go for the second, more
exciting method. He intends by the
further advance of the KBP to render
Fischer's kingside shaky.

13 . . .   R-B1
14 P-QN3   Q-R4
15 P-QR3   . . .

Continuing his ambitious program, he
readies P-QN4 to drive the queen
away at the right moment, thus
facilitating P-KB5.

15 . . .   P-R3
16 P-KB5   B-Q2

Of course, 16 ... PxP, 17 PxP
BxKBP, 18 RxB QxR, 19 B-Q3 wins the
queen.

17 P-QN4   Q-K4

Such a queen sortie is bold and risky, but it does give badly needed counterplay in the attack on the KP, while a passive retreat would surely abandon the game, since it would present no obstacle to White's smooth pursuit of his kingside onslaught. Also, the queen is better protected than first appears, for either 18 B-Q4 or 18 B-B4 would collapse against 18 ... NxP. Furthermore, it is difficult to guard the KP, because 18 B-Q3 loses to 18 ... N-N5, 18 B-B3 to 18 ... RxP, and 18 Q-B2 to 18 ... BxP. Not even the seemingly powerful 18 Q-Q3, threatening both B-Q4 and B-B4 in earnest, will do—18 ... PxP, 19 PxP RxP!, 20 QxR QxBch, 21 K-R1 R-B1, 22 R-B3 Q-K4, 23 Q-Q3 RxN, 24 QxR QxB, and White's rooks are no match for the three pieces.

18   QR-K1   . . .

By a beautiful combination, Larsen defends his KP. If 18 ... NxP, 19 NxN QxN, 20 R-B4 Q-B3, 21 R-R4 P-KR4, 22 BxP! PxB, 23 RxPch K-N1,

24 B-R6, and there is absolutely no defense.

18	. . .	B-B3
19	B-B4	NxP
20	NxN	QxN
21	B-Q3	Q-Q5ch
22	K-R1	QR-K1
23	B-K3	. . .

23 Q-QB2 would be answered by 23 ... K-R1, when White cannot go after the KNP without leaving his QB en prise. So he would have to continue 24 B-K3 Q-B6, 25 PxP PxP, 26 BxNP QxQ, 27 BxQ, with an equal game. It is already becoming clear that Fischer's defense denies White the chance to get anything.

23   . . .   Q-B6 .

There is no way to hold on to the stolen pawn, since 23 ... Q-K4, 24 Q-QB2 leaves Black helpless to protect simultaneously his threatened KR and KN pawns, with the result that he would start coming apart at the seams. Even more disastrous is 23 ... Q-R5, 24 R-B4 Q-R4, 25 Q-KB2, and there is no defense against R-R4, since 25 ... Q-N4 loses to 26 P-KR4 Q-B3, 27 PxPch, while 25 ... B-B3 yields to 26 B-K2 Q-N4, 27 P-KR4.

24	BxP	QxQ
25	BxQ	. . .

Attack and defense have balanced each other perfectly and the game could have quite correctly been abandoned as a draw here, except that Larsen's characteristic stubbornness leads him to continue pressing for a win. Now, that attitude has stood him in good stead in many a tournament, but all the same, this is a qualification match for the World Championship and his opponent is Fischer.

25	...	B-K4
26	B-B4	BxB
27	RxB	PxP
28	RxBP	K-N2

There are only shadow threats against the king: 29 R-K3 P-B3, 30 R-N3ch K-B2, 31 R-KR5 R-KN1, 32 R-R7ch K-K3, 33 B-N6 RxB, 34 RxR B-K5, 35 R/6-R6 BxR, 36 RxB R-QB1, 37 R-R4 P-QN4 only manages to give Black a pawn plus the game.

29	R-N5ch	K-R3
30	P-KR4	P-K3
31	R-KB1	P-B4
32	R-K1	R-B2
33	P-N5	...

All this straining after something gets him nowhere, but it is quite harmless, since it does not compromise his position either.

33	...	PxP
34	PxP	B-Q2
35	P-N4	...

The pawn cannot be captured because of 36 B-N6, but its advance should only have made the drawish character of the position more obvious.

35	...	R-QR1
36	PxP	PxP
37	B-B4?	...

Needless to say, had he seen the nasty point of Bobby's last rook move, he would have seized his last chance to draw by 37 R/1-KN1 R-R5, 38 R-N6ch K-R2, 39 RxP RxPch, 40 K-N2, for he is quite safe on 40 ... R-N2ch, 41 K-B2 R-B5ch, 42 K-K3.

| 37 | ... | R-R5! |
| 38 | R-QB1? | ... |

Blunder upon blunder, losing two pawns instead of one, although his chances of holding out after 38 BxR RxPch, 39 K-N1 KxR, 40 R-K7 BxP, 41 RxP B-Q6 were awfully meager.

38	...	BxP!
39	BxR	RxPch
40	K-N2	KxR

Now it is only a matter of technique and could have been given up right here.

41	B-Q5	B-R3
42	R-Q1	R-R5
43	B-B3	RxP
44	RxP	R-R7ch
45	K-N1	K-B5

46	B-N2	R-N7		51	R-QN8	B-K5
47	R-Q7	P-N3		52	B-R6	K-K6
48	R-Q8	B-K7		53	R-QB8	R-N8ch
49	B-R3	B-N5		54	K-R2	K-B5
50	B-B1	B-B6			Resigns	

GAME 3
Sicilian Defense

ROBERT FISCHER   BENT LARSEN

1 P-K4   P-QB4

Almost surely the French Defense of game one was to have been Larsen's preference for the match, but the reception it got forced a change in plans.

2 N-KB3   P-Q3

Even though Larsen intends a formation with . . . N-QB3, he does not play it at once, presumably because he wants to avoid 3 B-N5, which is one of his own favorites.

3	P-Q4	PxP
4	NxP	N-KB3
5	N-QB3	N-B3
6	B-QB4	P-K3
7	B-N3	B-K2
8	B-K3	O-O
9	P-B4	. . .

In his game with Larsen at the Interzonal, Palma de Majorca, Bobby tried Velimirovic's system: Q-K2, O-O-O and P-KN4. But Bent was all ready for it and won very decisively. The text move, leading to P-B5 to attack the KP and put pressure on the white squares in the center, is an earlier weapon of Fischer's, which, reintroduced here, may have come as a small surprise.

9	. . .	B-Q2
10	O-O	P-QR3
11	P-B5	Q-B1?

A blunder as serious as this, coming so early in the game, can only be explained by the demoralizing effect of his two successive losses. Otherwise, I think, anyone would instinctively avoid setting up QN3 as a fork square, especially when a knight has quick access to it. His idea, for what it is worth, is to put counterpressure on the KBP, hoping to compel resolution of the tension in the center. When he adopted the same plan in the fifth game, he was careful to omit the P-QR3.

12 PxP!   BxP

Recapturing with the pawn may look more natural, but it does not help— 12 . . . PxP, 13 N-B5 Q-B2, 14 B-KB4 N-K1, 15 Q-N4 and now: (i) 15 . . . Q-B1 drops the QP after 16 QR-Q1, or (ii) 15 . . . B-B3, 16 QR-Q1 N-K4, 17 BxN PxB (17 . . . BxB, 18 N-R6ch and mates), 18 RxB! QxR, 19 BxPch QxB, 20 N-R6ch, winning the queen, or (iii) 15 . . . R-B3, 16 B-N5 R-N3, 17 NxBch NxN, 18 BxN!, and the queen cannot be taken because of mate.

13	NxB	PxN
14	N-R4	. . .

Thus, Black is separated from his KP by his lack of any defense against N-N6, and the game is lost despite Larsen's determined efforts to hang on.

14	. . .	R-N1
15	N-N6	Q-K1
16	BxPch	K-R1
17	B-KB5!	. . .

Now, if Black lunges to get the pawn back by 17 ... P-N3, 18 B-R3 NxP, he gets tied in knots after 19 Q-Q5 N-B3, 20 Q-K6 N-K4, 21 B-R6 R-B2, 22 N-B8. Avoiding the knots by 19 ... RxRch, 20 RxR N-B3, 21 Q-K6 N-Q1, 22 Q-B4 N-B3, 23 B-Q4 is no improvement at all, since the terrible pin, in conjunction with N-Q7, will quickly prove fatal.

17	...	N-K4
18	Q-Q4	Q-R4
19	N-Q5	NxN
20	QxQN	Q-K7
21	B-R7	QR-K1
22	R-B2	Q-N4
23	P-B3	B-R5
24	P-KN3	QxQ

It is a heartless task to play out such a game, which, while won for White, still is not quite resignable by Black. Larsen decides on the endgame because his middle game is static, while White can go right on strengthening his with every move.

25	PxQ	B-B3
26	QR-KB1	N-B5
27	B-K6	R-R1

The attempt to rely on the drawing chances inherent in bishops of opposite colors—27 ... P-QN3, 28 R-B4 R-R1, 29 RxN RxB—would have failed after 30 R-B6, winning a second pawn.

28	B-Q4	BxB
29	PxB	RxR
30	RxR	...

Although it might appear that Black has improved his lot by doubling White's extra pawn, the price paid for that in White's domination of the KB file and the seventh rank, plus the resulting passivity of the rook and knight, outweighs the value received.

30	...	P-QN4
31	K-B1	P-N3
32	P-N3	N-R6
33	K-K2	R-R2
34	R-B8ch	K-N2
35	R-Q8	P-N5

It was equally hopeless to play 35 ... R-QB2, 36 RxP R-B7ch, 37 K-Q3 RxQRP, 38 R-Q7ch, followed by queening the QP.

36	RxP	N-N4
37	R-N6	NxPch
38	K-Q3	NxB

At this stage it does not matter how he chooses to be finished. 38 ... N-N4, 39 P-Q6 R-R1, 40 P-Q7 R-Q1, 41 B-R3 would allow White to capture all the queenside pawns.

39	RxN	...

Fischer's recapture is the correct one, since he thereby sets up the classical rook and pawn ending in which the defending king is cut off from the passed pawn and hence cannot stop it.

39	. . .	P-QR4
40	K-Q4	K-B2
41	R-K2	Resigns

Fischer Takes Larsen 6–0

The second half of the match saw further fruitless attempts by Larsen to win a game outright and salvage his honor. In the fourth encounter, he played an orthodox type of attack against Fischer's King's Indian, a Taimanov system which is supposed to give White some initiative, at least. But Bobby's accurate defense gave Larsen nothing at all and when Black got the chance for a kingside attack, Larsen was unable to backtrack to fend it off. Scratch one try. Correcting what he had done wrong in the third game, Larsen nicely provided theoretical justification for the strange ... Q-B1 idea in the fifth contest, taking the starch out of Fischer's pawn sacrifice and equalizing easily. But then he refused to accept his well-earned draw and, once again outplayed by Bobby, went down to defeat for the fifth straight time.

Still desperate for a redeeming point, Larsen shifted to the Bird's Opening in the sixth game, but even transposing into an irregular Sicilian failed to procure any particular chances for him. So, he ventured an unsound pawn sacrifice, stubbornly refused a drawing combination Fischer carelessly allowed him, and lost the game and match.

Now that the match is over, the chief advice I can give Larsen is what everyone knows: that, on this level, one can only win by sharply stalking the opponent, striving for a potent opening initiative, pressing it with all possible energy and leaving the rest to fate. On those occasions when one cannot obtain a fruitful position to press, there is nothing whatsoever to do except offer the draw and prepare to try harder in the next game. It does not matter whether one is behind in the match or not—there is no substitute for rational play.

I have no advice to give Fischer—has anyone? His play is unfailingly logical, holding an excellent balance between restraint and enterprise. If he keeps it up through two more matches, the world championship will surely be his. Certainly no one ever got off to a better start!

GAME 4
King's Indian Defense

BENT LARSEN   ROBERT FISCHER

1   P-QB4   P-KN3

More flexible than the 1 . . . P-QB4 of game two, this move also grants White various choices, among which is the possibility of transposing into the King's Indian toward which he heads at the third move.

2	N-KB3	B-N2
3	P-Q4	N-KB3
4	N-B3	O-O
5	P-K4	P-Q3
6	B-K2	. . .

Larsen usually prefers either the classical variation of the text or one of the offshoots from it, such as 6 P-KR3 or 6 B-K3. I remember no game at all in which he has ever used the Saemisch set-up.

6	. . .	P-K4
7	O-O	N-B3
8	P-Q5	N-K2
9	N-Q2	. . .

The idea behind this innovation of Taimanov's is to bolster a queenside pawn attack—P-QN4, P-B5—by bringing the knight to QB4 or QN3. This addition to the attack augments it to such a degree that Black dare not follow the usual strategy of ignoring the queenside to launch one of his own on the opposite wing, (which does work against 9 N-K1, for example). So, on his next move,

Fischer adopts a defensive blockade known from the games Taimanov–Kavalek (Beverwijk 1970), and Gligoric–R. Byrne (Lugano 1970), which ended in comfortable draws for Black.

9	. . .	P-B4
10	R-N1	N-K1

In the games mentioned in the previous note, both defenders deemed it important to play 10 . . . P-QR4 in order to eliminate one pair of pawns when White advances P-QN4, so that any queenside pawn weaknesses would be obviated. What is especially interesting to me is that Fischer has decided it is unnecessary to forestall tension on the queenside and that, with accurate defense, Black need fear nothing. The remainder of the game supports his judgment.

11   P-QN4   P-N3

If White exchanges on his QB5, the recapture will be with this pawn, so that White will be denied a passed QP and pressure on the resulting half-open QN file.

12	P-QR4	P-B4
13	P-R5	N-KB3
14	Q-R4	B-Q2
15	Q-R3	B-R3

This move, which was employed in the two games cited in the note to move nine, has as its strategic objective the exchange of a bishop fairly blocked by its own pawns for White's better one. Tactically, it ties down enemy pieces to the defense of the KP, since the pawn protection, P-B3, would give Black attacking chances after ... N-R4.

16	B-Q3	Q-B2
17	NPxP	NPxBP
18	PxP	PxP
19	B-B2	...

Preparing his ill-advised twentieth move, but it is remarkable that even at this early stage it is difficult to suggest a positive plan for White. He cannot aim for B-R4 to remove Black's QB, since the sequence, ... QxP, BxB QxQ, B-K6ch K-R1, BxQ BxN, wins a pawn for Black. Perhaps the best way to simplify would be 19 N-N5 BxN, 20 RxB, though Black would have some chance of taking over the QN file after 20 ... QR-N1, while a kingside attack by ... P-K5, ... N-N3, and either ... N-B5 or ... N-K4 would beckon too.

| 19 | ... | P-R3 |
| 20 | N/2-K4 | ... |

While this little exchanging combination only results in rapidly mobilizing the Black rooks for an attack on the king, it is not easy to find a secure way for White to try for a draw. He cannot get anywhere on the queenside, whereas Black controls the center and can use the half open KN file for a ready-made onslaught.

| 20 | ... | BxB |
| 21 | NxNch | RxN |

22	KRxB	QR-KB1
23	R-N6	B-B1
24	N-K2?	...

Completely underestimating the attack which follows on Fischer's next move. It was mandatory to play 24 P-B4 PxP, 25 N-K2 P-B6, 26 QxKBP P-B5, because even though Black has in view the powerful threat, ... N-N3-K4 and ... P-B6, White has more space for his pieces to fight back. On 27 ... N-N3, however, 28 BxN would permit 28 ... PxB, with the menace of ... P-N4-N5.

| 24 | ... | P-B5! |

Yes, White gets the K4 square—but Bobby's attack comes so quickly there is no chance to use it. The freeing P-B4 is ruled out and every last one of Black's pieces can be brought to bear on the king, while 25 ... P-B6 is the immediate threat.

| 25 | B-K4 | N-B4 |
| 26 | R-B6 | ... |

Trying to counterattack this way only gives Black an extra tempo. The best defense available was 26 K-R1 R-R3, 27 N-N1, but after 27 . . . Q-K2, threatening 28 . . . N-Q5 followed by 29 . . . Q-R5, White's chances of survival are small.

26   . . .   Q-KN2!

The queen can be brought to the attack at once because the offered pawn is taboo—27 BxN BxB, 28 RxRP R-N3, 29 P-N3 P-B6, 30 N-B3 Q-R3, 31 K-R1 Q-R6, 32 R-KN1 QxPch and mate next move.

27   R-N1   . . .

Consistent with his previous move, but a passive defense such as 27 K-R1 N-R5, 28 R-KN1 R-R3, 29 P-N3 would be a shambles after 29 . . . N-B6!, 30 BxN RxPch 31 KxR Q-R3ch, 32 B-R5 QxBch, 33 K-N2 B-R6ch, 34 K-R1 B-B8 mate. White could, of course, omit 29 P-N3, but what could he do about the threat of . . . N-B6! after the preparatory . . . K-R1? Anything involving P-R3 would be vulnerable to a breakthrough by . . . P-B6 or a sacrifice on R3, and P-B3 without P-R3 would only be asking for . . . Q-N4-R4, which forces the move anyhow.

27   . . .   N-R5!

Perhaps Larsen relied on 28 RxB RxR, 29 Q-R3, but the sequel would be 29 . . . R/1-KB1, 30 QxN R-R3, and his queen is trapped!

28   Q-Q3   . . .

Had he gone through with his 28 R-N8 idea, 28 . . . B-B4, 29 RxRch RxR, 30 Q-Q3 NxP, 31 BxB, N-K6ch would have finished effectively. Here 31 K-B1 BxB, 32 QxB P-B6, 33 N-N3 Q-R3, with the double threat of 34 . . . Q-B8, mating, and 34 . . . QxP, is just as conclusive.

28   . . .   B-B4

There is nothing to be done about the threats of 29 . . . NxP and 29 . . . QxPch, because 29 P-N3 PxP, 30 BPxP BxB, 31 QxB N-B6ch wins in the same way as the actual game continuation.

29	K-R1	P-B6!
30	N-N3	PxPch
31	K-N1	BxB
32	QxB	N-B6ch
33	KxP	N-Q7
	Resigns	

GAME 5
Sicilian Defense

ROBERT FISCHER   BENT LARSEN

1	P-K4	P-QB4
2	N-KB3	P-Q3
3	P-Q4	PxP
4	NxP	N-KB3
5	N-QB3	N-B3
6	B-QB4	P-K3
7	B-N3	B-K2
8	B-K3	O-O
9	O-O	B-Q2
10	P-B4	Q-B1

After White's tenth move the position is the same as in game three, but now Larsen tries his ... Q-B1 idea without erroneously preceding it with ... P-QR3.

11 P-B5!?   ...

An ingenious try, but Larsen brushes it off without any difficulty, so it would seem that White has nothing better than the orthodox Q-B3 or Q-K2.

11	...	NxN
12	BxN	PxP
13	Q-Q3	PxP

The alternative stubborn attempt to keep the pawn, 13 ... P-KN3, runs into insuperable difficulties after 14 QR-K1 B-Q1, 15 PxP BxP, 16 Q-N3 N-K1, 17 N-Q5 B-K3, 18 Q-B4 Q-Q2, 19 Q-R6 and there is no defense against R-B3-R3, since BxR is answered by RxN! Because the QB must stay where it is to prevent RxN, White can win in other ways, too, for example, 20 N-B4, threatening the simple but deadly 21 NxB, as well as 21 NxP!

14 ... R-K1, 15 PxP BxP, 16 RxB QxR, 17 QxQ PxQ, 18 RxB RxR, 19 BxN also gives White the winning advantage of three minor pieces to two rooks.

In the line I give in the first paragraph, Black's best is 16 ... B-N3, 17 BxB PxB, 18 QxP Q-B4ch, 19 QxQ PxQ, 20 R-K7, but White has a clear endgame advantage. Still another possibility is 16 ... Q-Q2, 17 B-R4 N-R4, 18 Q-B2 Q-B2, 19 P-KN4 BxNP, 20 N-Q5 Q-R4, 21 QxPch! RxQ, 22 R-K8ch and mates next move.

14	NxP	NxN
15	QxN	B-K3
16	R-B3	Q-B3!

Nipping White's chances in the bud, and avoiding 16 ... BxB?, 17 R-N3! P-B3, 18 RxB R-K1, 19 RxP with great advantage. Nor can Black risk 17 ... P-KN3, 18 QxB Q-K3, 19 Q-R4 B-Q4, 20 R-K3 Q-B4, 21 R-KB1 QxP, 22 QxPch, mating.

17 R-K1   ...

Bobby has to admit that he can get no further with his intended attack. 17 Q-K3 would have been tricky, as shown by 17 . . . P-Q4?, 18 R-N3 P-KN3, 19 R-K1 Q-Q3, 20 Q-R6 P-B3, 21 R/3-K3, winning a piece. But White stands worse after 17 . . . BxB, 18 QxB/7 BxBP, 19 R-KN3 B-N3.

17	. . .	QxQ
18	RxQ	P-Q4
19	R-N3	P-KN3

If 19 . . . PxR?, 20 RxPch K-R1, 21 RxPch B-B3, 22 BxBch K-N1, 23 R-N7ch K-R1, 24 B-B3 and Black is finished.

| 20 | BxQP | B-Q3? |

The draw was his for the asking after 20 . . . BxB, but this heroic adventure, by which he wins a slight material advantage, is too risky since White obtains considerable positional compensation.

21	RxB	BxR
22	R-K7	B-Q3
23	RxNP	. . .

Although White has only bishop plus one pawn for rook, the dominating position of his pieces and the possibility of getting connected passed pawns on the queenside give him all the winning chances. Why did Larsen choose to contest this at move twenty?

23	. . .	QR-B1
24	P-B4	P-QR4
25	R-R7	B-B2

25 . . . B-B4 was out of the question because of 26 BxB RxB, followed by K-B2-K3-Q4, winning the decisive pawn.

| 26 | P-KN3 | KR-K1 |
| 27 | K-B1 | R-K2 |

Hoping to free himself by . . . B-Q1.

| 28 | B-KB6 | R-K6 |
| 29 | B-QB3 | . . . |

Not really threatening to take the RP, because after the exchange of bishops, R/1-K1 would permit the Black rooks to penetrate too dangerously into the White position. But he threatens to threaten, meanwhile keeping up the pressure.

| 29 | . . . | P-R4 |

Black is in a position so passive that it almost amounts to Zugzwang, thus explaining this weakening advance, which aims at counterplay by . . . P-R5.

| 30 | R-R6! | . . . |

Threatening 31 RxPch as well as 31 R-QB6, with a powerful pin, and if 30 . . . K-B1, then 31 B-Q4 R/6-K1, 32 R-KB6 R-K2, 33 B-B5 wins. In this line, Black cannot escape by 31 . . . R-Q6, because the rook is trapped by 32 B-B5ch followed by 33 K-K2.

| 30 | . . . | B-K4 |
| 31 | B-Q2! | . . . |

The simplest and the best, compelling a decisive reduction of material.

31	...	R-Q6
32	K-K2	R-Q5
33	B-QB3	R/1xP

The alternative, 33 ... RxB, 34 PxR BxB, 35 PxB RxP is met by 36 R-QB6!, after which the Black rook cannot get back in time to prevent the QP from going all the way: 36 ... R-R6, 37 P-Q6 RxPch, 38 K-Q3 R-R8, 39 K-B2 R-R7ch, 40 K-B3 R-R8, 41 R-B8ch K-N2, 42 P-Q7. Also 33 ... R/5xP, 34 BxB R/5-B4, 35 RxPch K-R2, 36 R-Q6 R-K1, 37 B-K4ch K-N1, 38 B-Q4 RxBch, 39 K-Q3 RxBch, 40 RxR gives White a routine, winning rook and pawn ending.

34	KBxR	RxB
35	K-Q3!	...

Naturally not 35 BxB? R-K5ch and White won't win, but the text continues the relentless, decisive simplification.

35	...	R-B4
36	RxP	RxR
37	BxR	BxQNP

At last perfect material equilibrium has been reached, but, of course, Black cannot cope with the monster of a passed QRP.

38	P-QR4	K-B1
39	B-B3	BxB

Equally unavailing was 39 ... B-R6, 40 P-R5 B-Q3, 41 P-R6 B-N1, 42 B-K5 B-R2, 43 B-Q4, which exacts a piece for the pawn.

40	KxB	K-K2
41	K-Q4	K-Q3
42	P-R5	P-B3
43	P-R6	K-B3
44	P-R7	K-N2
45	K-Q5	P-R5
46	K-K6	Resigns

BENT LARSEN   ROBERT FISCHER

1 P-KB4   . . .

This oft-times favorite of Larsen's is every bit as sound as the more orthodox opening choices, although it is very difficult to gain the initiative with it.

1 . . .   P-QB4

Since Bird's idea is to set up a knight outpost at K5, it is useful to postpone the advance of the QP until it becomes clear whether gain of space or control of Black's K4 is more important.

2	N-KB3	P-KN3
3	P-K4	. . .

Transposing thusly into a kind of closed Sicilian is, in my opinion, merely exchanging one innocuous formation for another.

3	. . .	B-N2
4	B-K2	. . .

And varying in this way from the usual KB fianchetto can have no other advantage than that of novelty, but Larsen likes to be different for difference's sake.

4	. . .	N-QB3
5	O-O	P-Q3
6	P-Q3	P-K3
7	N-R3	KN-K2
8	P-B3	. . .

One difference between White's formation and the standard closed Sicilian is that this move can be played at once, denying Black his Q5 square for a knight outpost and serving as prop for a possible P-Q4. But White's otherwise tame development works against his using this difference to obtain anything really menacing.

8	. . .	O-O
9	B-K3	P-QR3
10	P-Q4	PxP
11	NxP	. . .

On 11 PxP Black gets a comfortable game by 11 . . . P-QN4, followed by 12 . . . B-N2, since 12 P-Q5? PxP, 13 PxP N-N5 gives up the QP.

11	. . .	P-QN4
12	NxN	NxN
13	Q-Q2	Q-B2

As so often in this type of position (by now an irregular open Sicilian), the Black QP is not weak, primarily because the enemy minor pieces cannot be brought to bear on it. But it does need some protection, so the last move clears for a rook to come to Q1.

14	QR-Q1	R-Q1
15	N-B2	R-N1
16	P-QR3	N-R4
17	P-K5?!	. . .

In allowing the center to be opened, White cannot get anywhere. If Larsen is all that intent on trying something, perhaps it should have been P-KN4.

And whether he should go in for forward marches from a position no stronger than his is another question altogether.

| 17 | . . . | B-B1 |
| 18 | P-QN4 | . . . |

The point of this is that the obvious reply, 18 . . . N-B5 is a complete lemon after 19 BxN QxB, 20 B-Q4 followed by N-K3-N4 which yields dangerous chances for a kingside attack.

| 18 | . . . | N-B3 |
| 19 | N-Q4?! | . . . |

Initiating a pawn sacrifice which is utterly unsound, but saving the pawn by 19 PxP BxP favors Black, who would then develop play against the QBP, while finding excellent squares in the center for his minor pieces (. . . N-K2-B4 or Q4).

19	. . .	PxP
20	PxP	NxKP
21	B-N5	R-Q4
22	Q-B4	R-N2?!

In awkwardly unpinning the knight this way, Bobby permits Larsen to escape his proper punishment and make a draw. Most accurate was 22 . . . B-KN2, 23 P-KR4 B-N2, 24 B-B6 BxB, 25 QxB Q-Q1, and there are no more draw swindles. However, 22 . . . QxP?, 23 B-B3! wins for White, since 23 . . . NxBch, 24 RxN leaves both king and queen en prise simultaneously.

| 23 | P-KR4 | B-N2 |

| 24 | B-B6 | BxB |
| 25 | QxB | QxP?! |

He should have played 25 . . . Q-K2 with the same consolidating idea as I suggest in the previous note.

| 26 | P-R5! | PxP |

26 . . . RxN, 27 QxN R-Q6, 28 Q-N5 RxR, 29 RxR P-B3, 30 Q-R6 R-Q2, 31 R-QB1 Q-Q5ch, 32 K-B1 B-N2, 33 R-Q1 is too much for Black. Nor could he improve by 30 . . . R-N2, 31 PxP PxP, 32 R-Q8ch K-B2, 33 Q-R8, since there is no perpetual check and no defense to the mate. 26 . . . Q-K6ch, 27 K-R1 RxN, 28 RxR QxR, 29 R-Q1 is just another way for Black to blow the defense.

| 27 | K-R1?! | . . . |

Had Larsen cared to, he could have taken the draw by 27 NxKP BxN, 28 RxR BxR, 29 Q-Q8ch K-N2, 30 Q-B6ch, etc.

27	. . .	N-N5!
28	BxN	PxB
29	Q-R6	. . .

29 R-B1 would have failed against 29 ... R-R4ch, 30 K-N1 Q-K6ch.

| 29 | ... | B-Q2 |
| 30 | R-B4 | ... |

Were it not for his do-or-die spirit, Larsen could once again make a draw—30 NxKP BxN, 31 RxR BxR, 32 Q-N5ch, etc.

| 30 | ... | P-B4 |
| 31 | Q-B6? | ... |

The only way to keep trying was 31 Q-N5ch K-B2, 32 QxNP which gives Black a difficult problem in finding shelter for the king.

| 31 | ... | B-B1 |

At last the QR can come to the defense and decide the issue for good.

| 32 | R/4-B1 | R-KB2 |
| 33 | Q-R6 | B-N2! |

33 ... RxN?, 34 R-B1 Q-Q7, 35 RxBch R-Q1, 36 QxQ wins Black's queen, and 34 ... Q-Q6 changes nothing—35 RxBch R-Q1, 36 Q-N5ch.

| 34 | NxKP | Q-KB3! |

Dashing any remaining White hopes.

35	Q-K3	R-K2
36	QR-K1	R-Q3
37	Q-N5ch	QxQ
38	NxQ	RxR
39	RxR	B-Q4
40	R-K8ch	K-N2
	Resigns	

Chapter III

FISCHER VS. PETROSIAN

After his glorious triumphs over Bent Larsen and Mark Taimanov, Bobby Fischer got off to a very rocky start in his final match against Tigran Petrosian. True, he did take the first game to run his match-game winning streak to 13, but that required some strong cooperation from Petrosian, who might still have been very much in awe of Bobby. For Petrosian came up with a brilliant opening innovation that refutes one of Fischer's favorite attacks, and only by very passive play, twice missing strong chances, did he allow Bobby to get on top in the game. Bobby seized the opportunity offered him, heading for a superior endgame which he won.

Game two was a shocker, not only because it brought Fischer's winning streak to an end, but because his opening play was so ill thought out that he was lost after sixteen moves. This time Petrosian played brilliantly, smashing his way to the point.

Game three was almost as much a shocker as the previous game, for again Bobby's opening play was unsound with the White pieces. Fortunately for him, Petrosian did not play sharply enough to score the point, allowing a threefold repetition of the position when he had a clear advantage.

In these first three games, Bobby's usually excellent opening preparation is nowhere to be seen. Did he take Petrosian too lightly after his 3-1 defeat of him in the 1970 Match USSR vs. the Rest of the World in Belgrade? Have his two previous fantastic match shut-outs blinded him to the danger of his present opponent? I don't know, but as of this writing, I am very worried about the outcome of the match.

GAME 1
Sicilian Defense

ROBERT FISCHER   TIGRAN PETROSIAN

1   P-K4   P-QB4

The first surprise—everyone anticipated only passive defense from
Petrosian, certainly not a Sicilian. But
he has done his homework very well,
and is all ready to refute some of
Fischer's favorite systems in this
match.

2   N-KB3   P-K3
3   P-Q4   PxP
4   NxP   N-QB3

In his World Championship Match
with Spassky, Petrosian relied on
4 . . . P-QR3 to avoid White's next
move. But now he has good reason
to permit it!

5   N-N5   . . .

Bobby has had phenomenal success
with this move, defeating Taimanov
twice with it in their match, but had
he foreseen Petrosian's powerful
eleventh move, he would surely have
sidestepped the whole line by
5 N-QB3.

5   . . .   P-Q3
6   B-KB4   . . .

Continuing in the same manner as in
the Taimanov games, this move
forces a weakness at Q5, since 6 . . .
N-K4?, 7 QN-R3 P-QR3, 8 BxN PxB,
9 QxQch KxQ, 10 O-O-Och B-Q2,
11 N-B4! is powerful for White.

6   . . .   P-K4
7   B-K3   N-B3
8   B-N5   B-K3

In game two of the Taimanov match,
Taimanov could not cope with the
gambit Fischer offered by 8 . . .
Q-R4ch, 9 Q-Q2 NxP, 10 QxQ NxQ,
11 B-K3 K-Q2, 12 QN-B3 NxN,
13 NxN, although the outcome would
be far from clear after the correct
13 . . . P-QN3, instead of 13 . . .
K-Q1?

9   QN-B3   P-QR3
10   BxN   PxB
11   N-R3   P-Q4!!

A smashing blow to White's opening
strategy! The sacrifice, which is only
temporary, develops Black's game at
an alarming rate, while putting great
difficulties in the way of White's
organization of his position. If 12
NxP KBxN, 13 PxB P-B4, 14 P-QB4
PxP and Black has recovered his
pawn with a powerful position. Here
14 P-KB3? PxP, 15 PxP Q-R5ch is
overwhelming, while 14 B-Q3 PxP,
15 BxKP Q-R4ch, 16 Q-Q2 QxQch,

17 KxQ, O-O-O is also awful for
White.

12	PxP	BxN
13	NPxB	Q-R4
14	Q-Q2	...

Nothing can be captured without
disaster: 14 PxB?? QxNch, 15 K-K2
N-Q5ch, or 14 PxN?? QxNch, 15 K-K2
B-B5ch.

14	...	O-O-O
15	B-B4	...

Safer was 15 B-Q3 BxP, 16 NxB QxN,
17 B-B5ch K-B2, 18 QxQ RxQ, although Black gets a workable four-to-
three kingside pawn majority, while
White has only queenside cripples.

15	...	KR-N1
16	R-Q1	B-B4

The simple and strong text move is
probably the best, as long as it is
followed up properly, while the
complications resulting from 16 ...
RxNP, although very inviting for a
tactical player, are not clear. 17 B-Q3,
my first suggestion, is not correct,
since 17 ... N-Q5!, 18 B-K4 R-N5!,
19 K-B1 RxB!, 20 NxR B-R6ch wins
the queen. 20 PxB is better, but
20 ... NxKP, 21 QxRch NxQ, 22
NxR favors Black, who should be able
to take advantage of White's unde-
veloped king's rook. However, 17 ...
BxP?, 18 NxB RxN, 19 QxQ RxQ,
20 BxKRP would give White a great
endgame, with an outside passed

pawn and a powerful bishop to back
it up.
17 Q-K3 does not work either: 17 ...
N-Q5, 18 K-B1 NxP!, 19 Q-Q3 R-N5,
20 QxN RxB, 21 PxB QxN, 22 P-K7
RxRch, 23 QxR Q-R6ch, 24 K-K1
Q-Q2 and wins.
But whether Black can get anything
after 17 N-K4 is a difficult question:
17 ... Q-N3, 18 Q-K3 QxQch,
19 PxQ B-N5, 20 R-QB1 B-B6, 21
NxP N-K2, 22 B-Q3 threatens 23 R-B1
with a consolidated position. White
can also win the Exchange by 18
Q-B3 B-B4!, 19 B-B1 BxN, 20 Q-R3ch
K-N1, 21 BxR, but after 21 ... BxBP,
22 R-QB1 N-Q5, the Black position
would be powerful.

17	B-Q3	BxB?

Simplification is to White's advantage, since the middle game complications favor Black. Excellent chances
in a two-edged game were offered by
17 ... P-K5!, 18 B-K2 RxNP, 19 Q-K3
N-K4, 20 K-B1 N-N5, 21 BxN RxB,
22 R-Q4. White cannot avoid the
pawn sacrifice by 18 B-B1, since he
could never develop a thing afterward. Nor can he accept the pawn
sacrifice—18 NxP BxN, 19 BxB
KR-K1, 20 P-KB3 P-B4 wins a piece.

18	QxB	N-Q5

18 ... RxNP loses a piece to 19
Q-R3ch.

19	O-O	K-N1
20	K-R1	...

Black threatened . . . QxN once his king moved away from the answering check.

20   . . .   QxRP?

Black would have better chances with 20 . . . P-B4, 21 P-B4 P-B3. Petrosian must play aggressively here but it seems nothing can get him to do it.

21   P-B4!   . . .

Now Black's positional weakness on the KB file stands out like a sore thumb. What is quite unusual is that Bobby has accurately judged that Petrosian's play on the QB file does not quite counterbalance his own chances.

21	. . .	R-QB1
22	N-K4	QxQ
23	PxQ	R-B7
24	R-Q2	RxR
25	NxR	P-B4!

It doesn't matter whether this finally holds the game or not—it's ingenious, and besides, nothing else has a chance.

26	PxP	R-K1
27	R-K1	N-B7
28	R-K2	. . .

29 R-QB1 is useless against 29 . . . N-N5.

28	. . .	N-Q5
29	R-K3	N-B7
30	R-R3!	. . .

This seemed to surprise Petrosian, who must have thought he could rely on a simple draw by repetition.

30	. . .	RxP
31	N-B3	RxP
32	RxP	RxP
33	P-KR4	N-K6
34	RxP	R-Q8ch
35	K-R2	R-QR8
36	P-R5	P-B5?

This loses at once since it overlooks Fischer's crushing thirty-eighth move. Had Petrosian played the simple and correct 36 . . . RxP, there is a real question whether the position is a win at all. For example: 37 N-R4 P-B5, 38 RxP R-R4, 39 P-N4 NxPch. Or 37 R-N7 P-B5, 38 P-R6 R-R4, 39 P-R7 R-R4ch, 40 K-N1 K-R2, 41 N-N5 P-R4, 42 R-N8 P-R5, 43 P-R8=Q RxQ, 44 RxR P-R6, 45 R-QB8 P-R7, 46 R-B1 N-B7. In this last line, if 38 R-N5 R-QB7, 39 N-K5 R-B2, 40 P-R6 R-R2, 41 N-B6ch PxN, 42 R-N8ch K-B2, 43 R-N7ch RxR, 44 PxR N-N5ch, 45 K-R3 N-B3, and Black even wins. But Petrosian was in time pressure and undoubtedly saw ghosts.

37	RxP	RxP
38	R-K4!	...

Winning outright, for if 38 ...
RxPch, 39 K-R3 R-K7, 40 P-R6.

38	...	NxP
39	K-N3	...

Trapping the knight.

39	...	R-R4
40	N-K5	Resigns

The rook is cut off.

GAME 2
Gruenfeld Defense

TIGRAN PETROSIAN   ROBERT FISCHER

1	P-Q4	N-KB3
2	P-QB4	P-KN3
3	N-QB3	P-Q4
4	B-B4	B-N2
5	P-K3	P-B4

The introduction to a very dangerous gambit which White could accept by 6 BxN RxB, 7 Q-R4ch B-Q2, 8 QxP BPxP, 9 QxQP O-O, 10 PxP Q-R4, 11 Q-Q2 P-QN4, as in Donner-Gheorghiu, IBM Tournament, Amsterdam 1969. Gheorghiu scored a smashing victory.

6	QPxP	Q-R4
7	R-B1	. . .

The attempt to hold the pawn by 7 Q-R4ch does not work out after 7 . . . QxQ, 8 NxQ B-Q2, 9 N-QB3 PxP, 10 BxP N-R3, 11 BxN PxB, 12 R-B1 R-QB1, 13 P-QN4 P-QR4, 14 P-QR3 PxP, 15 PxP P-QR4, 16 PxP RxP, with the better game for Black.

7	. . .	N-K5
8	PxP	NxN
9	Q-Q2	QxRP
10	PxN	Q-R4
11	B-B4	N-Q2
12	N-K2	. . .

12 P-B6 would have no other effect than to ruin White's pawn formation: 12 . . . PxP, 13 PxP N-B4, 14 N-K2 O-O, 15 O-O B-K3, with the better game for Black.

12	. . .	N-K4
13	B-R2	B-B4?

This aggressive-looking move is the real culprit behind Black's downfall. Correct was 13 . . . QxP/4, when the game would be about even.

14	BxN	BxB
15	N-Q4	QxP/4

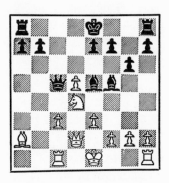

Is it really clear that Black cannot continue the sacrifice of the QBP? How would White proceed after 15 . . . B-Q2? If 16 N-N3 Q-R6, 17 O-O B-R5, 18 R-N1 O-O, White's pieces are very awkwardly placed as the price for the pawn. On the other hand, 16 P-B6 PxP, 17 PxP B-B1 leaves open the question whether the pawn can be permanently maintained, and even if it can, whether White can derive any real benefit from it.

16	NxB	PxN
17	O-O	. . .

It is very likely not an exaggeration to say that this position is already lost for Black. The forward KBP is all but impossible to defend and the Black king cannot find a haven anywhere.

And all because of the faulty but tempting 13 ... B-B4.

| 17 | ... | **Q-R4?** |

Come what may, he had to keep the direct frontal blockade of the QBP. The best was probably 17 ... B-Q3, though 18 Q-B2 is still terribly strong. For example, 18 ... P-B5, 19 PxP BxP, 20 R-N1 P-N3, 21 Q-B5 and the Black position looks wretched.

18	Q-B2	P-B5
19	P-B4	PxP
20	P-B5!	...

The mobile pawn majority, with the impending threat to open the bishop's diagonal by P-Q6, is easily worth the pawn sacrificed. If White's game was not won before, it certainly is now.

| 20 | ... | **Q-Q7** |

Fischer picks the only way to make trouble for his opponent. Perhaps he can divert him from his attack by tricky threats with the KP.

21	Q-R4ch	K-B1
22	QR-Q1	Q-K7
23	P-Q6	...

The threat is 24 PxPch followed by Q-Q7ch. White already has in mind the Exchange sacrifice of the next move.

| 23 | ... | **Q-R4** |
| 24 | P-B4! | ... |

Repulsing Black's demonstration with a fury. Best now would be 24 ... B-B3, but since that would never hold the game (24 R-Q5), Black burns his bridges behind him.

24	...	P-K7
25	PxB	PxQR=Q
26	RxQ	QxP
27	R-KB1	P-B3
28	Q-N3	K-N2

Equally hopeless was 28 ... P-K3, 29 QxNP R-K1, 30 P-B6 and there is nothing to be done.

| 29 | Q-B7ch | K-R3 |
| 30 | PxP | P-B4 |

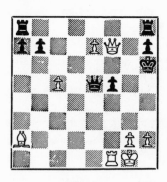

After 30 ... KR-KN1, there are several ways of finishing but one is enough: 31 B-N1 R-N3, 32 BxR PxB, 33 Q-B8ch. On 30 ... QR-KN1, 31 B-N1 wins again since there is nothing to be done about the threat of 32 RxPch. If 31 ... K-N4, 32 RxP QxR, 33 P-R4ch.

| 31 | RxP | **Q-Q5ch** |
| 32 | K-R1 | **Resigns** |

GAME 3
French Defense

ROBERT FISCHER   TIGRAN PETROSIAN

1	P-K4	P-K3
2	P-Q4	P-Q4
3	N-QB3	N-KB3
4	B-N5	PxP
5	NxP	B-K2
6	BxN	PxB

Although it is no surprise for Petrosian to employ the Rubinstein Variation, exchanging pawns at the fourth move, it is unusual for him to recapture in this way, getting doubled pawns. Occasionally, in the 1930s, Alekhine adopted it with the idea that if Black could defend his cramped position sharply, the two bishops might amount to something in the endgame.

7	P-KN3?	...

This is a bad mistake, but strangely enough, Bobby won with it against Minev in the Havana Tournament in 1967 and probably hadn't thought twice about it since then. Correct is 7 N-KB3, followed by 8 B-Q3 or 8 B-B4.

7	...	P-KB4
8	N-QB3	B-B3
9	KN-K2	N-B3!

Completely refuting White's seventh move, which Fischer now tries to justify by an unsound pawn sacrifice.

10	P-Q5	PxP
11	NxP	...

White could have backed out by 11 QxP, though Petrosian would have had a beautiful game after 11 ... BxNch, 12 NxB Q-K2ch, 13 B-K2 B-K3, 14 Q-Q2 R-Q1.

11	...	BxP
12	B-N2	O-O
13	O-O	B-R1

13 ... BxR, 14 QxB P-B3, 15 R-Q1 B-Q2, 16 N/2-B4 N-K4, 17 N-R5 P-B3, 18 N/Q5xPch RxN, 19 QxN R-B2, 20 R-Q6 is very likely too much for Black to handle. Here 15 ... N-K4, 16 N-N6 RPxN, 17 RxQ RxR, 18 P-KB4 N-N5, 19 P-KR3 N-K6, 20 QxP leaves Black so exposed that he couldn't even dream of playing for a win.

The text move is the right idea and gives Black the advantage, but 13 ... B-N2 was more accurate, since 14 N/2-B4 N-K4, 15 N-R5 P-QB3 only gives White a pawn-down endgame.

14	N/2-B4	N-K4
15	Q-R5	N-N3
16	QR-Q1	...

Here White should have chosen the tricky 16 N-R3 B-N2, 17 N-N5 P-KR3, 18 NxKBP, for if 18 ... KxN, 19 N-B4 Q-N4, 20 B-Q5ch K-B3, 21 P-KR4 (Suetin's clever little shot), Black is in deep trouble. For example, 21 ... QxQ, 22 NxQch K-K4, 23 QR-Q1 and Black cannot save his bishop without permitting the winning KR-K1ch. Suetin recommends 18 ... RxN, 19 QxN Q-N4, 20 QxQ PxQ, claiming that Black stands better, but White should have good chances of holding his own after 21 QR-K1 K-B1, 22 P-B4.

| 16 | ... | P-QB3 |
| 17 | N-K3 | Q-B3 |

Naturally, Black will not exchange knights and give White an open file against his king.

| 18 | K-R1 | ... |

White wishes to tie the enemy pieces down to the defense of the weak foremost KBP, but the immediate 18 B-R3 is met by 18 ... NxN, 19

PxN Q-N3ch, 20 Q-N5 B-B3, 21 Q-N3 K-R1.

18	...	B-N2
19	B-R3	N-K2
20	R-Q3	B-K3
21	KR-Q1	B-R3
22	R-Q4	BxN
23	RxB	QR-Q1

Petrosian has given up one of his bishops and now offers his pawn plus too, in order to get the queen file.

| 24 | RxR? | ... |

Too eager to reestablish material equality, Bobby overlooks the difficult consequences. Correct was 24 R-QN1 with about equal chances.

| 24 | ... | RxR |
| 25 | BxP | ... |

At first I thought this was a mistake and that 25 NxP was better, but Black can still answer 25 ... R-Q4, for if 26 NxNch? QxN, 27 Q-R6 R-Q8ch wins. So White would have to play 26 P-N4 anyway, under worse circumstances.

25	...	NxB
26	NxN	R-Q4
27	P-N4	BxN
28	PxB	P-KR3

Now Black has a considerable advantage, what with all of the White pawns broken up.

| 29 | P-KR3 | K-R2 |
| 30 | Q-K2 | Q-K4 |

31	Q-R5	Q-B3
32	Q-K2	R-K4
33	Q-Q3	R-Q4?

Petrosian did not seem to realize that he was allowing a three-time repetition of the position. Of course, what is confusing is that, in reaching the same position three times, Black's move was different each time, but that has no effect on the position repeated. Nor did it have any effect on Bobby who noticed it right away.

34	Q-K2	Drawn

Getting Ahead

After his unsettling start in the first three games, the openings of which were clearly to Petrosian's advantage, Bobby slowly began to get under way. It was Petrosian who backed away from the sharpest continuation in game four, either suspecting or discovering over the board that Fischer had a foolproof defense in hand. What it might have been, I suggest in my note to White's move twelve. Anyhow, Petrosian may have been a little rattled, since he made no serious attempt with the White pieces, acquiescing to wholesale liquidation and a quick draw.

The former world champion's super-cautious Petroff Defense in game five gave Bobby the chance for an opening advantage for the first time in the match. Unfortunately, he did not follow it up correctly, running into a great deal of trouble from which he just barely managed to escape. There was still no reason at this point in the series to be confident about Fischer's chances of ending up the victor.

But the sixth game was an altogether different story. Bobby answered Petrosian's offbeat Reti Opening very sharply, gaining a small but perfectly clear advantage. In the face of a lifeless game, in which he could only await possible attacks on both wings, Petrosian panicked, opening the queenside for no good reason. Bobby immediately jumped at the opportunity, breaking through on the QB file, obtaining a protected passed QP and powerful control of queenside terrain. After a beautifully played ending, Bobby went ahead in the match for the first time since game one.

GAME 4
English Opening

TIGRAN PETROSIAN   ROBERT FISCHER

1   P-QB4   . . .

Despite his success with 1 P-Q4 in
game two, Petrosian sticks to his
favorite strategy of varying his openings as much as possible.

1   . . .   P-QB4

And Fischer stays with the same defense he used in game two of the
Larsen match. He does not find it
necessary to go for an unbalanced
position by 1 . . . P-K4, but aims for
logical equality.

2   N-KB3   P-KN3

By playing this way, Bobby indicates
once again that he is not the least
bit concerned about the Maroczy
Bind which White can now head
directly into.

3   P-Q4   PxP

There is no way to avoid the exchange, since 3 . . . P-Q3, 4 PxP PxP,
5 QxQch KxQ leaves Black's king
without good shelter in the center,
and 3 . . . P-N3, 4 PxP PxP, 5 Q-Q5
compels an unsound pawn sacrifice.

4   NxP   N-QB3
5   P-K4   . . .

Opinions on this Maroczy formation
(pawns at K4 and QB4 versus pawn

at Q3) are still seesawing. Although
Fischer has been very successfully
pro-Maroczy in the past, lately he
has become contentedly anti-
Maroczy.

5   . . .   N-B3
6   N-QB3   P-Q3
7   P-B3   NxN

Since White's pawn bind restricts
Black's space, the exchange of a set
of minor pieces is advisable to avoid
getting cramped.

8   QxN   B-N2
9   B-K3   O-O
10   Q-Q2   Q-R4
11   R-B1   B-K3
12   P-QN3   . . .

The big question of this game is why
Petrosian did not play 12 N-Q5,
which Polugaevsky has been so
successful with. His game with
Ostojic, Belgrade 1970, went 12 . . .
QxQch, 13 KxQ BxN (13 . . . NxN,
14 BPxN and White will land a rook
on the seventh rank), 14 BPxB KR-B1,

15 RxRch RxR, 16 P-KN3! R-B2, 17
B-R3 N-Q2, 18 R-QB1 and White has
a tremendous endgame.

The answer, I think, is that no one
has tried 12 ... QxP! which leads to
an equal game after 13 NxPch K-R1,
14 B-K2 N-N1!, 15 NxN KxN, 16 B-Q4
BxB, 17 QxB Q-R4ch, 18 K-B2
Q-QB4, 19 KR-Q1 KR-Q1. Unless
Petrosian had spotted this, he would
have had no reason to hold back on
12 N-Q5.

The text move renews the threat of
N-Q5 by ruling out the reply ...
QxP.

12	...	KR-B1
13	B-K2	P-QR3
14	N-Q5	...

Now this move is nothing more
than a transparent draw offer, but
14 O-O would be answered by
14 ... P-QN4! with a free game. If
White wishes to retain any serious
chances for complications, he must
keep Black bottled up by P-QR4,
even though that weakens his own
queenside squares somewhat.

14	...	QxQch
15	KxQ	NxN
16	BPxN	B-Q2
17	RxRch	RxR
18	R-QB1	RxR
19	KxR	K-B1
20	K-B2	P-K3
	Drawn	

GAME 5
Petroff Defense

ROBERT FISCHER   TIGRAN PETROSIAN

1	**P-K4**	**P-K4**
2	**N-KB3**	**N-KB3**

Once again Petrosian switches defenses, although his two previous ones were a success for him. Without question, he could count on running into improvements from Bobby. Besides, he had perfect results with the present defense in his match with Spassky.

3	**NxP**	**P-Q3**

3 . . . NxP is an ancient blunder which loses a pawn after 4 Q-K2 P-Q4, 5 P-Q3 Q-K2, 6 PxN QxN, 7 PxP.

4	**N-KB3**	**NxP**
5	**P-Q4**	. . .

In the 1969 world championship match, Spassky relied on Lasker's favorite 5 Q-K2, but got nowhere with it after 5 . . . Q-K2, 6 P-Q3 N-KB3, 7 B-N5 QxQch, 8 BxQ B-K2, 9 N-B3 P-B3, 10 O-O-O N-R3!

5	. . .	**N-KB3**

By going before he is pushed, he makes it clear that he wants no part in the battle to maintain the knight outpost with 5 . . . P-Q4, which usually works out to a slight advantage for White. Petrosian never likes to be goaded into biting off more than he can chew.

6	**B-Q3**	**B-K2**

Najdorf criticized this, claiming that Black should hurry with 6 . . . B-N5 while he still has the chance. However, White would have a small advantage after 7 P-KR3 BxN, 8 QxB as well as after 7 . . . B-R4, 8 O-O B-K2, 9 R-K1 O-O, 10 QN-Q2 with the idea N-B1-N3.

7	**P-KR3**	**O-O**
8	**O-O**	**P-B3**

Fischer–Gheorghiu, Buenos Aires 1970, went 8 . . . R-K1, 9 P-B4 N-B3, 10 N-B3 P-KR3, 11 R-K1 B-B1, 12 RxR QxR, 13 B-B4 B-Q2, 14 Q-Q2 Q-B1, 15 P-Q5 N-QN5, 16 N-K4! with a very strong game for White.

With the text move, Petrosian aims for a compact position even though Black will remain somewhat short of maneuvering space. In such a position as this, it is unwise to play . . . P-Q4, since the result is a symmetrical setup, in which White is several tempos ahead.

9	**R-K1**	**QN-Q2**
10	**B-KB4**	**R-K1**
11	**P-B4**	**N-B1**
12	**N-B3**	**P-QR3**
13	**Q-N3?**	. . .

The queen is uselessly and awkwardly placed here, since the advance of the QNP cannot be prevented. To carry out his plan of doubling rooks on the king file, 13 Q-B2 was the move to retain his advantage.

Najdorf was strongly in favor of 13

P-Q5, which admittedly also favors White after 13 ... P-B4. But I think White's winning chances are greater by keeping the center fluid.

| 13 | ... | N-K3 |
| 14 | B-R2? | ... |

14 B-K3 was far better because now the bishop is out of action here, a matter which becomes increasingly dangerous as the game progresses. At K3 the bishop would stand in the way of White's projected doubled rooks on the king file, but that would be only a temporary hindrance, since the bishop would clear out whenever needed to unblock them.

| 14 | ... | B-B1 |
| 15 | R-K2 | P-QN4 |

A necessary and good way to free his position, carrying with it the possibility ... PxP, then ... P-Q4 and ... P-QB4!, for a sharp counterattack at the right moment.

16	Q-B2	B-N2
17	QR-K1	P-N3
18	P-QN4	...

Although this compels Black to break his queenside pawn front, in view of the threat to choke the QB by P-B5, it will be seen quickly enough that Petrosian is ready with some of the best defensive play of the match.

| 18 | ... | PxP |
| 19 | BxBP | ... |

| 19 | ... | N-B2 |

Accepting the pawn sacrifice by 19 ... P-Q4, 20 B-Q3 BxP is too dangerous, for 21 R-N1 BxN, 22 QxB R-R2, 23 Q-B1 not only leaves Black tied up on the queenside but threatens a king attack with Q-R6, B-K5, N-N5, etc. Nor would 21 ... Q-R4 work any better after 22 Q-N3 BxN, 23 QxQB NxP, 24 RxRch RxR, 25 N-N5 and the Black king cannot be defended since 25 ... R-B1 is useless in view of 26 B-Q6.
The text, however, is excellent, preparing ingenious counterplay.

20 B-QN3? ...

If Fischer was aware of what his opponent is up to, he would have driven back a knight by 20 RxR.

| 20 | ... | RxR |
| 21 | RxR | N/2-Q4! |

With an original attack on White's queenside pawns, Petrosian takes the initiative. It will quickly be seen why he does not fear doubled pawns on the queen file.

22　P-R3　　P-QR4!

And now he allows a passed QNP!

23　NxN　　　PxN
24　P-N5　　　. . .

White has alternatives, but Black's weird pawn formation gives him a grip of steel on the center squares.

24　. . .　　　P-R5!

Brilliantly demonstrating just how weak the White queenside really is. Now 25 BxRP is dangerous because . . . Q-R4, 26 B-N3 QxRP leaves the NP critically weak.

25　B-R2　　　Q-N3
26　Q-N1　　　. . .

The only move, for 26 Q-Q3? R-R4, 27 R-N2 B-QR3 had to be avoided.

26　. . .　　　R-R4

Najdorf criticized this move, claiming Petrosian's only chance to win lay in 26 . . . B-KR3, cutting off the White QB from reentering the game and threatening R-QB1-QB8ch. Still, I don't find the situation at all clear after 27 Q-N4! N-K5, 28 B-N1 when White threatens to consolidate by B-Q3 and R-B2.

27　R-N2　　　N-K5
28　B-KB4　　　N-B6
29　Q-B2　　　. . .

29　. . .　　　RxP

As difficult as Fischer's position looks, it seems he can defend it. 29 . . . NxB, 30 RxN QxNP, 31 R-N2 Q-Q2, 32 Q-N1 B-B3, 33 R-N8 R-N4, 34 QxR! BxQ, 35 B-R6 Q-K1, 36 RxQ BxR, 37 BxB KxB is a dead drawn endgame. On 32 . . . R-R2, White simply plays 33 R-N6 followed by Q-N4, and any thought of Black winning is a dream.

Also 29 . . . NxP, 30 B-Q2 R-R1, 31 Q-N1 B-B3, 32 BxP BxB, 33 RxN Q-B3, 34 R-N8 RxR, 35 QxR Q-R1, 36 QxQ BxQ is insufficient to win, although Black's bishops give him the edge. But Black must not try 34 . . . BxN?, 35 PxB QxP, 36 B-R6. The text move is virtually a draw offer.

30　RxR　　　NxR
31　QxP　　　Q-R3!

Getting rid of Fischer's only real weapon, the QRP.

32　QxQ　　　BxQ
33　B-K3　　　. . .

Neither B/2xP? nor P-QR4? nor B-B1? is playable since 33 ... N-B6! wins a piece.

| 33 | ... | NxRP |
| 34 | BxP | ... |

Petrosian offered a draw here, but Bobby insisted on playing a few more moves.

34	...	B-B5
35	B-B6	N-B7
36	B-Q2	B-K7
37	B-K4	BxN
38	BxN	Drawn

GAME 6
Nimzovich Opening

TIGRAN PETROSIAN   ROBERT FISCHER

1	N-KB3	P-QB4
2	P-QN3	P-Q4
3	B-N2	...

Petrosian won the ninth game of his match with Korchnoi using this rarely played opening, but the present game will do nothing for its popularity.

3	...	P-B3

This, the most aggressive reply, aims at a wholesale pawn advance in the center to jam the enemy QB. If there is to be a refutation of this opening, it can only be accomplished in this ambitious manner.

4	P-B4	...

As he did against Korchnoi, Petrosian transposes into a reversed Benoni, without accomplishing anything to improve the situation of the QB.

4	...	P-Q5
5	P-Q3	P-K4
6	P-K3	N-K2
7	B-K2	KN-B3

In case of PxP, BPxP, Black can bring the QN via Q2 to the powerful QB4 square, the reason for avoiding the routine QN-B3.

8	QN-Q2	B-K2
9	O-O	O-O
10	P-K4	...

There is no point in maintaining the center tension, since Black is too strong there.

10	...	P-QR3
11	N-K1	P-QN4

This advance is a preparation for Black to take the initiative on the queenside, but what is especially interesting is that Fischer does not bother to prevent the exchange of his better bishop by 11 ... B-K3, 12 B-N4 B-B2, instead relying on the fact that his remaining pieces will be superior to his opponent's because his pawns command more space.

12	B-N4	BxB
13	QxB	Q-B1
14	Q-K2	...

The exchange of queens would give Black a strong endgame since he could then operate immediately with such threats as QN-Q2, KR-N1, B-Q1-R4 and N-N3. In all this the awkward placement of White's QB is the culprit.

14	...	N-Q2
15	N-B2	R-N1
16	KR-B1	Q-K1
17	B-R3	...

This is a typical Petrosian do-nothing move. He wins a lot of games just fooling around, but here he has the wrong opponent for this kind of nonsense. However, his very passive opening makes it difficult for him to come up with any kind of positive plan.

17	...	**B-Q3**
18	**N-K1**	**P-N3**

Black is still not developed well enough for a kingside action, but he has all the time in the world to prepare further by Q-K3, K-R1, etc.

19 PxP? ...

Was this panic at the thought of what Fischer might do on the kingside, given enough time? Now Black's queenside qualitative pawn majority is mobilized for a breakthrough at QB5.

19	...	**PxP**
20	**B-N2**	**N-N3**
21	**N/1-B3**	**R-R1**
22	**P-QR3**	**Q-B2**
23	**Q-Q1**	**N-R4**
24	**P-QR4**	...

Best under the circumstances, since it would be absolutely fatal to wait for Black to develop further by KR-B1 before making his breakthrough.

24	...	**PxP**
25	**PxP**	**P-B5!**

Obtaining a passed QP as against White's weak isolated RP.

26	**PxP**	**N/3xBP**
27	**NxN**	**NxN**
28	**Q-K2**	...

The best defense because Black must now hurry his attack before having to contend with the strong consolidating N-K1-Q3.

28	...	**NxB**

Maybe Fischer would have done better to keep up the pressure by 28 ... KR-B1, since 29 N-K1 B-N5, 30 N-Q3 fails against 30 ... NxB!, and if 31 NxB, NxP should be an easy win.

29	**QxN**	**KR-N1**
30	**Q-R2**	...

Again the best defense because now Black can only play for a win by allowing White counterplay.

30	...	**B-N5**
31	**QxQch**	**KxQ**
32	**R-B7ch**	**K-K3!**

Now 33 RxP? loses to 33 ... B-B6, 34 R-KB1 RxP, followed by the exchange of rooks and the victorious march of the QP.

33 P-N4! ...

Opens air for the king, restrains ... P-KB4 and even threatens P-N5 in some variations. Petrosian is defending himself with might and main.

33	...	**B-B6**
34	**R-R2**	**R-QB1**

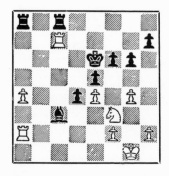

35	**RxR**	...

Najdorf and Suetin claim that 35 RxP draws, giving 35 ... R-B5, 36 R-QN7 R/5xP, 37 RxR RxR, 38 R-N6ch K-B2, 39 P-N5 P-Q6, 40 R-Q6! But 35 ... P-Q6, 36 R-QN7 B-R4, 37 R-N5 (not 37 R-N3? R-B7) R-B5, 38 R-Q5 RxKP, 39 RxP RxPch, 40 K-B1 R-QB1 is terrifically strong for Black.

35	...	RxR
36	P-R5	R-QR1
37	P-R6	R-R2
38	K-B1	P-N4

While the king runs after the QRP, he eliminates a pawn breakup by P-N5.

39	K-K2	K-Q3
40	K-Q3	K-B4
41	N-N1	K-N4
42	N-K2	...

This was the sealed move, leading to a fascinating endgame. The tricky point for Black is that he can never exchange rooks without permitting White a foolproof blockade of the position by bringing the knight to Q3.

| 42 | ... | B-R4 |
| 43 | R-N2ch | ... |

In my analysis at adjournment, I never even considered this move, but spent all my time on 43 N-B1 RxP, 44 N-N3 R-R1 (but not 44 ... K-N5, 45 N-R1 R-B3, 46 N-B2ch K-N6, 47 NxPch and draws. In this line, 46 ... K-N4, 47 N-R3ch K-B4, 48 N-B4 B-B6, 49 R-R1 also leaves Black tied up), 45 R-R1 R-R2, 46 R-R2 K-N5, 47 N-R1 R-QB2, 48 N-B2ch K-N6, 49 RxB R-B6ch, 50 K-Q2 RxNch, 51 K-K1 P-Q6, and wins.

43	...	KxP
44	R-N1	R-QB2
45	R-N2	B-K8

Simpler, I thought, was 45 ... R-B4 to break through to the sixth or eighth rank by ... B-N3, when the lone White rook cannot guard both the rook and knight files. The reply 46 R-B2 R-N4, 47 R-B6ch K-N2, 48 RxP fails against R-N6ch, 49 K-B4 P-Q6!

| 46 | P-B3 | K-R4 |

I still think this is needlessly complicated and stick by my suggestion in the previous note.

47	R-B2	R-QN2
48	R-R2ch	K-N4
49	R-N2ch	B-N5
50	R-R2	R-QB2
51	R-R1	R-B1
52	R-R7?	...

This gives Fischer just what he was playing for. White had nothing to do but hold his ground and wait for Black to reveal his plan.

52	. . .	B-R4
53	R-Q7	B-N3
54	R-Q5ch	B-B4
55	N-B1	K-R5
56	R-Q7	B-N5
57	N-K2	K-N6
58	R-QN7	R-QR1
59	RxP	. . .

This move is a preparation for resignation. He must have been counting on 59 N-B1ch K-N7, 60 N-K2, and saw at the last moment that 60 . . . R-R6ch!, 61 K-B4 P-Q6, 62 RxBch K-B7 queens the pawn by force.

59	. . .	R-R8
60	NxPch	. . .

60 N-N3 was useless—60 . . . R-R7, 61 N-B1 R-KB7 and it's all over.

60	. . .	PxN
61	KxP	R-Q8ch
62	K-K3	B-B4ch
63	K-K2	R-KR8
64	P-R4	K-B5
65	P-R5	R-R7ch
66	K-K1	K-Q6
	Resigns	

Wrapping It Up

Once Bobby was in gear nothing could stop him. Following on the heels of the excellent sixth game, he turned out a masterpiece in the seventh, the one that really won the match, breaking Petrosian's spirit and his resistance. The encounter was a fascinating confrontation which posed the question whether Petrosian, the strongest defensive player of our era, could hold a minimal disadvantage against Fischer, the winningest player of any era. Bobby's victory, therefore, was crushing, not only for its marvelous execution and not only because it gave him an overwhelming two-point lead in the match, but because it convinced Petrosian that he could no longer rely on holding such a position against him.

Before the eighth game, the Buenos Aires Armenian community staged a gala dinner party for their hero, attended by a thousand cheering people. That fired up Petrosian to such an extent that the usually smooth positional player went all out for attack, hoping desperately for a victory to put himself back into contention. But just when the grandmaster analysts in the press room were certain that he had something cooking, Bobby shot the whole thing down. Obviously dazed by the shattering turn of events, Petrosian failed even to hold the draw, futilely sacrificing a pawn to suffer his third defeat in a row. Fischer was as implacable in the defense as previously in the attack.

The ninth and last game clearly showed the after-effects of game seven. After Fischer had saddled Petrosian with doubled isolated pawns, the former World Champion was so sure he was staring the undertaker in the face that he refused even to consider passive defense, instead wildly sacrificing three pawns in a row for counterattack. Checkmates by the score were being hastily run up in the press room— but, of course, without consulting Bobby! Having gorged himself on the pawns, he sneered at the threats, steering his way deftly into a lopsidely won endgame for point and match.

Neither Petrosian's match temperament nor his experience in matches was up to taming America's young chess genius. The question to be answered in late spring is: Will Spassky fare any better?

GAME 7
Sicilian Defense

ROBERT FISCHER   TIGRAN PETROSIAN

1	P-K4	P-QB4
2	N-KB3	P-K3
3	P-Q4	PxP
4	NxP	P-QR3

Despite his successful opening with 4 ... N-QB3 in game one, Petrosian shies away from it a second time, not eager to see what new system Fischer has readied for him. I was curious too, but in the safe role of reporter, I could afford to be. Petrosian used the present Paulsen Variation in his 1969 match with Spassky, who could not find a way to obtain any initiative against it.

5	B-Q3	N-QB3
6	NxN	NPxN

By recapturing in this way, Black intends to set up a solid bulwark of center pawns for defense. Whether they will be an asset or an unwieldly burden is the problem this opening sets.

The recapture with the QP has the disadvantage of entering a symmetrical position two tempos behind.

7	O-O	P-Q4
8	P-QB4	. . .

This predilection of Fischer's is far stronger than Spassky's tame and ineffectual 8 N-Q2, since it puts the enemy center under fire at once. For Black to exchange a pawn now in order to exchange queens would be to undertake an inferior endgame with broken pawns.

8	. . .	N-B3
9	BPxP	BPxP
10	PxP	PxP

Neither of the piece recaptures to avoid the isolated pawn is satisfactory. 10 ... QxP, 11 N-B3 Q-B3, 12 B-K2! gives Black great problems in development. 10 ... NxP, 11 B-K4 B-N2, 12 N-B3 B-K2, 13 Q-R3ch Q-Q2, 14 QxQch KxQ, 15 R-Q1 wins a pawn. In the latter line, Najdorf claimed an improvement by 11 ... R-R2, but I have little confidence in the Black game after 12 Q-B3 R-Q2, 13 N-Q2, with the idea N-B4-K5.

11	N-B3	B-K2
12	Q-R4ch	Q-Q2?!

Better was 12 ... B-Q2, 13 Q-Q4 B-K3, 14 B-KB4 O-O, 15 QR-B1, with a small but clear advantage for White. Fischer's original queen maneuver puts teeth into the whole variation.

13 R-K1! . . .

Bobby refuses to be inveigled into the unclear consequences of snatching the Exchange: 13 B-QN5 PxB, 14 QxR O-O, 15 Q-R5 P-Q5, 16 NxP B-N2.

The text move is positionally powerful, practically forcing the queen exchange which gives the knight a tempo to bear down on the weak QB5 and QN6 squares. In such a choice as this, one can clearly observe the Capablanca-like quality of Fischer's chess.

In reply, 13 ... P-Q5 would merely lose a pawn after 14 QxQch BxQ, 15 N-K2 B-QN5, 16 R-Q1 B-QB4, 17 B-KB4, followed by 18 B-K5.

13	...	QxQ
14	NxQ	B-K3
15	B-K3	O-O
16	B-QB5	...

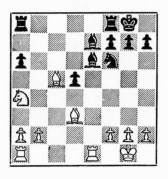

Once again Fischer prefers the simple and clear positional theme of removing the defender of the weak dark squares to the obscure complications resulting from pawn grabbing. According to my analysis, his judgment was perfect, since 16 N-N6 QR-N1, 17 BxP N-N5!, 18 N-R4 (18 B-Q4? B-Q1, 19 N-R4 R-N5, 20 B-B5 RxN, 21 BxR KxB, 22 B-K2 B-B3 is too strong for Black, who already has two pieces for rook and pawn and a

dangerous initiative) 18 ... R-R1, 19 B-QN5 KR-N1, 20 B-B6 (20 N-B3?! B-B3!, 21 B-B6! P-Q5!, 22 BxR PxN!, 23 B-K4 PxP, 24 QR-Q1 NxB, 25 RxN BxP, 26 B-N1, and, to say the least, White has no winning chances at all) 20 ... R-R3, 21 QR-B1 NxB, 22 PxN (22 RxN? B-N4) B-N4 (threatening ... P-Q5!), 23 R-B5 R-QB1, 24 B-N5 RxR, 25 NxR RxP, and White will be glad to have a draw.

16	...	KR-K1
17	BxB	RxB
18	P-QN4	...

More accurate than 18 N-B5, which would have allowed ... P-QR4. Since Black cannot now play that without allowing P-N5, producing a terrible passed pawn, he is stuck with two weak isolated pawns.

18	...	K-B1
19	N-B5	B-B1
20	P-B3	...

Fischer is setting up the decisive king march, K-B2-K3-Q4.

| 20 | ... | R/2-R2? |

This attempt to develop the bishop is refuted at once. Black's only chance to hold this game.is 20 ... RxRch, 21 RxR N-K1. Then the king can hold K2 and the knight QB2 to keep the rook out, and Black can hope for ... N-B2-K3 and ... K-K2-Q3. But Petrosian does not realize how badly off he is.

| 21 | R-K5! | ... |

Preventing the knight maneuver which was Petrosian's only slim hope.

21   ...   B-Q2

22   NxBch!   ...

This exchange, which wins the game, was completely overlooked by the press room group of grandmaster analysts. Najdorf, in fact, criticized it(!), suggesting instead the incomparably weaker 22 P-QR4.
Now, in addition to his potential outside passed pawn, Bobby has a bishop vastly superior to the knight and his rooks will possess the only open files.

22   ...   RxN
23   R-QB1   R-Q3

Allowing Fischer to gain the seventh rank was a painful decision, but the alternatives were equally grim. If 23 ... P-N3 (defending against BxQRP!), 24 R-B6 followed by P-N4 and P-KN5, winning the QP. Fischer's

fantastic efficiency shows itself clearly here.

24   R-B7   N-Q2
25   R-K2   P-N3
26   K-B2   P-KR4

This and the next move are merely additional weaknesses, but Petrosian is in Zugzwang. If 26 ... R-K1, 27 RxRch, KxR, 28 R-R7, N-N3, 29 P-QR3, N-N1, 30 K-K3 and the king will get to QB5 since Black's N-B3ch can be nullified by R-R8 at the right moment.

27   P-B4   P-R5
28   K-B3!   ...

By threatening to pick up the KRP with the king, Bobby forces the following pawn advance, which totally wrecks the defense of both the sixth and seventh ranks.

28   ...   P-B4
29   K-K3   P-Q5ch

It was either this, which allows the bishop to rake the white squares, or permit the king to reach the dominating Q4 square.

30   K-Q2   N-N3

Going down with his boots on, but what point was there in passively awaiting B-B4, K-Q3, R-K6, etc.?

31   R/2-K7   N-Q4
32   R-B7ch   K-K1
33   R-QN7   NxBP

This is delirious desperation, but 33
... R-N3, 34 RxR NxR, 35 R-KN7
K-B1, 36 RxP N-Q4, 37 B-B4 wins
easily, as does 34 ... KxR, 35 B-B4.

34 B-B4   Resigns

There is nothing to be done about
the threat of R-KN7 or R-KR7, completing the mating net.

GAME 8
Tarrasch Defense

TIGRAN PETROSIAN   ROBERT FISCHER

1	P-Q4	N-KB3
2	P-QB4	P-K3
3	N-KB3	P-Q4

With a two-point lead and the match virtually in the bag, a staid classical defense is more in order than the more ambitious Gruenfeld or King's Indian.

4	N-B3	P-B4
5	P-K3	...

On 5 BPxP, Fischer would undoubtedly have replied 5 ... NxP, heading for the semi-classical Queen's Gambit, which has long been a favorite of his. The text move brings the game into the Tarrasch Defense symmetrical variation, which is as hoary a line as can be found these days. Tarrasch considered it the ideal Queen's Gambit, but he never got anyone to agree. Why didn't Petrosian have something more potent ready for such an occasion?

5	...	N-B3
6	P-QR3	N-K5?!

But this is somewhat risky, helping White build up a center that can be used for attack. Maintaining symmetry by 6 ... P-QR3 is simpler and adequate.

7	Q-B2	NxN
8	PxN	...

Against Korchnoi, Petrosian played the weaker 8 QxN and drew very quickly, but the text move should give attacking chances.

8	...	B-K2
9	B-N2	O-O
10	B-Q3	P-KR3
11	O-O	N-R4
12	N-Q2?!	...

With every piece exchange, the attacking possibilities are diminished. Correct in this type of position is 12 BPxP KPxP, 13 N-K5 B-Q3, 14 P-KB4 with excellent chances.

12	...	PxBP
13	NxP	NxN
14	BxN	P-QN3
15	P-K4	...

Here 15 Q-K4 R-N1, 16 B-Q3 P-B4, 17 Q-B4 B-Q3, 18 Q-B3 B-N2, 19 Q-K2 P-K4 rebounds to White's disadvantage. 15 QR-Q1 was suggested too, but 15 ... PxP, 16 BPxP B-N2, 17 Q-K2 R-B1, 18 B-N3 B-Q4 leads nowhere.

15	...	B-N2
16	Q-K2	R-B1
17	B-N3	P-QN4!

Petrosian's buildup is beginning to look menacing, but Fischer is already gearing to meet it. The point of this is revealed on the twentieth move.

18 P-KB4 . . .

Everyone, including me, was worried now about how Fischer could defend against the terrible threat of P-B5, bringing everything but the kitchen sink to bear on Black's KB2 after . . . PxP, RxP.

18 . . . Q-N3!

This stops Petrosian's attack for one move, since 19 P-B5? PxQP, 20 PxQP P-K4 seals the KB file and also wins the QP.

| 19 | K-R1 | PxP |
| 20 | PxP | P-N5!! |

And this brings Petrosian's attack to a screeching halt with the nasty threat of 21 . . . B-R3 as well as 21 . . . PxP.

| 21 | PxP | BxNP |
| 22 | P-Q5 | . . . |

This move was unjustly criticized, but it should be sufficient to hold the draw, 22 R-B3 was no better since 23 . . . B-B6!, 24 BxB QxB, 25 B-K1 Q-B7 also gives Black a small edge.

| 22 | . . . | B-B6 |
| 23 | BxB | RxB |

24 B-B2? . . .

He could not help losing the attack against Bobby's sharp defensive play, but he need not lose his head too. This pawn sacrifice just loses the game, whereas 24 B-R2 PxP, 25 BxP BxB, 26 PxB, while not beautiful, should suffice to halve the point. On 24 . . . R-K6, Najdorf pointed out that 25 Q-Q2 RxP, 26 PxP PxP, 27 P-B5 would be good enough to draw.

| 24 | . . . | PxP |
| 25 | P-K5 | R-K6 |

Bobby does not miss the finesse. If at once 25 . . . P-Q5, then 26 B-Q3 keeps the Black pieces at bay and may lead to some attacking chances.

26	Q-Q2	P-Q5
27	QR-N1	Q-R3
28	R-B2	. . .

If 28 QxP BxPch, 29 KxB R-K7ch, 30 R-B2 Q-B3ch, 31 K-N1 QxB, the ending should be an easy win because of the exposed White king.

28	. . .	R-Q1
29	K-N1	B-K5

The exchange clears the way for the passed pawn.

30	BxB	RxB
31	P-R3	P-Q6
32	R-N3	Q-B5
33	R-N2	. . .

Petrosian spots the trap: 33 R-QB3 Q-Q5, 34 K-B1 R-K7!, and wins at least a rook.

33	. . .	R/1-Q5!

Forcing 34 P-N3 and the consequent exposure of the king, which makes the win effortless.

34	P-N3	R-Q4
35	K-R2	R-N4
36	R-R2	R-N8
37	P-N4	. . .

37 RxP?? R-K7, 38 RxR PxR, 39 Q-Q8ch K-R2, 40 R-R8 R-R8ch! gives mate in two. The text move is an unfortunate necessity to meet the threat of mate by 37 . . . R/5-K8.

37	. . .	R-K7!

The sharpest, quickest finish.

38	RxR	PxR
39	QxP	QxPch
40	K-N2	R-N6!
	Resigns	

The king is now helpless, for 41 Q-KB2 Q-K5ch, 42 K-R2 R-KB6!, 43 Q-KN2 Q-B5ch, 44 K-N1 (44 K-R1 R-B8ch) 44 . . . R-KN6 wins the queen. Here 42 K-N1 R-N8ch, 43 K-R2 Q-R8ch, 44 K-N3 R-N8ch, 45 K-B4 (45 K-R4 P-N4ch and mate in two) 45 . . . R-KB8 leads only to the same result.

GAME 9
French Defense

ROBERT FISCHER   TIGRAN PETROSIAN

1 P-K4	P-K3
2 P-Q4	P-Q4
3 N-QB3	N-QB3

This is really a variation of the old Nimzovich Defense by transposition: 1 P-K4 N-QB3, 2 P-Q4 P-Q4, 3 N-QB3 P-K3. Its idea is to get White to advance P-K5 and then to counter with ... P-KB3.

4 N-B3	N-B3
5 PxP	. . .

Fischer's ultra-dry classicism shows itself once again. He is going to base his game strategy on giving Black doubled QB pawns.

5 . . .	PxP
6 B-QN5	B-KN5
7 P-KR3	BxN

Of course 7 ... B-R4, 8 P-KN4 B-N3, 9 N-K5 would be powerful for White.

8 QxB	B-K2
9 B-N5	. . .

9 . . .	P-QR3

This was criticized as an unnecessary waste of a tempo, but is it? 9 ... O-O, 10 O-O-O (10 BxKN BxB, 11 NxP NxP, 12 NxBch K-R1!! gets White nowhere, except into trouble) 10 ... N-K5, 11 BxB QxB, 12 NxP Q-N4ch, 13 N-B4 NxBP, 14 BxN NxKR, 15 BxP QR-N1, 16 RxN RxB, 17 QxR QxNch, 18 K-N1 QxP, 19 QxBP leaves White a pawn ahead. 16 ... Q-N4 can be tried, but after 17 B-Q5 QxPch, 18 K-Q2 QxQPch, 19 N-Q3 QR-Q1, 20 B-N3 P-B4, 21 P-B3, the pieces are to be preferred to the rook plus pawn. Also, 10 ... P-QR3, 11 B-QR4 P-N4, 12 B-N3 P-N5, 13 BxN PxN, 14 QxBP BxB, 15 QxN, and White will be two pawns ahead with an easy win.

10 BxNch	PxB
11 O-O	O-O
12 KR-K1	P-R3
13 B-R4	Q-Q2

Instead, 13 ... R-K1 only gets Black into a bad pin after 14 R-K3 N-K5, 15 BxB QxB, 16 QR-K1.

14 R-K2	P-QR4
15 QR-K1	B-Q1
16 P-QN3	R-N1
17 N-R4	N-K5
18 BxB	QRxB
19 Q-B4!	. . .

Although it looked superficially as though Petrosian was freeing his position, Bobby has kept the bind. P-KB3 followed by R-K7 or N-B5 or both is the threat.

19	. . .	Q-Q3
20	QxQ	PxQ
21	P-QB4!	. . .

Just when it appeared that Petrosian had fixed up his pawn weaknesses, Bobby forces a new doubleton that is even worse.

21	. . .	N-B3
22	R-QB1	R-N1

Black cannot avoid weak pawns by 22 . . . R-QB1, since 23 R/2-B2 is unanswerable.

23	PxP	PxP
24	P-B3	N-R4

Petrosian's pawn position is too awful to look at, much less defend, so he gambles everything on a coffe-house kingside demonstration. He can hardly be blamed for that.

25	R-B6	N-B5
26	R-Q2	KR-K1
27	RxP	R-K8ch
28	K-B2	R-KR8
29	K-N3	. . .

He must anticipate . . . R-K1, when . . . NxPch would become a threat.

29	. . .	N-R4ch
30	K-R4	P-N3
31	RxP	R-K1
32	RxP	R/1-K8
33	N-B3	N-B5
34	K-N4	N-K3
35	R-K5	P-B4ch
36	K-N3	P-B5ch
37	K-R4	K-R2
38	N-K4	P-N4ch
39	K-N4	N-N2

At last Petrosian has conjured up some real threats: 40 . . . K-N3 and 41 . . . P-R4 mate, or 40 . . . RxP, and if 41 KxR R-R8ch, 42 K-N4 R-R5 mate. But it's all too late.

40   NxPch!   . . .

This winds up everything neatly.

40	. . .	` PxN
41	RxR	RxR
42	KxP	N-K3ch
43	K-B5	R-K7
44	RxR	NxPch
45	K-K5	NxR
46	P-QR4	Resigns

Chapter IV

FISCHER VS. SPASSKY

Fischer Falls Behind—Then Catches Up

The match of the century was supposed to have started Sunday, July 2nd, but it did not. Fischer had failed to show up in Reykjavik after two abortive attempts to board Loftleidir flights earlier in the week. Both times, press photographers had driven a camera-shy challenger back to New York City following brief appearances at Kennedy International Airport.

Then Bobby announced he was holding out for 30 percent of the gate receipts for both himself and Spassky. The Icelanders could not agree, since they had earmarked that anticipated income for expenses connected with the staging of the match.

Suddenly, a British chess promoter and financier, James Slater, came forward with a dazzling surprise $125,000 donation to the prize fund, matching the amount the Icelandic Chess Federation had put up, and setting the winner's slice of the purse at $156,250 and the loser's at $93,750.

But even this record purse did not bring Bobby to Reykjavik, although it more than made up for what the share of the admissions would have come to. For whatever reason, it took hours of persuasion by William Lombardy, Fischer's last-minute choice as second, and attorney Paul Marshall to get Bobby to go through with the match.

After successive postponements granted, first to Fischer, then to Spassky, the first game finally began July 11th. With the Black pieces, Fischer adopted the Nimzo-Indian Defense, equalizing easily by an innovation on his fourteenth move. But he went haywire on his twenty-ninth, snatching a pawn which permitted Spassky to trap and win his bishop. The two pawns he got for the piece should have given him considerable drawing chances, but he handled the defense weakly and, in the adjourned session, Spassky put away the point with effortless technique to lead 1–0.

Chief Referee Lothar Schmid stopped Fischer's clock, which registered one elapsed hour, and awarded the second game to Spassky by forfeit. Bobby had boycotted the game over the noise he claimed the television cameras were making. With the score 2–0 against him, nobody expected Bobby to continue the match which he had been so reluctant to enter in the first place. But a massive telegram campaign, a phone call from presidential advisor Henry Kissinger, and redoubled efforts by his friends and advisors here made him change his mind and cancel his plane reservation home.

Although he had had little sleep, he shifted to the belligerent Benoni as Black in the third game and ran Spassky off the board. After Bobby's radically powerful 11 ... N-R4, he shortly began wrapping up one of the most one-sided victories in a championship match. It was his first defeat of Boris in his career; previously Spassky had beaten him four times, including the match opener. The score was now 2–1 for Spassky.

Spassky got off a surprise Sicilian in the fourth game, for which his analysis team had prepared him well. A brilliant pawn sacrifice at the sixteenth move gave him a raging attack, but he still could not find a decisive way through the challenger's trenchant defense. The game is still the subject of continuing debate, no one yet having found a clear conclusion as to what the result should have been. After the players agreed to a draw, the score was 2½–1½ with Spassky still leading.

In the fifth game, Bobby again chose the Nimzo-Indian, varying with Huebner's 6 ... BxNch, which dogmatically offers chances to both sides. Once again, as in the third contest, an unexpected and unusual knight move at Fischer's eleventh turn brought down Spassky's ambitious attempt to seize the initiative. Spassky was slowly being pushed back on the defensive, but no immediate win was in sight when the champion blundered under the pressure at his twenty-seventh move. Fischer hit him with instant crunch, levelling the match at 2½–2½.

To overcome a two-point deficit against the World Champion in only three games is fantastic. But Fischer's play is too sharp for Boris. Fischer's do-it-yourself opening analysis has been vastly superior to what the entire army of Soviet analysts could give Boris. The one time the Russian had a success in the opening, in the fourth game, Fischer's remarkable defensive middle game play denied him the point.

When Bobby gets going, the colors do not matter. Spassky will not be able to hang on in this match unless he can find some way of defending against Fischer's defenses. Despite the first two minus points, I am still sticking to my earlier prediction of 12½–8½ for Fischer. *(R.B.)*

The first encounter in a match has its special significance. After their long period of preparation and intensive, thorough theoretical work, both players have the chance to try out everything in practice for the first time. The World Champion has to decide right at the first move whether to choose a close game by advancing his queen's pawn two squares, or whether to strive, by 1 P-K4, for spirited piece play in the opening stage.

In either case, Fischer's previous openings repertory was not particularly suited for a match for the World Championship. Against 1 P-Q4, the challenger always preferred to defend by the super-sharp King's Indian or the Modern Benoni variations, while against 1 P-K4, his predilection was to let himself in for neck-breaking Sicilian adventures. In tournaments with participants of various playing strengths, these tactics brought him many successes. However, when confronted by a well-prepared opponent of his own caliber, his striving for complications at any price could be very dangerous.

The chess world waited tensely to see what tactics Fischer would choose in the opening. Would he remain true to his narrow repertory, well known also to his opponent, or would he show more flexibility in his selection of openings this time? As we know now, the challenger took the second alternative and, a number of times, ventured on what were for him completely new directions.

The first match game was not characteristic of the Reykjavik series. Perhaps it was because of the complications before the start and the nerve-wearing situations associated with them that both grandmasters played the opening of the game so carefully. After about twenty moves, several reporters already had their stories on the "short draw" finished. However, it didn't go that way. About ten years ago, when the attempt was made to eliminate peaceful, gutless draws by the infamous 30-move rule, ex-World Champion Mikhail Tal said, "If two chessmasters do not want to do battle with each other, then a brigade of flame-throwers would not help." Fortunately for chess, it also works the other way around: In the event both players are interested in a fight, they each can often find new possibilities even in so called "dead draw positions," setting new problems for the opponent. From the point of view of fighting chess, the match in Iceland was unique. *(I.N.)*

GAME 1
July 11, 1972
Nimzo–Indian Defense

BORIS SPASSKY   BOBBY FISCHER

1   P-Q4   . . .

Whoever has a choice has worries!
One of the problems which confronted the champion was: From
which could he hope for a more
long-enduring initiative, 1 P-K4 or
1 P-Q4? *(I.N.)*
The consensus was that this would
be Spassky's choice to open. If a
Fischer opponent opens 1 P-K4, he
must be prepared for all the tortuous
labyrinths of the Najdorf Sicilian,
which Bobby knows better than
anyone. *(R.B.)*

1   . . .   N-KB3

More than 3,000 spectators waited
seven long minutes for this knight
move, which finally opened the
"match of the century." As in almost
every game, Spassky was on time, but
Fischer regularly came several
minutes late. *(I.N.)*

2   P-QB4   P-K3

Before this game, Spassky and
Fischer had met five times and twice
the American had chosen the Gruenfeld Defense with the Black pieces.
Spassky won both contests, although
Black stood well in the opening
phase in Santa Monica 1966 as well
as in Siegen 1970. Perhaps this type

of position does not especially suit
Fischer—in Reykjavik the challenger
did not want to fight a duel with
Gruenfeld weapons. *(I.N.)*
Many of the fans, including me, were
excitedly expecting a Gruenfeld, with
which Bobby had lost to Spassky two
times running, at the Siegen
Olympiad 1970 and at the Piatigorsky
Cup 1966. At least in the Siegen
game, Bobby had the opening advantage and only went astray later. But,
for this opening game, Bobby adopts
a straightforward defensive strategy,
perhaps saving a "grudge Gruenfeld"
for later. *(R.B.)*

3   N-KB3   . . .

An invitation to 3 . . . P-QN3 and the
Queen's Indian Defense. *(I.N.)*

3   . . .   P-Q4

No! *(I.N.)*
White's last move leads to a more
leisurely game than 3 N-QB3, and
Black can equalize against it with the
text reply or with 3 . . . P-QN3,
envisaging a Queen's Indian. *(R.B.)*

4   N-B3   B-N5

A second little surprise; ordinarily
Fischer prefers to head into the
so-called "improved" Tarrasch Defense, 4 . . . P-B4. *(I.N.)*
In the past Fischer has often played
the Semi-Tarrasch, 4 . . . P-B4, with
excellent results, but the Nimzo-
Indian which arises after the text

move is possibly the safest defense in the Queen's Pawn openings. *(R.B.)*

5   P-K3   . . .

According to theory, 5 PxP PxP, 6 B-N5 is more active, but naturally the choice of this or that continuation in so early a stage of play is a matter of taste. *(I.N.)*

5	. . .	O-O
6	B-Q3	P-B4
7	O-O	N-B3

7 . . . QPxP, 8 BxP QN-Q2 is also played here, but the text move is more usual and leads to positions which are thoroughly analysed in many books on the openings. *(I.N.)* What has been called the normal main line of the Nimzo-Indian has now been reached. Everything is symmetrical except the positions of the opposing king bishops, but that difference is quite enough to create exciting possibilities for the middle game. *(R.B.)*

8   P-QR3   B-R4

This retreat can lead to more complicated variations than the popular 8 . . . BxN. *(I.N.)*
The chief continuation used to be 8 . . . BxN, ceding the two bishops to White in the hope that his unwieldy pawn position would prevent him from developing any real initiative, but 8 . . . B-R4, which has been popularized in the last few years by Olafsson and Larsen, has a different

objective. By keeping all the tension in the position, Black challenges White to find a smooth way to complete his mobilization. Playing the text move at once, instead of interpolating 8 . . . PxBP, 9 BxP, may be an improvement over Larsen's line proper, which allows White a greater range of choices. *(R.B.)*

9   N-K2   . . .

The main variation continues 9 PxQP KPxP, 10 PxP BxN, 11 PxB B-N5. Spassky prefers, however, to make so called "second best" moves in the opening from time to time, in order to avoid twenty moves of a well-trodden path. According to so-called general principles, it is not correct to move an already developed piece again, and especially not to remove it from the center. On the other hand, the knight move is based on the consideration that, since the Black dark-squared bishop is absent from the defense of the king's wing, White might be able to organize a successful attack there under favorable circumstances. In this event, the knight would be excellently placed at KN3. *(I.N.)*
For the first time, White is really threatening to win a pawn by PxBP, which earlier was answerable by . . . BxN, PxB Q-R4. The attempt to set up an attacking formation by 9 PxQP KPxP, 10 N-K5 would have worked out badly after 10 . . . R-K1, 11 P-B4? PxP, 12 NxN NPxN, 13 PxP

B-N3, when the QP is awkward to protect and Black controls all the good squares. *(R.B.)*

9	. . .	PxBP
10	BxP	B-N3

Fischer wants to clarify the situation and is willing to lose a tempo for that purpose. Botvinnik suggests 10 . . . PxP, 11 PxP B-B2, while the elastic 10 . . . Q-K2 also comes strongly into consideration (11 PxP QxP and the White king bishop hangs). *(I.N.)*

11 PxP!   . . .

Regardless of the simplification, this is the correct method, for White is better developed and has more space. He can justifiably try to exploit these advantages even after the exchange of queens. *(I.N.)*

11 . . .   QxQ

The exchange of queens, even though furthering White's development, was the only course possible. After 11 . . . BxP, White has at his disposal the strong continuation, 12 Q-B2. *(I.N.)*

12	RxQ	BxP
13	P-QN4	B-K2

The Black king bishop has made 5 out of the first 13 moves! Therefore, it is no wonder that Black has to struggle with difficulties. *(I.N.)*

14 B-N2   B-Q2!

The best counter, tactically based on the variation 15 BxN BxB, 16 RxB? BxR. Only with this move does the real game begin, for up to White's fourteenth move, this game repeats the order of moves of Spassky–Krogius, Riga 1958, in which Black continued with 14 . . . P-QN3 and lost in the end. *(I.N.)*
This innovation improves on Krogius's 14 . . . P-QN3, which is not only too slow, but weakens the squares on the queenside. It seems that White's slightly better endgame development might lead to something, but Bobby shows that the Black formation is unbreachable. *(R.B.)*

15 QR-B1?   . . .

Too quiet. Botvinnik suggests 15 K-B1, which, naturally, is quite logical (in the endgame the king belongs in the center, as a rule). However, the most energetic was 15 P-K4! KR-Q1, 16 P-K5 N-K1, 17 N-N3 and his advantage in space assures White a persistent initiative. *(I.N.)*

| 15 | ... | KR-Q1 |
| 16 | N/2-Q4 | ... |

Now the position becomes totally simplified, but after the tame fifteenth move, White had no more active a plan at his disposal. *(I.N.)*

16	...	NxN
17	NxN	B-R5
18	B-N3	BxB

Inaccurate would be 18 ... RxN, 19 BxB and, with the two bishops, White would stand better. *(I.N.)*

19	NxB	RxRch
20	RxR	R-QB1
21	K-B1	K-B1
22	K-K2	...

Also possible was 22 BxN BxB, 23 R-Q7 R-B6, and now, not 24 N-B5 P-QN3, but 24 N-Q2. Naturally, the balance of the position would remain undisturbed. *(I.N.)*

| 22 | ... | N-K5 |

Further simplification is virtually forced by this move, which makes the drawish character of the position evident. *(R.B.)*
The text move is somewhat more active than 22 ... R-B7ch, 23 R-Q2 RxRch. *(I.N.)*

| 23 | R-QB1 | RxR |
| 24 | BxR | P-B3 |

This move seems to be superfluous here; a shade more accurate was 24 ... K-K1 *(I.N.)*

| 25 | N-R5 | ... |

According to Botvinnik, White could also play 25 P-B3 N-Q3, 26 N-B5, but that's all a question of taste. *(I.N.)*

25	...	N-Q3
26	K-Q3	B-Q1
27	N-B4	...

White could also quietly play 27 B-N2 here, because 27 ... BxN, 28 PxB rather favors White. *(I.N.)*

27	...	B-B2
28	NxN	BxN
29	P-N5	...

It is a good idea to put as many pawns as possible on squares the opposite color of the bishop. There is really nothing to play for now and the offer of a draw would have been quite appropriate. But ... *(R.B.)*
A good positional move, preventing ... P-QN4. *(I.N.)*

| 29 | ... | BxKRP? |

ncredible! Fischer made this move very quickly, and it may be assumed that he erred in his precalculations. Even if a draw is still to be found by later analysis, this move must be stamped as an outright blunder. The routine continuation, 29 ... K-K2, leads to a completely equal position. *(I.N.)*

Bobby played this blunder hastily and nervously, probably basing it on a miscalculation at the thirty-second move. The wonder is that, even though he now loses the bishop for two pawns, he would have been able to draw had it not been for his later mistakes. *(R.B.)*

30   P-N3   . . .

The bishop is now lost and the only question is whether Black can activate his king during the time which White must expend hunting the piece down. *(I.N.)*

30	. . .	P-KR4
31	K-K2	P-R5
32	K-B3	K-K2

The other possibility, 32 ... P-R6, 33 K-N4 B-N8, 34 KxP BxP, only costs time, because after 35 B-Q2!, Black cannot rescue the bishop. *(I.N. & R.B.)*

A spirited attempt to save the game is 32 ... P-N4, 33 K-N2 P-N5, 34 KxB P-R6 and the strong passed KRP demands continual surveillance. The resulting position is, nevertheless, won for White, though not without difficulty, for example: 35 B-N2 P-B4, 36 P-B3 K-K2, 37 PxP PxP, 38 B-K5 P-R3, 39 P-R4 PxP, 40 PxP K-Q2, 41 P-K4 K-K2, 42 K-N1 K-Q2, 43 K-B2 K-K2, 44 B-Q4 K-Q3, 45 K-B1, P-K4, 46 B-N1 K-B2 and White can make no progress.
Correct is 35 P-K4! K-K2, 36 P-B3 P-B4, 37 P-K5 P-R3, 38 P-R4 RPxP, 39 RPxP K-B2, 40 K-N1 K-N3, 41 K-B2 K-B2, 42 B-K3 K-N3, 43 K-B1 K-R4 (43 ... PxP, 44 B-N1), 44 B-N1 K-N4, 45 B-R2 K-N3, 46 K-K2 and Black's defensive resources are exhausted. *(I.N.)*

33	K-N2	PxP
34	PxP	BxP
35	KxB	K-Q3

In the resulting position, a win for White is still not simple to prove. The World Champion maneuvers very skilfully and increases his advantage with every move. *(I.N.)*

36	P-R4	K-Q4

Black has no time to attack the White pawns on the queen's wing, for example: 36 ... K-B4, 37 B-R3ch K-B5, 38 B-B8 P-KN3, 39 B-K7 K-N6, 40 P-R5 K-R5, 41 P-N6 P-R3, 42 BxP KxP, 43 K-B4 KxP, 44 K-K5 P-R4, 45 KxP, or 39 ... P-B4, 40 K-B4 K-N6, 41 P-R5 K-R5, 42 P-N6 P-R3, 43 K-N5 KxP, 44 KxP KxP, 45 K-B6, and, in both cases, the king's pawn guarantees the win. *(I.N.)*

37 B-R3   K-K5?

37 ... K-B5 leads only into the variations dealt with in the previous note. It appears more difficult for White to win after 37 ... P-K4. Nevertheless, the positions arising from this thrust should also be won for White. For example: 38 K-N4 P-KN3, 39 B-K7 P-B4ch, 40 K-N5 P-B5 (40 ... K-K5, 41 B-B5 P-R3, 42 P-N6 K-Q4, 43 B-N4 achieves nothing), 41 PxP PxP, 42 KxBP K-B5, 43 K-K4 K-N6, 44 K-Q5 KxP, 45 K-B4 K-R4, 46 B-B5 P-R3, 47 P-N6

P-N4, 48 B-K3 P-N5, 49 K-B5, with the capture of the QNP. However, 37 ... P-R3! will enable Black to rescue himself, for after 38 P-N6 Black can successfully attack the queenside pawns, while on any other move he can exchange pawns, relying on the reduced material to keep the draw. For example, 38 P-N6 K-B3, 39 P-R5 K-Q4, and White cannot win. *(I.N.)*

38 B-B5   P-R3

If 38 ... P-QN3?, 39 BxP! PxB, 40 P-R5 and the game is White's. *(R.B. & I.N.)*

39 P-N6!   ...

Without this pawn, White cannot hope for a win. *(I.N.)*
This is the only chance for further play. If White exchanges pawns, he will be left with a RP of the wrong color, since Black can always liquidate the kingside pawns by ... P-K4, ... P-B4 and ... P-B5. If White allows ... PxP, PxP, the drawing method is as follows: Black eliminates the kingside pawns as before and plays ... K-Q4-B5, forcing White's last pawn to N6. Then Black continues ... K-Q4-B3-Q2-B1 and White can do no more than stalemate him. *(R.B.)*

39 ...   P-B4

Tougher resistance was possible by 39 ... P-K4, 40 K-N4 P-N3. *(I.N.)*

40 K-R4!   P-B5?

The playing hall being prepared for the Match of the Century between American challenger Bobby Fischer and world champion Boris Spassky.

The Russian contingent leaves a press conference at the Loftleidir Hotel on July 1st after hearing of Fischer's delay in arriving in Iceland. (l. to r., Ivo Nei, Boris Spassky, Nikolai Krogius, Efim Geller).

exclusive photographs by Chester Fox

Dr. Max Euwe formally apologizes to the Russian contingent for Fischer, who did not arrive for the 1st game. (l. to r., Nei, Euwe, Geller).

a tense moment during the 4th game Spassky awaits Fischer's move.

cher looks at audience during the 1st game. He later claimed somebody was unwrapping candy and mally complained to the referee.

Before the start of the 6th game Spassky awaits Fischer's incessantly late arrival.

At game #14 Spassky brings orange juice the chessboard.

Fischer, accompanied by his second, Father William Lombardy, leaves the hall after the 12th game.

Fatigue and determination vie in the 13th game.

During the 14th game Fischer calls for the referee because someone's chair squeaked.

During the 15th game, Fischer takes a recess.

During the 19th game, Spassky moves as Fis notes it down.

Fischer takes a pawn as Spassky notes the m during the 19th game.

In the press room, Harold Schonberg of *The New York Times*, International Master Ingi Johansson of Iceland, and Robert Byrne cover the match (July 18th).

Two to three hours before the start of each match, the audience starts cueing in front of the hall (Aug. 15th).

Fischer and Spassky at the closing ceremony analyze the last game on Bobby's pocket set as Boris' wife, Larissa Spassky, looks on.

Dr. Euwe, head of FIDE, congratulates the new world champion with a laurel wreath at the closing ceremony (September 3).

Once again Black could place greater difficulties before his opponent by 40 ... K-Q4, 41 B-B8! (after 41 B-Q4 P-K4, 42 B-B3 P-B5!, White cannot win) 41 ... P-N3, although White would gradually win by 42 K-N5 P-K4, 42 B-K7! *(I.N.)*
This is the final blunder which makes things easy for Spassky. On 40 ... K-Q4!, it is extremely hard to find a win for White, for example: 41 B-K7 K-K5, 42 B-N5 P-N3!, 43 B-R6 P-K4, 44 K-N5 KxP, 45 KxPch P-B5, 46 K-B5 K-Q5! draws without trouble; nor would 44 B-N7 improve this line, for after 44 ... K-Q4!, 45 B-B6 P-B5, 46 PxP PxP, 47 K-N4 K-B4, 48 B-Q8 P-N4!, 49 B-B7 K-N5, 50 KxP P-B6, 51 B-N3 KxP, the position is a draw. Nevertheless, Jeffrey Kastner of the Manhattan Chess Club has come up with an ingenious winning idea which seems foolproof. His main idea is 41 B-N4! P-K4, 42 K-N5 P-B5, 43 PxP PxP, 44 KxP K-B3, 45 B-R5! winning. His analysis considers 41 ... K-K5, 42 B-Q2 K-Q6, 43 B-B1 K-B7, 44 B-R3 K-Q6 (here, he points

out that 44 ... K-N6, 45 B-B8 KxP, 46 BxP K-N4, 47 K-N5 K-B3, 48 K-B4 will quickly put Black in Zugzwang), 45 B-B5! K-B5, 46 B-B8 K-Q6, (if 46 ... P-N3, 47 K-N5 P-K4, 48 K-B6! P-B5, 49 PxP PxP, 50 B-Q6 wins; or 49 ... P-K5, 50 B-R3 P-K6, 51 B-B1 K-Q6, 52 BxP KxB, 53 KxP KxP, 54 K-B6, winning the king and pawn ending. On 48 ... K-Q4, however, Kastner erroneously gives 49 K-K7?, when Black can draw by 49 ... P-N4, 50 B-R6 P-N5, 51 B-N5 K-K5, 52 K-Q6 P-B5, 53 PxP PxP, 54 K-B7 P-N6, 55 B-R4 K-K6, 56 KxP P-N7, 57 B-K7 P-B6, 58 KxP P-B7, 59 B-B5ch K-B6, etc. Instead, White wins by 49 B-R6! P-B5, 50 BxP! PxB, 51 PxP K-K5, 52 KxP KxP, 53 K-B6, transposing into the previous line), 47 BxP KxP, 48 K-N5, and now, if 48 ... P-B5, 49 B-B3 K-Q6, 50 B-K1 (but not 50 KxP? which Kastner gives, for 50 ... KxB, 51 K-K5 K-N5!, **52** K-Q6 [KxP? K-R4! wins for Black] 52 ... P-K4!, 53 K-B7 P-K5, 54 KxP P-K6, etc. is only a draw) 50 ... P-K4, 51 K-B5 K-Q5, 52 B-B2ch K-Q4, 53 B-N1 wins. The best defense Bent Larsen, Kastner and I could find is 48 ... K-K5, 49 B-B3 K-Q4, 50 B-K1!! K-B4, 51 B-B2ch K-N5, 52 K-B6 KxP, 53 KxP K-N4, 54 K-Q6 P-R4, 55 K-B7 K-R3, 56 B-K3! P-R5, 57 B-B1, and once again White wins through Zugzwang. An extraordinary endgame! *(R.B.)*
Why is it that White is unwilling to play P-R5 in this ending? The answer is that once he does, Black can bring his king to QB1 or QR1 and

draw by stalemate. But if the White
pawn is still on QR4, Black is not
stalemated, but must advance his RP
and lose it and the game. *(I.N. & R.B.)*

41   PxP   . . .

The sealed move. Spassky took about
35 minutes on his clock in order to
adjourn, so that he could find the
winning continuation in the peace of
his room. Our analysis showed that
the position is won for White with
correct play. *(I.N.)*

41	. . .	KxP
42	K-R5!	K-B4

Also hopeless is 42 . . . P-N4, 43
K-N6 P-N5, 44 B-Q6ch P-K4, 45 K-B6,
etc. *(I.N. & R.B.)*
He tries to keep the enemy king out
of action. If 42 . . . K-K5, 43 K-N6
K-Q4, 44 B-N1 K-B5, 45 K-B7! K-N5,
46 KxKP KxP, 47 K-Q7 K-N4, 48 K-B7
and wins. *(R.B.)*

43	B-K3	K-K5
44	B-B2	K-B4

Black has no time to play for the
capture of the QRP, because that
would allow the White king to penetrate to QB7 with decisive effect.
(R.B.)

45	B-R4	P-K4
46	B-N5	P-K5
47	B-K3	. . .

The simplest, for Black is now caught
in Zugzwang. *(I.N.)*
White now has the opposition, by
which he forces his king into the
game, winning in a simple, direct
way. *(R.B.)*

47	. . .	K-B3
48	K-N4	K-K4
49	K-N5	K-Q4
50	K-B5	P-R4
51	B-B2	P-N4
52	KxP	K-B5
53	K-B5	K-N5
54	KxP	KxP
55	K-Q5	K-N4
56	K-Q6	**Resigns**

GAME 2

July 13, 1972

Thousands of chess fans and Boris Spassky waited in vain for Robert Fischer. Unfortunately, the American grandmaster found no other method to resolve his conflict with the Fox Film Company than simply not to play. Thus was produced the shortest game in the history of world chess championship battles. After no moves and one hour of waiting time, the Chief Referee, Grandmaster Lothar Schmid, pronounced the game lost for White. *(I.N.)*

GAME 3

July 15, 1972

The World Championship match had once again become uncertain and for a second time Spassky came up against the caprice of the challenger—he was extraordinarily determined to play the 3d game in a small, uncomfortable table-tennis room. This game began about 10 minutes after the usual 5:00 P.M. starting time. It was very quiet in the main auditorium. Thousands of chess fans watched the pantomime of the debating trio, Robert Fischer, Lothar Schmid and Boris Spassky on closed-circuit television. After the first few moves, everyone breathed more easily. From now on to the end of the match one could devote himself almost exclusively to the tension on the chessboard. *(I.N.)*

Modern Benoni Defense

BORIS SPASSKY ROBERT FISCHER

1	P-Q4	N-KB3
2	P-QB4	P-K3
3	N-KB3	P-B4

With a two-point deficit, one of which was lost by Bobby when he failed to show up for the second game, he goes after the point by heading into the aggressive, unbalanced Benoni. *(R.B.)*
With the score 0–2, Fischer is intrested in a sharp battle. *(I.N.)*

| 4 | P-Q5 | . . . |

The principal continuation. Only in this way is it possible for White to try to show the seamy side of the buildup chosen by Black. Quiet and solid, but without pretension is 4 P-K3. *(I.N.)*

4	. . .	PxP
5	PxP	P-Q3
6	N-B3	P-KN3
7	N-Q2	. . .

An old development, introduced into tournament practice by Nimzovich. Usual here is 7 P-K4, but intresting is 7 B-B4 B-N2, 8 Q-R4ch B-Q2, 9 Q-N3 Q-B2, 10 P-K4 O-O, 11 B-K2 P-QR3, 12 P-K5! which gives White a promising position, as in Portisch–Fischer, Palma de Majorca 1970. *(I.N.)*
White plans P-K4, but he moves the knight first to avoid the pin . . . B-N5. Very often in the Benoni, White's king knight is his most effective minor piece, especially when it can be stationed on QB4. *(R.B.)*

| 7 | . . . | QN-Q2 |

Also possible is 7 . . . B-N2, 8 N-B4 O-O, 9 B-B4 N-K1, because 10 N-N5? B-Q2!, 11 N/5xQP P-QN4, 12 NxN BxN, 13 N-K5 Q-Q3 is clearly favorable for Black. *(I.N.)*

| 8 | P-K4 | . . . |

8 N-B4 N-N3, 9 P-K4 NxN, gives White no advantage (Gligoric–Petrosian, Zurich 1953). *(I.N.)*

| 8 | ... | B-N2 |
| 9 | B-K2 | ... |

Here, however, 9 N-B4 comes strongly into consideration, in order, after 9 ... N-N3, to lead the play into the stem game of the variation, Nimzovich–Marshall, New York 1927. *(I.N.)*

9	...	O-O
10	O-O	R-K1
11	Q-B2	...

The alternative, preferred by Gligoric, Petrosian and me, is 11 P-B3, to forestall all counterplay against the KP and to release the knights from defensive duty as soon as possible. Still, Bobby has always been able to create counterchances against that move, too. *(R.B.)*

In the game Gligoric–Fischer, Palma de Majorca 1970, 11 P-QR4 N-K4, 12 Q-B2 P-KN4! led to a complicated, two-edged position. *(I.N.)*

| 11 | ... | N-R4!? |

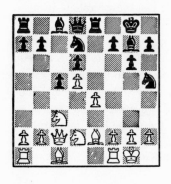

Spassky was caught off guard by this super-sharp knight sally and took over half an hour deliberating what to do about it. 12 N-B4 N-K4, 13 NxN BxN, 14 P-B4 B-Q5ch, 15 K-R1 P-B4 gives Black a beautiful game, as does 12 P-B4 P-B4!, 13 BxN (13 PxP? BxN loses a piece) 13 ... PxB, 14 PxP N-B3, because Black cannot be prevented from recovering the BP, while there are also threats of ... N-N5, followed by ... B-Q5ch and ... Q-R5. *(R.B.)*

An interesting knight diversion, introduced by Yugoslav players, which puts concrete and unusual problems before White. *(I.N.)*

| 12 | BxN! (I.N.) | ... |

The only correct move. On 12 P-B4 B-Q5ch, 13 K-R1 QN-B3 threatens 14 ... N-N5 and Black is actively placed, while it is perfectly understandable that White does not want to allow the knight into his KB4. *(I.N.)*

| 12 | ... | PxB |
| 13 | N-B4 | ... |

Instead of this, White could try to develop his bishop on the long diagonal. *(I.N.)*

| 13 | ... | N-K4 |
| 14 | N-K3 | ... |

14 NxN BxN, 15 P-B4 B-Q5ch, 16 K-R1 deserves attention, because 16 ... P-B4 can be answered by 17 P-K5! *(I.N.)*

| 14 | ... | Q-R5! (R.B.) |

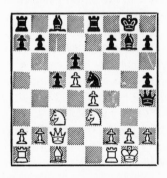

Feinting an attack this way forces White to keep a watchful eye on his kingside. 15 N-B5?, for example, loses to 15 ... BxN, 16 PxB N-B6ch!!, 17 PxN B-K4, 18 P-B4 Q-N5ch, 19 K-R1 Q-B6ch, 20 K-N1 K-R1, 21 R-K1 B-Q5, 22 N-K4 (22 B-K3 BxB, 23 RxB RxR and wins) 22 ... R-K2!, 23 R-K3 BxR, 24 Q-B3ch P-B3, 25 BxB QxN, 26 QxPch R-N2ch, 27 K-B1 Q-R8ch, 28 K-K2 QxR. *(R.B.)*

Black has achieved good piece play to compensate for his pawn weaknesses. The chances on both sides are about equal. Instead of the next move, 15 N-N5 would not get anywhere because of 15 ... Q-K2, 16 P-QR4 P-QR3, 17 N-B3 P-N3 and Black will not be stopped from getting in ... P-N4. *(I.N.)*

15   B-Q2   ...

The prophylactic 15 P-B3 was to be considered. *(I.N.)*

| 15 | ... | N-N5 |
| 16 | NxN | PxN |

Now that the Black pawns are straightened out, his two bishops give him a clear advantage. *(R.B.)*

17   B-B4   ...

Ex-World Champion Vassily Smyslov suggested that 17 N-K2 would have been stronger here, giving the variation 17 ... P-B4, 18 N-N3 PxP, 19 KR-K1, with recovery of the pawn under favorable circumstances, or better 17 ... B-B4, 18 N-N3 B-N3, 19 QR-K1 P-KR4, 20 B-B3 with a position full of tension and chances for both sides. The bishop move of the text is, however, in no way bad, and is, perhaps, the most logical continuation for the completion of White's development. *(I.N.)*

| 17 | ... | Q-B3 |
| 18 | P-KN3? (I.N.) | ... |

A mistake with sad consequences. The white squares around the White king are now chronically weak. The correct continuation was 18 B-N3, followed by P-B4. To 18 ... P-KR4, White can reply strongly with 19 N-N5. *(I.N.)*

This move was criticized on the grounds that White needs to keep his pawn chain intact so he can later defend his KP by P-B3. Such a defense, however, would certainly expose the White king dangerously, perhaps proving to be one of those cures that is worse than the disease. *(R.B.)*

| 18 | ... | **B-Q2** |
| **19** | **P-QR4** | **P-N3** |

If Black omits this preparation for P-QN4 in favor of 19 ... P-QR3, White can block the queenside expansion by 20 P-R5. *(R.B.)*

| **20** | **KR-K1** | **P-QR3** |

After the mistake on move 18, White has gotten into a very uncomfortable position and can only passively await whatever Black undertakes on the queenside. The only active attempt, breaking through by P-K5, is impossible, granted prudent play on the part of Black. *(I.N.)*

| **21** | **R-K2** | **P-N4!** |

Just at the right moment. White cannot now go into 22 PxP PxP, 23 RxR RxR, 24 P-K5, because 24 ... R-R8ch, 25 K-N2 PxP, 26 RxP P-N5, 27 N-K4 Q-QR3 wins. *(I.N.)*

| **22** | **QR-K1** | **Q-N3** |

Directed against P-K5. *(I.N.)*

| **23** | **P-N3** | ... |

Should Spassky have tried for an active defense based on getting in P-K5? On the unpinning, 23 Q-Q1 BxN, 24 PxB PxP, 25 P-K5, Black's extra pawn would have been far outweighed by White's attacking chances. But Black has a simpler and superior continuation: 23 ... B-K4, 24 BxB RxB, 25 Q-B2 QR-K1, which leaves him with powerful pressure against the KP, which can be exploited by ... P-B4 at the right moment. In addition, White would have to be on guard against an attack on the KR file by ... R-R4 and ... Q-R3. Probably White already has no more than a choice of miseries. *(R.B.)*

| **23** | ... | **R-K2** |

The pressure against the KP begins, and Spassky has no recourse but passive defense. *(R.B.)*

| **24** | **Q-Q3** | **R-N1** |

Black stands superior and has the choice here between the game continuation and 24 ... PxP, 25 PxP R-N1. *(I.N.)*
Combining attack with defense, Fischer threatens to exchange at QR5, for if the knight recaptures, then ... B-N4 x-rays a rook, while if the pawn retakes, ... R-N6 puts White in a fatal bind. *(R.B.)*

| **25** | **PxP** | **PxP** |
| **26** | **P-N4** | **P-B5!** |

26 ... PxP, 27 N-R2 gives White more possibilities to organize a line of defense. *(I.N.)*

The protected passed pawn Bobby now gains is very strong. It would have been an error to play 26 ... PxP, since White would have gotten new life after N-R2 and NxP. *(R.B.)*

27	Q-Q2	QR-K1
28	R-K3	P-R4

Black can prepare himself at his leisure for decisive action. It is not worth it to go after a pawn immediately by 28 ... BxN, 29 QxB RxP, 30 RxR RxR, 31 RxR QxR, 32 Q-B6. *(I.N.)*

29	R/3-K2	K-R2
30	R-K3	K-N1
31	R/3-K2	...

Spassky must resign himself to the loss of the KP and look for drawing chances with the bishops of opposite color. *(R.B.)*

31	...	BxN

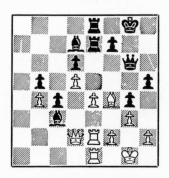

Fischer does decide on the win of the pawn. It is not easy to see how Black could get more out of his good position. On 31 ... R-R1, White can free himself somewhat by 32 P-K5, for example: 32 ... Q-Q6, 33 PxP RxR, 34 NxR. Black still stands excellently here, but a direct way to success is in no way easy to discover, especially in the last hour of play. *(I.N.)*

32	QxB	RxP
33	RxR	RxR
34	RxR	QxR
35	B-R6	...

Perhaps the best chance, for White can answer 35 Q-B6 by 35 ... B-B4. *(I.N.)*

Not 35 BxP?? as 35 ... QxP, 36 B-B4 Q-Q8ch, 37 K-N2 B-B3ch leads to mate. *(I.N. & R.B.)*

35	...	Q-N3
36	B-B1	Q-N8
37	K-B1	B-B4
38	K-K2	...

If White could only exchange queens, the ending would be a draw, even though Black were to go two pawns ahead by winning the QP. However, White's precarious king's position, which cannot be improved, the necessity for defending the QNP, and the many weak squares difficult to cover, make his situation untenable. 38 K-K1 was recommended as safer, but then he remains virtually in Zugzwang. *(R.B.)*

38	...	**Q-K5ch**
39	**Q-K3**	**Q-B7ch**
40	**Q-Q2**	...

On 40 K-K1 P-B6, Black would also win. *(I.N.)*

40 ... Q-N6! (R.B.)

Against the threat of 41 ... P-B6, White cannot play 41 B-N2 because 41 ... Q-B6ch, 42 K-K1 Q-R8ch, 43 K-K2 B-Q6ch, 44 K-K3 Q-K5 is mate. Also, on 41 Q-N5ch B-N3, 42 Q-Q8ch K-R2, 43 QxP Q-B7ch, 44 B-Q2 P-B6 wins the bishop. *(R.B.)*

41 Q-Q4 ...

This makes Black's task easier. Tougher was 41 K-K1 and Black would still have some trouble utilizing his plus pawn. However, after 41 ... Q-KB6, White's position is not enviable. *(I.N.)*

41 ... B-Q6ch! (R.B.)

The sealed move. It is easy to see that White is lost, and Spassky gave up the next day without play. A boldly played game by Fischer. *(I.N.)* Spassky was expecting this conclusive shot when he showed up for the adjournment session, merely gave it a glance and resigned. If 42 K-K3 Q-Q8, 43 B-N2 (43 B-Q2 Q-B6 mate) 44 ... Q-B6ch, 44 K-Q2 Q-K7ch, 45 K-B3 Q-B7 mate. Or 43 Q-N2 Q-B6ch, 44 K-Q4 Q-K5ch, 45 K-B3 Q-K8ch, and after White blocks with either queen or bishop, 46 ... Q-K4 mate. *(R.B.)*

GAME 4

July 18, 1972

From this game on to the end of the match, the play took place in the main auditorium under normal conditions. Although there were further problems for the arbiter and the organizers (on account of the filming, how far back the spectators should sit, etc.), the remainder of the match was not again threatened by catastrophe.

The challenger arrived six minutes late and opened the game with the king's pawn, as expected. Rather surprisingly, Spassky chose the Sicilian Defense, Fischer's own favorite. Bobby played his preferred variation, featuring the development of the king's bishop to QB4, but Black was well prepared for it. On the thirteenth move, he sacrificed a pawn and obtained dangerous attacking chances after it was accepted. Fischer put up a tough defense but, nevertheless, Black could have maintained good winning chances had he avoided the exchange of queens. The endgame gave Black no serious hopes of success. *(I.N.)*

Sicilian Defense

ROBERT FISCHER   BORIS SPASSKY

1 P-K4   P-QB4

Using Bobby's own favorite weapon against him comes as a terrific surprise. Still, with Sicilian connoisseur

Geller on his analysis team, Spassky's opening choice is not as far out as it seems. It is Fischer who quickly runs into trouble! *(R.B.)*

2	**N-KB3**	**P-Q3**
3	**P-Q4**	**PxP**
4	**NxP**	**N-KB3**
5	**N-QB3**	**N-B3**

After 5 . . . P-QR3, the Najdorf Variation arises, in which Fischer is one of the greatest specialists with Black. *(I.N.)*

6 B-QB4   . . .

The American grandmaster has preferred this bishop development against the Sicilian Defense since his earliest tournaments. *(I.N.)*
The hallmark of Fischer's anti-Sicilian play, this Leonhardt–Sozin Variation looks toward an attack on Black's center by P-B4-5 after . . . P-K3. If the Black KP can be eliminated by exchange, or forced forward to K4, White's Q5 square would become useful as a knight outpost and the KB's diagonal would be opened. *(R.B.)*

6	**. . .**	**P-K3**
7	**B-N3**	**B-K2**
8	**B-K3**	**O-O**
9	**O-O**	**. . .**

For a while, Velimirovic persuaded everybody to play Q-K2 followed by queenside castling. But then Larsen

showed that Black's attack on the
White king was at least as strong as
White's, so Bobby returns to the
older text move. *(R.B.)*
9 Q-K2 and 10 O-O-O leads to very
sharp play, as in Fischer–Larsen,
Palma de Majorca 1970. *(I.N.)*

9 ...   P-QR3

In the game Fischer–Korchnoi,
Zagreb 1970, 9 ... NxN, 10 BxN
P-QN4, 11 NxP B-R3, 12 P-QB4 BxN,
13 PxB NxP, 14 Q-B3 N-B3, 15 Q-K2
gave White the better prospects.
(I.N.)

10 P-B4   ...

The idea of the Sozin Variation lies
in attack on the point K6 by means
of the advance of the KBP. In the
event White succeeds in provoking
... P-K4 and afterward wins control
of the Q5 square, he usually stands
better. The following Black maneuvers are directed against this positional threat. *(I.N.)*

10 ...   NxN

Larsen played 10 ... B-Q2 against
Fischer in their match. However,
Black's white-square bishop is more
active on the long diagonal. *(I.N.)*

11	BxN	P-QN4
12	P-QR3	B-N2
13	Q-Q3	P-QR4!

Logically played! The Black play lies
on the queen's wing. *(I.N.)*
As Spassky demonstrates in this
game, the pawn sacrifice involved
here is exteremely·powerful. It must
be accepted, for otherwise, ... P-N5
gives Black too good a position.
(R.B.)

14 P-K5   ...

On the ideal continuation, 14 P-B5,
Black has the very strong reply
14 ... P-N5! Then the piece sacrifice, 15 PxP PxN, 16 PxPch K-R1 is
unsound, while on the retreat of the
knight, Black stands very well. Therefore White decides to go for the win
of a pawn. *(I.N.)*

14	...	PxP
15	PxP	N-Q2
16	NxP	...

I always marvel at how quickly and
fearlessly the American grandmaster
takes such "poisoned" pawns at
times. More prudent was 16 N-K4.
(I.N.)

16 ...   N-B4

17   BxN   ...

Practically forced. *(I.N.)*
Giving Black the two bishops is not a happy choice, but 17 Q-K3 NxB, 18 QxN (18 PxN? Q-Q4, 19 Q-K2 B-R3 wins a piece) 18 ... P-R5, 19 Q-Q3 B-R3, 20 QR-Q1 Q-R4, 21 P-B4 BxN, 22 PxB QR-N1, 23 P-N6 B-B4 only results in Black's obtaining the better pawn position. *(R.B.)*

17   ...   BxBch
18   K-R1   Q-N4!

18 ... QxQ, 19 PxQ B-B3! is sufficient for equality, but the queen sortie is more dangerous for White. *(I.N.)*
18 ... QxQ, 19 PxQ B-R3 is in White's favor after 20 N-B7 BxQP, 21 KR-B1 QR-N1, 22 NxP!, but the move played is excellent. *(R.B.)*

19   Q-K2   ...

Too optimistically played. White had his last opportunity to achieve about

an equal position here through 19 Q-N3 QxQ, 20 PxQ B-R3, 21 P-R4 BxN, 22 PxB B-Q5. Now the Black attack becomes very strong. *(I.N.)*
19 Q-N3 is safer, but gives nothing after 19 ... QxQ, 20 PxQ B-R3, 21 B-B4 BxN, 22 BxB B-Q5, 23 P-B3 BxKP. Bobby courageously tries to refute Spassky's gambit and spends the rest of the game suffering for his unwise decision. *(R.B.)*

19   ...   QR-Q1
20   QR-Q1   RxR
21   RxR   P-R4! (R.B.)

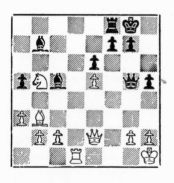

The pawn threatens to travel to KR6, shredding the last of the White defenses. *(R.B.)*
Here Black had a very good alternative, namely 21 ... R-Q1. Then White could not play 22 N-Q6 because of 22 ... BxPch, 23 QxB QxP, when the White position is hopeless. After the better 22 RxRch QxR, 23 P-B3 Q-N4, 24 N-Q4 (24 N-Q6 BxPch!, etc.) 24 ... Q-B8ch, 25 B-Q1

B-Q4, Black has more than sufficient compensation for the pawn. *(I.N.)*

22 N-Q6   B-R1

Now Fischer faces very difficult problems. The Black bishop-pair is dangerous directed toward the White kingside and the further march of the KRP threatens. *(I.N.)*

23 B-B4   P-KR5
24 P-R3   . . .

After 24 N-K4 QxP, 25 NxB QxN, material equality is restablished but, positionally, Black is clearly superior (good bishop, active play on both wings). *(I.N.)*

The only defense, for 24 B-Q3 P-R6, 25 B-K4 QxP, 26 B-R7ch KxB, 27 QxQ PxP is mate. However, the squares in the vicinity of the White king are now pitifully weak. *(R.B.)*

24 . . .   B-K6!

Spassky is justified in playing for a win. On 24 . . . Q-N6, White does not reply 25 R-Q3? BxPch!, but 25 N-K4 QxKP, 26 NxB QxN gives good prospects of a draw. *(I.N.)*

25 Q-N4   . . .

What else can White do? Black was threatening Q-N6, followed by . . . QxRP mate, as well as . . . B-B5 to seize the KP. *(R.B. & I.N.)*

25 . . .   QxP

25 . . . QxQ, 26 PxQ P-R6, 27 B-B1 P-B3, 28 N-B4 is nothing for Fischer to worry about. *(R.B.)*

The exchange of queens seems to be good; for example, 25 . . . QxQ, 26 PxQ B-B5, 27 R-K1 (or 27 R-KB1 BxP, 28 NxP P-R6!) 27 . . . P-R6, 28 B-B1 P-B3 with great advantage. However, 27 B-K2! is much stronger, enabling White to maintain himself. *(I.N.)*

26 QxRP   . . .

Interesting is the sacrifice, 26 NxP!? KxN, 27 BxPch! because 27 . . . QxB, 28 R-Q7ch is favorable for White. Still, after 27 . . . K-B3, it is not obvious how White can get any further with his attack. *(I.N.)*

26 . . .   P-N4!

Again well played. After 26 . . . B-N4, 27 Q-Q4 Q-N6, 28 N-K4 BxN, 29 QxB B-B5, 30 K-N1 White can defend himself. *(I.N.)*

27 Q-N4   . . .

It is necessary to keep both the KN3 square and the rook defended. To reply 27 . . . P-B4 is impossible, for 28 Q-R5 threatens perpetual check, and 28 . . . K-N2 loses after 29 N-K8ch K-N1 (29 . . . RxN, 30 R-Q7ch and mates), 30 Q-N6ch K-R1, 31 Q-R6ch K-N1, 32 BxPch R-B2, 33 N-B6ch. *(R.B.)*

27 . . .   B-B4

There is no win after 27 ... R-Q1, since 28 NxP! RxRch, 29 QxR KxN, 30 Q-Q7ch K-B3, 31 Q-Q8ch recovers the bishop. Nor is 29 ... Q-N6 good for anything more than a draw, since 30 N-R6ch! K-N2, 31 Q-Q7ch leads to perpetual check. It's amazing that Fischer is still alive here. (R.B.)

Also good was 27 ... K-N2. On the other hand, 27 ... R-Q1 allows White to escape with a whole skin after 28 NxP! RxRch, 29 QxR Q-N6, 30 Q-Q8ch with perpetual check. Moreover, continuations other than 29 ... Q-N6 do not offer Black anything. (I.N.)

28   N-N5   K-N2

Spassky menaces the crushing ... R-R1-R5. (R.B.)

29   N-Q4   ...

Without this knight, White cannot defend his weakened king's wing. (I.N.)

29   ...   R-R1

Gligoric and Olafsson maintained that Black can win here by 29 ... R-Q1, since 30 NxPch PxN, 31 RxR Q-K8ch is mate in three. Also, on 30 N-B5ch K-B3, 31 N-R6 RxRch, 32 QxR K-N3, 33 N-N4 QxP, Black has an overwhelming position.

But the situation is not clear after 30 P-B3. If 30 ... B-Q3, 31 K-N1 R-R1, 32 N-B5ch! PxN, 33 QxPch K-B1, 34 Q-Q8ch, White draws. If 30 ... R-R1, 31 N-B3 BxN, 32 QxB B-Q3, 33 K-N1 R-R5 wins for Black. But here 31 R-KB1! R-R5, 32 N-B5ch! QxN, 33 RxQ RxQ, 34 RxB RxP, 35 RxP B-B6, 36 B-B1 is still perhaps tenable. In this last line, if 31 ... B-Q3, 32 N-B5ch at least draws by perpetual check. (R.B.)

On 29 ... B-Q3, White has the strong move 30 N-B5ch! Many commentators recommended the other rook move, 29 ... R-Q1. Now White would lose the straying knight after 30 N-B5ch K-B3, 31 N-R6 K-N3. Very complicated variations can arise after 30 P-B3 R-R1 (30 ... B-Q3, 31 K-N1 R-R1, 32 N-B5ch!). Let us investigate the resulting position more closely: (1) 31 N-B3 BxN, 32 QxB B-Q3 and White lacks the move Q-B3. (2) 31 BxP!? BxN!, 32 PxB QxB, 33 QxPch Q-N3, 34 Q-K5ch P-B3!, 35 Q-B7ch K-R3, 36 P-Q5 R-KN1, 37 Q-B4ch Q-N4, 38 Q-B3 R-Q1 and Black has justifiable hopes of winning. (3) 31 R-KB1 R-R5, 32 N-B5ch!? QxN!, 33 RxQ RxQ, 34 RxB RxP, 35 RxP (35 B-Q5? BxB, 36 RxB PxR, 37 KxR P-R5! loses at once) 35 ... B-B6! with the

better game. (4) 31 B-Q3 K-B1!?, 32
R-KB1! B-Q3, 33 NxPch K-K1, 34
B-N5ch QxB, 35 R-K1 with a very
strong attack. Instead of 31 ... K-B1,
better is 31 ... B-N3!
In all variations, Black has good
chances, but the text move is also
good. *(I.N.)*

30	N-B3	BxN
31	QxB	B-Q3?

For the first time, this error in time
pressure lets White breathe. After the
correct continuation of the attack by
means of 31 ... R-R5, White would
scarcely have been able to find a
liberating defense. *(I.N.)*

32	Q-B3	...

At last Bobby can catch his breath,
now that the shooting is over. *(R.B.)*
Now White has nothing to fear. The
conclusion is clear without commentary. *(I.N.)*

32	...	QxQ
33	PxQ	B-K4
34	R-Q7	K-B3
35	K-N1	BxP
36	B-K2	B-K4
37	K-B1	R-QB1
38	B-R5	...

By forcing the exchange of rooks,
this move eliminates even the minute
chance of Black's exploiting the frag-
mented pawn position and makes
the game an obvious draw. *(R.B.)*

38	...	R-B2
39	RxR	BxR
40	P-QR4	K-K2
41	K-K2	P-B4
42	K-Q3	B-K4
43	P-B4	K-Q3
44	B-B7	B-N6
45	P-B5ch	Drawn

This hard-fought game has theoretical
significance. *(I.N.)*

GAME 5

July 20, 1972

The fifth game followed a zigzag course. In the opening, the World Champion played boldly and a complicated strategic situation arose. However, Spassky handled the middle game with marked unsureness. Fischer, on the other hand, gave an excellent strategic performance and outplayed his opponent move by move. In a difficult position, Spassky made a gross blunder, very rare for him, and had to strike his weapons even before the 30th move. From this game on, Spassky's long series of disasters began—out of six games, he could only score two half points. This phase practically decided the match for the World Championship. *(I.N.)*

Nimzo–Indian Defense

BORIS SPASSKY	BOBBY FISCHER
1 P-Q4	N-KB3
2 P-QB4	P-K3
3 N-QB3	B-N5

This time the defense originated by the Dano–Russian grandmaster Aron Nimzovich arises by the direct route. *(I.N.)*

4 N-B3 ...

The most popular continuation here is 4 P-K3, while Spassky has often played 4 B-N5. *(I.N.)*

4 ...	P-B4
5 P-K3	N-B3
6 B-Q3	BxNch
7 PxB	P-Q3

Fischer plays according to the Nimzovich formula against the doubled QBP's without even waiting for the provocative P-QR3. In the last few years, the young German grandmaster Robert Huebner has had considerable success with this line of play. *(R.B. & I.N.)*

The point is to take advantage of the placement of White's knight at KB3, where it is considerably weaker than at K2 in Saemisch-type formations. Huebner's recipe also calls for O-O-O, although the placement of the Black king cannot be determined until White reveals what formation he will set up. *(R.B.)*

8 P-K4 ...

Ex-World Champion Mikhail Botvinnik prefers, in similar situations, to keep the central square K4 free for his pieces. *(I.N.)*

An alternative is to keep the king bishop's diagonal open by 8 N-Q2, but after 8 ... P-K4, it is not apparent how White is to obtain the initiative. *(R.B.)*

8 ...	P-K4
9 P-Q5	N-K2

Huebner's idea is to use the Black minor pieces for maneuvering on the kingside. In any case, 9 ... N-QR4 would be a mistake, since 10 N-Q2, followed by N-N3 virtually compels ... NxN, mending the White pawn position after PxN. *(R.B.)*

10   N-R4   P-KR3

Black wishes to give the game a closed character in order to limit the activity of White's bishop pair. With his next move, Spassky stirs up interesting complications. *(I.N.)*

11   P-B4!?   . . .

Spassky thought for a long time about this committing move. 11 P-B3 or 11 P-N3 can be recommended for more cautious souls. *(I.N.)*

Two alternatives tried here are 11 P-N3 B-R6, 12 R-KN1 P-KN4, 13 N-N2 and 11 P-B3 P-KN4, 12 N-B5 NxN, 13 PxN N-R4. Neither one has worked out satisfactorily for White.

The text move appears to be tremendous, since 11 ... PxP, 12 BxP P-KN4?, 13 P-K5! N-Q2, 14 P-K6 PxB, 15 PxNch QxP, 16 O-O yields White an overwhelming position. *(R.B.)*

11   . . .   N-N3!

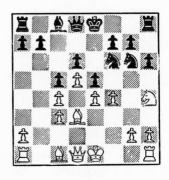

Playing for material gain with 11 ... PxP, 12 BxP P-KN4, 13 P-K5 N-N5 would be punished: 14 P-K6 N-KB3, 15 O-O! and now Black loses no matter which piece he takes—15 ... PxB, 16 RxP N/2-N1, 17 PxPch KxP, 18 Q-R5ch or 15 ... PxN, 16 PxPch KxP (16 ... K-B1, 17 Q-Q2 KxP, 18 BxRP), 17 B-K5! PxB, 18 Q-R5ch K-N2, 19 RxN. *(I.N.)*

But this weird reply stops White cold. 12 N-B5? BxN, 13 PxB, NxBP, 14 BxN PxB, 15 O-O O-O, 16 RxP recovers the pawn, but at the expense of a winning position for Black, who has a good knight against a bad bishop and control of the king file. 12 PxP? is even worse after 12 ... NxN, 13 PxN QxP leaving White in a disorganized mess. *(R.B.)*

12   NxN   PxN
13   PxP   . . .

The first inaccuracy. The exchange of the central pawns relieves Black of many troubles and gives the Black knight the good blockading square Q3 in several variations. Better was 13 O-O O-O immediately and now, according to Tal, 14 P-KR3 or 14 R-N1 with the plan R-N2-KB2. *(I.N.)*

13   . . .   PxP
14   B-K3? (I.N.)   . . .

Not a successful move, after which Black stands rather better. The black-squared bishop belongs on B1. After the inaccurate exchange of the center pawns, White still has a good position and could now face the future calmly after 14 O-O O-O, 15 P-QR4 P-QR4, 16 R-N1. *(I.N.)*

A first glance might give the impression that White stands well here, with the two bishops and a protected passed pawn. But the king bishop has the purely passive role of guarding the KP and QBP, while the pawn formation on the kingside is such that White is denied his normal attacking chances there. It is Black, with his maneuvering possibilities against the fixed enemy pawn weaknesses, who has the upper hand. *(R.B.)*

14	. . .	P-N3
15	O-O	O-O
16	P-QR4	. . .

Spassky still hopes for an active game on the queen's wing, but that is too optimistic. The advanced White QRP will prove a permanent weakness in the further course of the game. More prudent was 16 R-N1. *(I.N.)*

16	. . .	P-QR4

There was no possibility of avoiding this, since P-R5 would have followed, giving White two queenside files to play on. Black's backward QNP is a drawback, but not a serious one, because White's pressure against it is limited by his lack of mobility. *(R.B.)*

17	R-N1	. . .

One can find no plan in White's play. If White wishes to get this rook to KB2, he could have saved a move by 17 R-R2. *(I.N.)*

17	. . .	B-Q2
18	R-N2	R-N1
19	QR-KB2	. . .

This is a nothing move, but it is not clear how White can proceed in any event. In order to scare up a real threat against the QNP, White must be able to triple on the QN file. That would require a long-winded maneuver beginning with Q-R1, which would give Black a chance to attack on the other wing. If Black was really worried about anything after 19 Q-R1, he could always get rid of a pair of rooks by . . . N-N5. *(R.B.)*

19	. . .	Q-K2

In such positions, in which his opponent lacks active counterplay, Fischer is very dangerous. Once again in this game, he maneuvers very skillfully. *(I.N.)*

20	B-B2	P-KN4
21	B-Q2	Q-K1
22	B-K1	Q-N3
23	Q-Q3	N-R4

An important decision. After the exchange of rooks, the position is simplified considerably, yet the American grandmaster is on the right path. First, it is not to be seen how Black can strengthen his position without this exchange and, second, after it he maintains good chances for success. *(I.N.)*

24	RxRch	RxR
25	RxRch	KxR
26	B-Q1	...

According to Tal, 26 P-N3 offered better possibilities of defense. Objectively that is correct, but practically it scarcely alters anything. After the journey of the Black king to QB2 and the knight to Q3, it would be very uncomfortable for White to defend his pawn weaknesses at QB4 and QR4. Moreover, taking Spassky's time pressure into consideration, it is hard to believe that this position could still be rescued. *(I.N.)*

26 ... N-B5

Now Black's advantage is glaringly obvious, but is it enough to win by

force? Grandmaster Fridrik Olafsson thinks so, but it is not perfectly clear. After 27 Q-N1 (best), Black can continue by ... K-K2-Q1-B2 and then start a kingside attack with ... P-R4-5, ... Q-R3 and ... P-N5. It is difficult to suggest countermeasures and, unfortunately, we are deprived of seeing the thing worked out, because Boris makes his biggest blunder of the match right here. *(R.B.)*

27 Q-B2?? ...

What can the commentator say after this move? In the practice of the World Champion, such oversights almost never occur (I can only remember Spassky blundering a piece to Bent Larsen in the U.S.S.R. *versus* The Rest-of-the-World match in Belgrade 1970). Objectively, however, the position was already untenable. After 27 Q-N1, Black brings his king to QB2 and then starts operations on the king's wing. *(I.N.)*

27 ... BxP!

After this simple tactical shot, Spassky gave up, because after 28 QxB QxP, the mate cannot be parried. *(I.N.)*

The sacrifice cannot be accepted, for 28 QxB? QxP threatens two mates at once, and 29 K-B2 N-Q6ch, 30 K-N3 Q-R5ch, 31 K-B3 Q-B5ch, 32 K-K2 N-B8 is mate. Declining is also hopeless, because 29 Q-N1 BxB, 30 QxB QxP leaves White two pawns down to begin with, and the prospect of losing more stares him in the face. *(R.B.)*

Fischer Pulls Away

Just as he did in the second week of play, Bobby dominated the third week's contests, racking up 2½ points out of 3 for a 2-point lead in the match. Some are saying that Boris is playing badly. It isn't true—he's not getting a chance to play at all. Fischer pounces on him so sharply, usually in the opening, that he is unable to show what he can do. How can a marvelous attacking player reveal his stuff when he cannot get a position that permits him to fire even one salvo? It may have looked as though Boris has something going for him in the seventh game, but it was all sophisticated teasing on Fischer's part. He marched confidently through the complex labyrinth of his prepared analysis, which allowed Boris assorted pot-shots to prevent Black from castling, but nothing else of more than ephemeral value. Soon Boris found himself in full retreat, a pawn down and with a lost game. Had Fischer not fallen prey to overconfidence, he would have won easily for a total shutout week, instead of giving up a half point.

The biggest blow to Spassky's self-assurance was game six. For the first time in his life, Bobby played the Queen's Gambit, having always maintained that it was "dull and a draw." And he beat Spassky, who had never lost a game with his favorite Tarta-kower Variation! The bare facts are so dazzling they need no embellishment. Just play over the game.

By game eight the tension of almost continuous defensive play showed up in two Spassky errors. There is some question whether the first was a piece of mistaken judgment or an oversight, but the second was a naive blunder which denied Boris any chance to put up resistance. Otherwise, the game was notable for Bobby's second use of a queenside opening, the English. It would have been fascinating to see how he intended to proceed from the Maroczy Bind he had set up, but Spassky's mistakes took the game out of normal channels. *(R.B.)*

July 22, 1972

Before the match there was a lot of talk that it is comparatively easy to prepare for Fischer, because he is very conservative in his choice of openings. Especially with White, Fischer plays 1 P-K4 almost without exception. Only once, against Polugaevsky in Palma de Majorca 1970, did he open with 1 P-QB4. Naturally Fischer knows all the half-open defenses and the Ruy Lopez with White superbly well, but nevertheless, his limited preference helps his opponents anticipate him. Thus, the Soviet grandmasters Petrosian and Keres enjoyed success against the young Fischer with the Caro–Kann Defense, as did the World Champion's second, Yefim Geller, with sharp variations of the Sicilian Defense. But, as this game shows, Spassky did not have their luck in his choice of defense. It was to be taken for granted that the American was all ready for the Tartakower–Bondarevsky Variation, because this line of play has previously been part of the World Champion's repertory. Even worse for Spassky was that, during the game, he forgot the latest stand of theory and played inaccurately. The challenger, who gave one of his best performances of the match in this game, was now in the lead. *(I.N.)*

Queen's Gambit Declined

ROBERT FISCHER   BORIS SPASSKY

| 1 | P-QB4 | ... |

To my knowledge, Fischer has played this only once before, against Polugaevsky in Palma de Majorca 1970. The great advantage of his going to queenside openings is that, without any history to rely on, it was impossible for Spassky to know what to prepare. *(R.B.)*

1	...	P-K3
2	N-KB3	P-Q4
3	P-Q4	N-KB3
4	N-B3	B-K2

Spassky has often played the Tarrasch Defense, 4 ... P-B4, with success. *(I.N.)*

With the Black pieces in game 1, Fischer played 4 ... B-N5, transposing into the Nimzo–Indian, but Boris, as in his match with Petrosian three years earlier, prefers to stay with the normal lines of the Queen's Gambit Declined. *(R.B.)*

5	B-N5	O-O
6	P-K3	P-KR3
7	B-R4	P-QN3

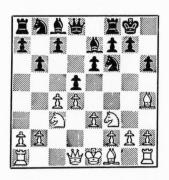

Boris has been responsible for reviving this old Tartakower Variation and had never lost a game with it prior to this encounter. *(R.B.)*

8	PxP	NxP
9	BxB	QxB
10	NxN	PxN
11	R-B1	B-K3

The first moves are all well-known theory, found in countless opening books, and need no commentary. It should be observed that the bishop is better placed at K3 than on N2, where it is blocked by its own QP. *(I.N.)*

12 Q-R4   P-QB4

Black gets maneuvering space and a free game by this advance, which, however, creates some problems guarding against possible pawn weaknesses. In the old days, it was Capablanca who forced this defense into eclipse. Will Bobby do the same now? *(R.B.)*

13	Q-R3	R-B1
14	B-N5!	...

This move of Soviet Grandmaster Furman is more dangerous for Black than 14 B-K2 N-Q2. *(I.N.)*

14 ...   P-R3

The idea of the White bishop development lies in provoking a weakening of Black's QN3 square. It is not one hundred percent certain that such a weakening is necessary, but on the other hand, it is understandable that Black will not tolerate the bishop in its present position for long, where it considerably disturbs the development of the Black queen's wing. *(I.N.)*

15 PxP   PxP

Naturally, on 15 ... RxP, White would not exchange rooks, but would simply castle, with considerable advantage. *(I.N.)*

16 O-O   R-R2

Compelling the bishop to retreat, but for this purpose Geller's suggestion, 16 ... Q-N2, 17 B-K2 N-Q2, was better. *(I.N.)*

16 ... Q-N2 has been suggested as an improvement, unpinning the BP and preventing Fischer's 18th move. After White's necessary bishop retreat, he would most likely continue with R-B3, followed by doubling rooks. *(R.B.)*

17 B-K2   N-Q2

In the game Furman–Geller, 1970, after 17 ... P-QR4, 18 R-B3!, White had a clear advantage. However, Petrosian's idea, 17 ... P-B5, is worthy of attention. Of course, the control of the central point Q4 would give White justifiable hopes for the initiative, but the position is by no means clear. For example, 18 QxQ RxQ, and on 19 N-Q4, Black can play 19 ... N-B3. In case White avoids the exchange of queens with 18 Q-B3, Black will obtain play on the half-open QN file. Also better than the knight move was 17 ... Q-B1. *(I.N.)*

18   N-Q4!   ...

This simple positional move is quite strong, because after the exchange of a set of minor pieces, the cramping effect of the Black QP and QBP virtually disappears, while their vulnerability remains. *(R.B.)*
Black should not have allowed this knight move. *(I.N.)*

18   ...   Q-B1?

Black is intent on resolving the tension, but this move is a loss of time and perhaps already the fatal mistake. Dr. Euwe recommended 18 .. N-B1, but White retains a small advantage in any case. *(R.B.)*
Bad luck seldom strikes but once. Now White can exchange the bishop under favorable circumstances. After 18 ... N-B3, the exchange on K6 gives White little. However, 19 N-N3 N-Q2, 20 R-B3 yields White the

better game, for the pressure on the QB file is uncomfortable. *(I.N.)*

19   NxB   ...

Here White could also play 19 N-N3, but the text move is more active and better expresses Fischer's taste—he loves to fight with a white-squared bishop against an opponent's knight. *(I.N.)*

19   ...   PxN
20   P-K4!   ...

Here is the point of the previous exchange, which only seemed to strengthen the Black pawns. But they are now weaker than ever. Dr. Euwe considers that the lesser of Black's evils would be the reply 20 ... PxP. Nevertheless, 21 B-B4 Q-K2, 22 KR-K1 N-B3, 23 P-B3 K-R1, 24 PxP P-K4, 25 QR-Q1 gives White a clear advantage, since the scattered Black pawns are all targets, and tending them prevents Black from disputing the queen file. *(R.B.)*

Now Black's situation in the center is critical. *(I.N.)*

20   ...   P-Q5

Again Black chooses a second-best defense. Tougher was 20 ... N-B3 or even 20 ... PxP. Tal analyzes the very interesting variation, 20 ... P-B5, 21 Q-R3 Q-B2, 22 B-N4 R-K1, 23 PxP PxP, 24 KR-K1 and now, not 24 ... N-K4, 25 B-R5 P-N3, 26 Q-KN3 QR-K2, 27 P-B4 N-Q6, 28 RxR RxR, 29 BxP QxP, 30 B-B7ch! KxB, 31 R-KB1 QxRch, 32 KxQ R-K8ch, 33 QxR NxQ, 34 KxN, with a won king-and-pawn ending for White, but better—24 ... RxRch, 25 RxR N-B1, with a secure position. It seems to me, however, that instead of 23 PxP, 23 B-R5! P-N3, 24 B-K2 is correct. Although the material is even, the Black position is very critical. *(I.N.)*

21   P-B4   ...

While Black's pawns are immobile on the queenside, White's will spearhead a decisive attack on the other wing. 21 ... P-K4?, 22 PxP Q-K2, 23 P-K6 is ruinous for Black. *(R.B.)*

21   ...   Q-K2
22   P-K5   ...

Now Fischer is in his element. The pawn majority on the king's wing and the strong bishop are good weapons for a successful attack on the king. *(I.N.)*

22   ...   R-N1

On 22 ... N-N3, 23 P-B5 is very strong, because Black cannot capture the pawn on account of Q-N3ch. *(I.N.)*

23   B-B4   K-R1

After 23 ... N-N3?, 24 Q-QN3 wins a pawn for White at once. *(R.B. & I.N.)*

24   Q-R3   N-B1

After 24 ... RxP, 25 *B* RxKP, there is no way to reinforce the lone rook on the seventh rank, while the advance of the White pawn spearhead will quickly wreck the enemy king position. Now that White is shifting to the kingside onslaught, Black is lost anyway. *(R.B.)*

Black's position after 24 ... RxP, 25 BxKP is by no means enviable, but perhaps that was still the last possibility for obtaining some practical counterbalance. *(I.N.)*

25   P-QN3   P-QR4
26   P-B5!   PxP
27   RxP   ...

The KB file will be the main route of the attack. The threat is R-B7, winning the queen for rook and bishop. *(R.B.)*

27   ...   N-R2
28   QR-B1   ...

Fischer's play is a model for execution of an attack. Of course, he does not fall into the trap, 28 R-B7? N-N4, but now R-B7 is again a real threat. *(I.N. & R.B.)*

28	...	Q-Q1
29	Q-N3	R-K2
30	P-KR4	...

The Black knight has now practically no squares at its disposal. *(I.N.)*

| 30 | ... | R/1-N2 |
| 31 | P-K6 | ... |

The pressure mounts. All Spassky can do about it is to crouch in terror on the second rank. He cannot use White's last move to get in 31 ... N-B3, because Bobby is just waiting to sacrifice the Exchange at KB6, thus fatally denuding the Black king. If 31 ... Q-B2, White mates in four starting with 32 R-B8ch. *(R.B.)*

| 31 | ... | R/N2-B2 |

31 ... P-Q6 doesn't work on account of 32 R-Q5. *(I.N.)*

| 32 | Q-K5 | Q-K1 |

After 32 ... P-Q6, 33 R/5-B3, the QP is lost. *(I.N.)*

| 33 | P-R4 | Q-Q1 |

Black has no more reasonable moves: 33 ... N-B3, 34 RxN, or 33 ... K-N1, 34 R-B7 loses quickly. *(I.N.)*

34	R/1-B2	Q-K1
35	R/2-B3	Q-Q1
36	B-Q3	...

Fischer's last three moves did nothing but mark time, for what reason, I don't know, except perhaps to demonstrate sadistically that Black is almost in Zugzwang. The present move, however, threatens Q-K4, to which there is no defense. *(R.B.)*
It was also possible to win with 36 R-B7. *(I.N.)*

| 36 | ... | Q-K1 |
| 37 | Q-K4 | N-B3 |

A quicker way to go was 37 ... RxP?, 38 R-B8ch NxR, 39 RxNch QxR, 40 Q-R7 mate. *(R.B.)*

| 38 | RxN! | ... |

This sets the seal on the win, leaving only a few grisly details. *(R.B.)*

38	...	PxR
39	RxP	K-N1
40	B-B4	K-R1
41	Q-B4	Resigns

On 41 ... R-B1, 42 RxPch K-N1, 43 Q-N4ch R-N2, 44 P-K7ch Q-B2, 45 QxR mate, or, if 41 ... K-N1, 42 QxRP leaves Black no recourse against 43 R-N6ch. *(R.B.)*

This game had, in addition to its sporting significance, without doubt a psychological influence—Fischer showed that he was also very much at home in closed openings, thus forcing the World Champion to extend his theoretical preparation. *(I.N.)*

Game 7

July 25, 1972

For the first time, Boris Spassky tried his chief weapon in Reykjavik, the opening move P-K4. Robert Fischer defended himself with his favorite variation of the Sicilian Defense. While according to theory this pawn snatching line is very dangerous for Black, the New York grandmaster is like a fish in water in the complications arising from it and he has chalked up many successes with it. In this encounter, White played very adventurously, sacrificing three pawns, one after the other, and then even a bishop. However, Fischer defended himself very coldbloodedly, gave most of the material back, and remained with a plus pawn with a good position. But, in the middle game, he made a few inaccuracies and gave his ingenious opponent chances. At the time of adjournment, the game was already a draw. The organizers placed at the disposal of the World Champion an upholstered leather chair for the 7th game, identical to the one Fischer uses. *(I.N.)*

Sicilian Defense

BORIS SPASSKY   ROBERT FISCHER

1 P-K4   ...

Fischer's terrific defenses to 1 P-Q4 have driven the champion to this. *(R.B.)*

1	...	P-QB4
2	N-KB3	P-Q3
3	P-Q4	PxP
4	NxP	N-KB3
5	N-QB3	P-QR3

The Najdorf Sicilian is such a favorite with Bobby that he is quite willing to forego the surprise value of something else for the opportunity of using it. *(R.B.)*

6	B-N5	P-K3
7	P-B4	Q-N3

Beginners' books are always spouting a lot of nonsense about the evils of snatching the QNP with the queen, but he who wins a pawn and runs away has a won endgame. Though stormed at with shot and shell, the "poisoned pawn" variation still holds its own, as Fischer demonstrates in this game. *(R.B.)*

In addition to this variation, Fischer also plays 7 ... B-K2, 8 Q-B3 Q-B2, 9 O-O-O QN-Q2. *(I.N.)*

8 Q-Q2   ...

Of course, White can avoid the sharp variations with 8 N-N3, but he can only hope for opening advantage with the text move. *(I.N.)*

8	...	QxP
9	N-N3	...

The most popular alternative is 9 R-N1; naturally, the choice of this or that continuation is a matter of taste. *(I.N.)*

9	...	Q-R6

Long preferred has been 9 ... N-B3, but the idea contained in this move may be stronger. As will be seen, Black must have his QP defended at the fourteenth move in order to carry out a sharp combination. *(R.B.)*

10	B-Q3	...

The exchange at KB6, which, as will be seen, was played in the eleventh game, offers more for White. *(I.N. & R.B.)*

10	...	B-K2!

This seems more accurate than the theoretical 10 ... QN-Q2, because Black's queen knight can be very effectively developed at QB3 in several variations. *(I.N.)*

11	O-O	P-R3!

Virtually forcing White into an unfavorable combination, since 12 BxN, BxB yields him nothing for the sacrificed pawn. *(R.B.)*

12	B-R4!? (I.N.)	...

More prudent was 12 BxN BxB, 13 P-K5! PxP, 14 N-K4, and the White initiative compensates for the sacrificed material. White can scarcely hope for more. *(I.N.)*

12	...	NxP!

The success of this little combination depends on the status of the respective positions after Fischer's seventeenth move. *(R.B.)*

13	NxN	BxB
14	P-B5! (I.N.)	...

White has achieved a great advantage in development and plays now for line-opening in the good old style of the previous century. However, the technique of successful defense has improved enormously in recent decades. *(I.N.)*
The only chance to put Black's defense to the test. 14 NxPch? QxN, 15 B-N5ch K-K2 merely throws away stuff for nothing. *(R.B.)*

14	...	PxP!

After 14 ... O-O, the White kingside attack is irresistible. *(I.N.)*

15	B-N5ch!?	...

Nobody can say he isn't trying, but succeeding is another matter. *(R.B.)*
This enticing continuation is, in the long run, not sufficient. Better practical chances lay, perhaps, in 15 Q-B4 B-K2, 16 N-B3, or 15 N-B3, but even

then, White's advantage in development does not fully compensate for the sacrificed pawn. *(I.N.)*

15	...	**PxB**
16	**NxPch**	**K-B1!**

The only correct move, for after 16 ... K-K2?, 17 NxNP/5 Q-R3, 18 Q-N4ch the White attack would be annihilating. *(I.N.)*
Unreliable is 16 ... K-K2: 17 Q-K3ch KxN, 18 QR-Q1ch K-B2, 19 Q-K5ch K-N3, 20 Q-Q4ch and White has at least a perpetual check.
Another possibility to be avoided is 17 ... K-B3, 18 NxBP/5! BxN, 19 RxBch KxR, 20 R-B1ch K-N3, 21 Q-K4ch K-R4, 22 P-N4ch K-N4, 23 Q-B5 mate. *(R.B.)*

17	**NxB**	**N-B3!**

Black's position looks quite dangerous, but still Fischer succeeds in parrying the direct threats with a few accurate moves. *(I.N.)*

18	**N-Q6**	...

This is a clear admission of bankruptcy, but the more threatening-looking 18 Q-Q7 will not save Spassky's game either: 18 ... P-KN3, 19 N-Q6 B-K2, 20 NxNP/5 Q-R3, 21 Q-Q3 is a clear pawn-down position for Spassky, with nothing to show for it. In this line, 20 NxBP/5 Q-R2ch, 21 N/5-Q4 (21 K-R1 R-Q1, 22 Q-B7 PxN, is an unsound piece sacrifice), 21 ... NxN, 22 QxN QxQch, 23 NxQ B-B4 is also a hopeless endgame. After 18 Q-Q7 P-KN3, White can try 19 QxNP. But then 19 ... Q-R3 compels the exchange of queens, once again giving Bobby an easily won endgame. *(R.B.)*
White has no better continuation at his disposal. On 18 Q-B4 RxN, 19 QxB Q-K2 can be played, while after 18 Q-Q7 P-KN3, 19 N-Q6, Tal gives, in addition to the quiet 19 ... B-K2, the spectacular 19 ... N-K4, 20 QxNP/7 QxN/3, 21 QxRch K-N2, 22 Q-N7 R-QN1, 23 QR-Q1 (or 23 Q-R7 N-N5, 24 P-N3 BxP, etc.) 23 ... B-B7ch!! and Black wins by force (24 K-R1 QxR). *(I.N.)*

18	...	**R-Q1**

Fischer has very skillfully refuted the risky play of the World Champion and now grasps the initiative while retaining material advantage. If we take into consideration that Spassky had only a half-hour for the next 22 moves, while Fischer had an hour and a half, it is a mystery that he escapes from the affair with a whole hide. *(I.N.)*

19 NxNP/5 Q-K2

The text move, which is, I guess, still part of Bobby's prepared analysis, is stronger than 19 . . . RxQ, 20 NxQ R-Q4, 21 N-B4 P-KN3, 22 QR-Q1 RxR, 23 RxR, K-K2, 24 N-B5, which gives White some chances to hold the ending. *(R.B.)*

Black stands materially and positionally better and can choose various roads to his goal. The simplest seems 19 . . . RxQ, 20 NxQ R-Q4, 21 P-B4 R-K4, or 21 N-B4 P-KN3, 22 QR-Q1 RxR, 23 RxR K-K2, 24 N-B5 R-Q1, and the endgame arrived at is won for Black. *(I.N.)*

20 Q-B4 P-KN3
21 P-R4 . . .

If White can exchange the QRP, he will eliminate a weakness and develop some queenside play. *(R.B.)*

21 . . . B-N4

The bishop stood beautifully on R5; better was 21 . . . K-N2, in order to mobilize the king rook. *(I.N.)*

22 Q-B4 B-K6ch

Again here 22 . . . K-N2, 23 QR-K1 Q-N5 was strong. *(I.N.)*

23 K-R1 P-B5
24 P-N3 . . .

White tries to obtain counterplay at any price. *(I.N.)*

24 . . . P-N4

Tal's suggested continuation looks very good: 24 . . . N-K4, 25 Q-K4 P-B4, with the idea of . . . P-B6. In case of 25 Q-K2, then 25 . . . P-N4. *(I.N.)*

25 QR-K1 Q-N5

Now, on 25 . . . N-K4, White had the answer 26 Q-K4. Also the try, 25 . . . R-Q5? turns out to be only a fatal blunder after 26 N/5xR Q-K5ch, 27 R-B3. *(I.N.)*

The exchange of queens is forced under very favorable conditions. 26 Q-K2 Q-K5ch, 27 R-B3? P-N5 is out of the question. *(R.B.)*

26 QxQ NxQ
27 R-K2 K-N2

This is a good move, but 27 . . . N-B3 would have been equally effective in denying Spassky counterplay. *(R.B. & I.N.)*

28 N-R5 P-N3
29 N-B4 N-Q4
30 N/4-Q6 B-B4?

Bobby made the last three moves at a blitz clip, for no reason at all. It was unnecessary to retreat the bishop from its strong position, since 30 ... K-N3 would have eliminated the threat of P-B4 followed by N-B5ch. Then 31 NxP? KxN, 32 P-B4 K-N3, 33 PxN RxP would have left White without a prayer. Now Spassky gets the opportunity to trade off the bishop and escape from the bind of the kingside pawns. *(R.B.)* Good was 30 ... K-N3, 31 P-B4 N-B3. *(I.N.)*

31 N-N7   R-QB1?

After this move, White is past the worst. Correct was 31 ... N-K6 and, regardless of the previous tough defense, the White position is very difficult. On 32 NxR, Black can play either 32 ... NxR or 32 ... RxN, while 32 R/1-K1 P-B6!, 33 NxR RxN, 34 R-B2 N-N5, 35 RxP R-Q7 is also no bouquet of roses for White. *(I.N.)*

32	P-B4!	N-K6
33	R-B3	NxP
34	PxP	P-N5
35	R-Q3	P-R4

As a result of his sloppy play, it is difficult for Bobby to organize his game hereabouts. *(R.B.)*

36 P-R3!   . . .

White grasps his chances truly skillfully. First he reduces the material, and then takes advantage of the open lines to put the Black king position in jeopardy. *(I.N.)*

36	. . .	N-R4
37	N/7-Q6	BxN
38	NxB	R-B8ch
39	K-N2	N-B5
40	N-K8ch	. . .

Also possible was 40 R-Q5 NxN, 41 RxN and, in the four-rook end-game, the Black plus pawn can scarcely be utilized. *(I.N.)*

40	. . .	K-N3
41	P-R4!	. . .

A brilliant sealed move by the champion, which sets up a bind around the king and assures a draw. For a while, Najdorf was running around telling people that the move even wins for White. But it isn't that good. *(R.B.)*

The sealed move is the strongest. Spassky thought over it for a long time, leaving himself only 20 minutes for the next 15 moves. *(I.N.)*

41	. . .	P-B3

There was no way of omitting this in view of the threat R-Q5-N5ch and N-B6. *(R.B.)*

42   R-K6   . . .

The interesting possibility, 42 R-Q8 R-B7, 43 P-B5ch K-R3, 44 RxR N-K6ch, 45 K-N3 NxR gets White nowhere. Good enough for a draw seems 42 R-Q5 R-B6, 43 P-B5ch K-R3, 44 N-Q6 R-KB1! (44 . . . N-K6ch, 45 RxN RxR, 46 N-B7ch offers Black no real chances), 45 NxN RxN, 46 R-K7. However, Black still has good winning chances here with 46 . . . P-N6, 47 R/5-Q7 RxKRP, 48 R-KN7 R-KN5, 49 RxR PxR, 50 KxP R-KN1! *(I.N.)*

42   . . .   R-B7ch
43   K-N1   . . .

The active 43 K-N3 doesn't work after 43 . . . R-KB1, 44 R-Q7 N-Q7. *(I.N.)*

43   . . .   K-B4

43 . . . K-B2 could have led to an amusing perpetual check by 44 P-B5 RxN, 45 R-Q7ch K-B1, 46 RxPch, etc. *(R.B.)*
Black could have given his opponent more practical difficulties by the Exchange sacrifice, 43 . . . RxN, 44 RxR K-B4 (on 44 . . . N-Q7, White has the choice of 45 R/8-Q8 N-B6ch, 46 RxN PxR, 47 R-Q5 or equally 45 R-K2 N-B6ch, 46 K-B2), 45 R-QB8 K-K5. At this point the White position could become critical on 46 R-Q6

P-N6! However, 46 R-QN3 is better, allowing White to maintain himself. *(I.N.)*

44   N-N7ch   KxP

On the retreat, 44 . . . K-N3, White does not need to repeat the position with 45 N-K8, but he can proceed with 45 P-B5ch! *(I.N.)*

45   ₁R-Q4ch   K-N6
46   N-B5ch   K-B6

47   R/6-K4   . . .

At this point, White could even make make a try to win: 47 R-K1, which threatens 48 R-B1ch K-K7, 49 R-B2ch, picking up a rook. But Black still has a sufficient defense in 47 . . . R-N7ch!, 48 K-R1 P-N6, with a draw. On 47 R-Q1, Black once again plays 47 . . . R-N7ch and, after 48 K-R1 N-K4, White can get no further. E. Woska of Potsdam has suggested some interesting variations: 47 R-Q3ch K-B5, 48 N-N3! and, in his opinion, the position is won for Spassky. For example, 48 . . . P-B4,

49 N-K2ch RxN, 50 RxR P-N6, 51 K-N2, or 48 ... N-Q7, 49 N-K2ch K-B4, 50 N-Q4ch, or 48 ... R-B8ch, 49 K-B2 R-B7ch, 50 K-K1 R-B8ch, 51 K-K2 P-B4, 52 K-B2 R-B7ch, 53 N-K2ch RxN, 54 RxR P-N6ch, 55 K-N2, etc. Still, in this last variation, Black can play 51 ... R-B7ch, 52 K-Q1 R-Q7ch! and one cannot even begin to speak of White winning. *(I.N.)*

The Black king has run out the string and anything but the perpetual check would be suicidal for Black. A point thrown away for Bobby. *(R.B.)*

Far from faultless, but a very interesting fighting game. In the final position, the resources of both sides are completely exhausted. *(I.N.)*

47	...	**R-B8ch**
48	**K-R2**	**R-B7ch**
49	**K-N1**	**Drawn**

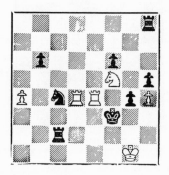

GAME 8

July 27, 1972

With the eighth encounter, Spassky continued his series of disasters in Reykjavik. In a symmetrical variation of the English Opening, Fischer placed on the table a new formation for debate. From a theoretical viewpoint, the White formation is scarcely dangerous for Black, but the psychological effect was enormous. The World Champion took about an hour on his eleventh move before choosing the logical standard plan, which, as a matter of fact, is the best continuation. After White's fifteenth move, however, after reaching a very comfortable position, Spassky sacrificed the Exchange without any reason. Only 4 moves later, there followed a serious misstep by the champion and the game was practically all over. Grandmaster Gligoric designated this game as "the worst in Spassky's career." The rational manner of the challenger's play notched a new success. *(I.N.)*

English Opening

ROBERT FISCHER   BORIS SPASSKY

1 P-QB4   ...

There are probably several reasons for Fischer's adoption of this opening move. In his study of Spassky's games, he must have discovered weak points in some of the champion's favorite defenses and wished to exploit them. In game 4, with his favorite 1 P-K4, Bobby ran into trouble against the Sicilian and, perhaps, therefore desired a breather so he could think up something new for it. *(R.B.)*

1 ...   P-QB4

Boris doesn't usually play this move, preferring 1 ... P-K4. By now he must be so leery of what Fischer has up his sleeve against his known favorites, that he is willing to venture only what he is known not to care for. *(R.B.)*

2	N-QB3	N-QB3
3	N-B3	N-B3
4	P-KN3	P-KN3
5	B-N2	B-N2
6	O-O	O-O

Spassky defends himself with a specialty of the American's. *(I.N.)*

7 P-Q4   PxP

Permitting White to set up the Maroczy Bind is not something of which I approve, though Walter Browne and a few others swear by it. The most solid reply is 7 ... P-Q3, heading into the Yugoslav Variation of the King's Indian Defense, but I am not sure Boris is familiar with that. *(R.B.)*

Possible is also 7 ... P-Q3. After the text move White has more space but, in return for that, Black has chances on the queen's wing. *(I.N.)*

8	NxP	NxN
9	QxN	P-Q3
10	B-N5	...

The idea of this bishop development lies in provoking the weakening ... P-KR3, after which White could play 11 B-Q2, but Black is not forced to that. According to theory, either 10 Q-Q3 or 10 B-Q2 offers more for White. *(I.N.)*

10 ...   B-K3

Now the White queen must move away because of the threat, ... N-Q4. *(I.N. & R.B.)*

11   Q-B4   ...

The most popular retreats are to Q3 or KR4, but the less usual text is not inferior to them. Anyhow, it puzzled Boris, who took a whole hour to determine if it concealed any gimmicks. *(R.B.)*

Original, but nothing more. After 11 Q-R4 Q-R4, 12 QR-B1 QR-B1, 13 P-N3 R-B4, 14 B-Q2 R-R4, 15 Q-B4 B-R3, practical experience indicates the position is equal. *(I.N.)*

11   ...   Q-R4

The soundest formation for Black.

The move prepares the freeing advance, ... P-QN4, and eventually the Black queen can become active on the king's wing. Scarcely to be recommended is 11 ... Q-Q2, 12 KR-Q1 QR-B1, 13 P-N3, when White exerts uncomfortable pressure in the center. Possible, but not necessary, is the sharp variation, 11 ... P-KR3, 12 BxRP BxB, 14 QxB BxP. In the further course of play, the weakened Black king position can give him trouble. *(I.N.)*

12   QR-B1   QR-N1

It was still not necessary to defend the QNP, which could not be taken without White having to give up his own in return, but Black is preparing the freeing ... P-QN4. *(R.B.)*

13   P-N3   KR-B1

Fischer had used a half hour, Spassky three times as much, up to this point. *(I.N.)*

14   Q-Q2   P-QR3
15   B-K3   P-QN4?

Dr. Euwe thought this was a deliberate sacrifice, since Black does get some compensation for the Exchange. Gligoric disagreed, contending that only White has any winning chances now.

The main question is how well Black stands after 15 . . . R-B2, recommended by Euwe and Najdorf. 16 B-R7 R-R1, 17 Q-K3! N-Q2, 18 B-Q4 improves the White game, delaying . . . P-QN4 and aiming to get rid of the fianchettoed bishop. 17 . . . N-N5, 18 Q-N6 QxQ, 19 BxQ R-Q2, 20 N-Q5 gives White a clear advantage. Here, 18 . . . BxN, 19 RxB QxR, 20 QxR gives White such an enormous advantage that it has to be classed as a forced win (20 . . . RxB, 21 Q-N8ch wins).

So, in response to the immortal chess question of the late Oscar Tenner—"Did he fall, or was he pushed?"—I tend to favor the latter alternative. The Maroczy Bind is not without teeth. (R.B.)

A sacrifice or an oversight? I also asked myself this question during the game. Black has achieved a good position (in comparison with the ordinary situation, White has lost a few tempi) and does not need to avail himself of extraordinary resources. He has the choice of several plans here. Into consideration comes 15 . . . B-Q2, 16 B-R7 R-R1, 17 B-Q4 B-B3, 28 P-K4 P-QN4. Perhaps the most logical is the preparatory 15 . . . R-B2 or 15 . . . Q-R4. (I.N.)

16	B-R7	PxP

Now it became clear to me that Black's previous move was a blunder. It would have been consistent to give up the Exchange for the white-squared bishop, in order to develop some initiative on the white squares. Nevertheless, White would have had a good counter: 16 . . . R-R1, 17 BxR RxB, 18 B-Q4! PxP, 19 N-K4 QxQ, 20 NxQ, and the endgame is clearly favorable for White. (I.N.)

17	BxR	RxB
18	PxP	BxP
19	KR-Q1	N-Q2?

This is an incredible tactical blunder, after which the game is a flat win for White. Still, it is very difficult to suggest anything for Black against N-Q5, with its terrible threat to exchange two minor pieces and thus capitalize on the advantage of the Exchange. (R.B.)

Misfortune seldom strikes but once! Spassky is depressed by his oversight on the fifteenth move and loses with-

out play. After 19 ... K-B1, 19 ...
B-K3, or 19 ... Q-R4, Fischer would
have to work hard to eliminate
Black's initiative, so that he could
cash in on his small preponderance
in material. *(I.N.)*

20 N-Q5! ...

Spassky has overlooked this simple
reply completely. *(I.N.)*

20 ... QxQ
21 NxPch! ...

Spassky must have overlooked this
interpolation. *(R.B.)*

21 ... K-B1
22 RxQ KxN
23 RxB ...

In addition to his material advantage,
White stands better positionally,
too. *(I.N.)*

23 ... R-N8ch
24 B-B1 N-B4
25 K-N2 P-QR4

Black undertakes a last try to obtain
counterplay against the enemy QRP.
(I.N.)

26 P-K4 ...

Also good was 26 P-K3 P-R5, 27 B-Q3
R-QR8, 28 B-K4 P-R6, 29 B-Q5.
Already at this point, various roads
lead to Rome. *(I.N.)*

26 ... B-R8
27 P-B4 P-B3
28 R-K2 ...

This seems awkward. At the time, I
preferred 28 B-K2, to be followed by
K-B3 and R-Q1. With the text, Bobby
threatens P-K5. *(R.B.)*

28 ... K-K3
29 R/2-QB2 B-N7
30 B-K2 P-R4

This new pawn weakness makes
possible a quicker decision. There is,
however, no satisfactory defense.
(I.N.)

31 R-Q2 B-R6
32 P-B5ch! ...

Decisively opening the position for
the rooks and allowing the bishop to
join the party. *(R.B. & I.N.)*

32 ... PxP
33 PxPch K-K4
34 R/4-Q4 ...

The threat is mate by 35 R-Q5ch
K-K5, 36 B-B3ch K-K6, 37 R-K2. *(R.B.)*

34 ... KxP
35 R-Q5ch K-K3

36	RxPch	K-K2
37	R-B6	Resigns

A fine performance by Fischer. *(I.N.)*

Spassky Makes a Stand

With the tide running swiftly against him in the previous seven games, Boris was finally able to make a stand in the next stage of the match. True, damming the current will not enable him to save the match, but an even keel is better than a sinking boat. And it could inspire him to continue under sail to get back the minus points which have given Fischer a 6½–4½ lead.

Game 9 was the shortest, quietest draw of the match so far. After the blunders of round 8, perhaps Spassky needed to demonstrate to himself that he could not be just bowled over. Many grandmasters aim for a draw in the next contest after a bad loss to fight the feeling that they will never do anything right again. Nevertheless, the opening is of considerable interest to theory, for Fischer introduced an enterprising pawn shot at his ninth move, transplanting an idea from the Gruenfeld Defense. Boris made some attempt to demonstrate weaknesses on Fischer's queenside, but without getting anywhere against Fischer's accurate tactical defense. That left no other conclusion but a split point.

For game 10, Bobby returned to 1 P-K4, but Boris did not try a repeat performance of the Sicilian Defense which worked so well for him in game 4, undoubtedly fearing that

Fischer was ready with something new. The fans, including me, were dying to find out what it might be. However, Spassky did not want to risk his hide to satisfy our curiosity. Instead, he went to the Breyer Defense to the Ruy Lopez, which has been his foremost favorite in recent years. It led to some of the most exciting chess of the match. Spassky broke out of a bind with a pawn sacrifice, obtaining enough play to induce the challenger to give back the pawn at once. Bobby then offered a pawn of his own to begin the sharpest combination of the match, finally winning the Exchange at the expense of allowing his opponent two dangerous connected passed pawns. His excellent streamlined technique cut through the endgame problems for a convincing win after adjournment.

Now 3 points down, Boris fought back at once, again taking on the "poisoned pawn" variation of the Najdorf Sicilian, with which he had obtained a lost position in round 7, drawing only through Fischer's careless endgame play. This time he improved by 10 BxN and 11 B-K2, leading to a far more preferable system than the 10 B-Q3 of game 7. But it was his spectacular 14 N-N1 that made the game. Gligoric, who showered it with exclamation points, came running into the press room, declaring, "It turns the entire 'poisoned pawn' variation upside down! Fantastic! There's nothing to do about it!" Nevertheless, the dust hasn't settled on it yet. Bent Larsen and Fridrik Olafsson are not convinced that it deserved the success that it achieved.

Bobby went wildly astray against it, however, sacrificing a pawn, the acceptance of which gave Spassky an overwhelming position immediately. Realizing that there was no long-range way to fix up his game, Fischer swung into a desperate, unsound attack, which Boris brushed off effortlessly, winning a queen for a minor piece and making short shrift of what remained of Fischer's position.

Before this game, Boris had gone nine straight rounds without taking a single point over the board. Now the question was raised: Will this win build up his morale so that he can make a serious bid to get back into the match? *(R.B.)*

GAME 9

August 1, 1972

After his painful defeat in the previous game the World Champion took time out for the first time in the match. Two points behind, Spassky had to decide what tactics to choose in the next game. The course of the encounter showed that the champion had still not recuperated, for he made only very careful attempts to seize the initiative.

Fischer demonstrated again that he was employing flexible tactics in this match. Formerly it was considered a failing of Fischer's tournament tactics that he was so transparent: his work in the openings was good, but everyone knew in advance what variations he would choose. Also, he played almost every game stubbornly for a win, without regard for the tournament situation. With good preparation, one could turn these circumstances to good account in a long match. But in Reykjavik, Fischer revealed himself as a mature campaigner, who utilized diverse weapons for diverse situations. Among other things, he made successful raids on Spassky's openings repertory. *(I.N.)*

Queen's Gambit Declined

BORIS SPASSKY	ROBERT FISCHER
1 P-Q4	N-KB3
2 P-QB4	P-K3
3 N-KB3	P-Q4

Fischer no longer has need of such extraordinary measures as the 3 . . . P-B4 of the third game. *(I.N.)*

4	N-B3	P-B4

While this move has been accepted as the equalizer for about forty years, recently Spassky (in his 1969 match with Petrosian) and Polugaevsky have brought it under the hammer once again. In the match opener, Bobby went for the Nimzo–Indian, . . . B-N5, instead, but the text move has always ranked high in his estimation. *(R.B.)*

Once again Black varies his play, foregoing the Nimzo–Indian, 4 . . . B-N5, of game 1. *(I.N.)*

5	BPxP	NxP
6	P-K4	. . .

The alternative, favored by Najdorf and a number of others, is 6 P-K3, which leads to positions roughly characteristic of the Queen's Gambit Accepted. Not since his game with me in the 1962 U.S. Championship has Bobby been in any trouble against it. Spassky, with his Tarrasch-like play, prefers the classical pawn center arising from the text. *(R.B.)*

Spassky is partial to this manner of play; also popular here is 6 P-K3. *(I.N.)*

6	. . .	NxN
7	PxN	PxP
8	PxP	N-B3

The prelude to an innovation. Spassky perhaps hoped to repeat his fifth match game with Petrosian (Moscow 1969): 8 ... B-N5ch, 9 B-Q2 BxBch, 10 QxB O-O, 11 B-B4 N-B3, 12 O-O P-QN3, 13 QR-Q1 B-N2, 14 KR-K1 R-B1, 15 P-Q5!, with a dangerous initiative. *(I.N.)*

9   B-QB4   ...

Premature would be 9 P-Q5 PxP, 10 PxP B-N5ch! However, 9 P-QR3 B-K2, 10 B-Q3 O-O, 11 B-N2, as in Keres–Geller, Moscow 1962, results in a sharp game with good perspectives for White. *(I.N.)*

9   ...   P-QN4!?

It makes a lot of sense strategically to get the Black queenside in motion, since his compensation for the enemy center is the pawn majority on that wing in the endgame. Tactically, however, it looks dangerous to advance like this without first completing development. The next 6 moves demonstrate that Bobby's innovation

has been well prepared. Of course, the pawn cannot be taken at once because of 10 ... Q-R4ch. *(R.B.)* The new idea, whereby Black hopes to win a tempo for the development of the queen's wing. *(I.N.)*

10   B-Q3   ...

The pawn naturally cannot be taken on account of the queen check at R4 and, on 10 B-N3, Black can win another tempo by ... N-R4. However, 10 B-K2 deserved attention, for then White could more quickly begin action on the queen file. *(I.N.)*

10	...	B-N5ch
11	B-Q2	BxBch
12	QxB	P-QR3
13	P-QR4	...

This move does not achieve its aim because of Black's strong reply. More enterprising was 13 O-O O-O, 14 P-Q5! PxP, 15 PxP N-K2, 16 QR-Q1 and Black cannot take the QP (16 ... QxP, 17 Q-N4 and Black loses material). Also interesting is the immediate 13 P-Q5 PxP, 14 PxP QxP, 15 O-O. *(I.N.)*

13   ...   O-O!

The first of Bobby's tactical points is that 14 PxP NxP, 15 PxP?? N-N6 is disastrous for White. *(R.B. & I.N.)*

14   Q-B3   ...

The queen sticks out like a sore thumb on the open file, but 14 Q-N2 Q-R4ch, 15 N-Q2 Q-N5 is too strong for Black. Perhaps 15 K-K2 P-N5 can be tried, though that just about rules out any aggression in the center on White's part. *(R.B.)*

14	. . .	B-N2
15	PxP	PxP

The pawn is without visible means of support, but its defense is there, although indirect. The advantage is Black's on 16 RxR QxR, 17 BxP N-R2, followed by the capture of the KP. The same result occurs on 16 BxP RxRch, 17 QxR N-N5, 18 Q-R4 Q-K2, because it is impossible for White to defend the KP and threat of 19 . . . R-R1 and 20 . . . R-R8ch simultaneously. *(R.B.)*

16   O-O   . . .

White must think of his development. The pawn-snatch, 16 BxP RxRch, 17 QxR Q-N3 or 16 RxR QxR, 17 BxP N-R2! is too dangerous. *(I.N.)*

16   . . .   Q-N3

By means of this move, Black takes his QB4 square away from the White queen. However, it was more prudent to exchange rooks first. *(I.N.)*

17   QR-N1   . . .

Probably Dr. Euwe is right in claiming that the only way for White to try for sharp play is QR-Q1, followed by B-N1 with the idea of a kingside attack. However, Boris has undoubtedly judged the position as equal and is reconciled to a draw with the least fuss. After the text move, the weakness of the Black QNP and the White QP are in balance. *(R.B.)*

17	. . .	P-N5
18	Q-Q2	. . .

There is some difference of opinion about the endgame resulting from 18 P-Q5 PxP, 19 PxP PxQ, 20 RxQ N-R4, 21 P-Q6. Gligoric feels that White stands better, while Euwe believes it to be a draw. I don't think there is anything in it for White after 21 ... B-Q4. *(R.B.)*

Now the game levels out quickly to a draw. White should have tried the active move, 18 P-Q5! After the possible 18 ... PxP, 19 PxP Q-Q1, 20 Q-B2! QxP, 21 BxPch K-R1, 22 B-K4 Q-QN4, 23 KR-B1 N-R4, 24 BxB NxB, 25 Q-K4, White stands clearly better. However, 19 ... PxQ is better: 20 RxQ and now not 20 ... N-R4, 21 P-Q6, when White has good chances for success, but stronger, 20 ... N-Q1, 21 P-Q6 BxN, 22 PxB N-K3, and Black can hold the endgame. In this variation, White could try 21 B-B4 but, after 21 ... R-B1, 22 B-N3 R-B4, White can scarcely improve his position. *(I.N.)*

18   ...   NxP

Liquidation is now practically forced, since 18 ... KR-Q1 runs into 19 P-Q5!, which wins the QNP and the game. *(R.B.)*

19	NxN	QxN
20	RxP	Q-Q2
21	Q-K3	KR-Q1

The game could be given up as a draw here, except that throughout

this match both players insist on playing everything out to the bitter end. Nor was there a chance in 21 ... R-R6, 22 Q-N6. *(R.B.)*

22   KR-N1   ...

The simplest. *(I.N.)*

22	...	QxB
23	QxQ	RxQ
24	RxB	P-N4
25	R-N8ch	RxR
26	RxRch	K-N2
27	P-B3	R-Q7
28	P-R4	P-R3
29	PxP	PxP
	Drawn	

The most quiet game of an exciting match. *(I.N.)*

GAME 10

August 3, 1972

Both grandmasters are partisans of the open game and, therefore, it was expected that the "king of the open games," the Ruy Lopez, would enjoy heavy employment and enrichment. This was not the case, however, because Fischer did not stick exclusively to 1 P-K4 as anticipated and because Spassky preferred to use the sharper Sicilian Defense. The tenth game was interesting also from the point of view of opening theory. Black defended himself with the Breyer Variation and both opponents showed an excellent grasp of its thematic finesses. There arose a position in which Fischer strove to encircle his adversary on the queen's wing, while Spassky countered with combinative resources. By means of a sacrifice of the Exchange, Black achieved counterplay, but he was unable to realize his chances in time-pressure. Fischer once again demonstrated his steady play in the last hour of the game. *(I.N.)*

Ruy Lopez

ROBERT FISCHER   BORIS SPASSKY

1   P-K4   . . .

After two wins with 1 P-QB4, that move has lost its surprise value, while Bobby has undoubtedly come up with something against Spassky's round 4 Sicilian. *(R.B.)*

1	. . .	P-K4
2	N-KB3	N-QB3
3	B-N5	P-QR3
4	B-R4	N-B3
5	O-O	B-K2
6	R-K1	P-QN4
7	B-N3	P-Q3

Spassky has also used the super-sharp Marshall Gambit quite frequently in recent years. For example, the opening moves in the Fischer–Spassky encounter in Santa Monica, 1966, were: 7 . . . O-O, 8 P-B3 P-Q4, 9 PxP NxP, 10 NxP NxN, 11 RxN P-QB3, 12 P-N3 N-B3, with chances for both sides. *(I.N.)*

8	P-B3	O-O
9	P-KR3	N-N1

The famous retreat of Julius Breyer is based on the idea that the knight is more flexible posted at Q2, where it does not impede the advance of the QBP, nor obstruct the diagonal of the QB when it plays to QN2, laying siege to the KP. Long a favorite of Spassky's, this variation has been one of the most successful Lopez defenses in recent years. *(R.B.)*

10	P-Q4	QN-Q2
11	QN-Q2	. . .

Fischer has very often preferred 11 N-R4, which I played against Boris in the Alekhine Memorial Tournament in Moscow, November 1971. That game was a draw in which I was unable to achieve any opening initiative against the champion's accurate defense. Perhaps that encouraged

Bobby to look for another approach. (R.B.)

11	...	B-N2
12	B-B2	R-K1
13	P-QN4	...

When Spassky has the White pieces in this system, he invariably goes for 13 N-B1 and N-N3. It does not give much, but Spassky has never needed much. The text move is intended to make ... P-B4 difficult to achieve and looks toward a further queen's wing expansion by White. (R.B. & I.N.)

13 ... B-KB1

This retreat belongs to the system; now White must keep the KP protected. (I.N.)

14 P-QR4 ...

More usual here is 14 B-N2 N-N3, 15 P-R3, with P-B4 to follow. (I.N.)

14 ... N-N3

Granted the premise of this defense, the idea of compelling White to resolve the queenside tension must be good. Because 15 PxNP would be too leveling, the following move is as good as forced. (R.B.)
Black is willing to yield a tempo for the sake of stabilizing the pawn formation on the queenside. The counter-thrust, 14 ... P-B4, also seems reasonable, but Spassky ordinarily tries to get along in the Ruy Lopez without this move. (I.N.)

15 P-R5 ...

After 15 PxNP PxNP, Black's only weakness, the QNP, can easily be defended. (I.N.)

| 15 | ... | QN-Q2 |
| 16 | B-N2 | ... |

Here, and on the next move, Black can answer P-Q5 with ... P-B3, obtaining dynamic play against the White center. (I.N.)

16 ... Q-N1

There are two useful points to this move: one is to keep the enemy QNP under direct surveillance (anticipating White's P-B4); the other is to protect his K4 so he can aim for the liberating ... P-B4. (R.B.)
Black is somewhat cramped and must sooner or later decide on ... P-B4; the original queen move provides another protection for the KP. Worthy of consideration is also 16 ... P-N3, to be followed by 17 ... B-N2. (I.N.)

17 R-N1 ...

Thus the QNP is indirectly defended so that White can proceed with B-Q3, Q-B2 and P-B4. It is also important to have the QB protected, as the following sharp play shows. *(R.B.)*
This move is very enticing because of the vis-à-vis of queen and rook. Because of the threat, 18 P-B4, Black must now undertake something, and 17 ... P-N3, 18 B-N3, or 17 ... Q-R2, 18 P-B4 are both favorable for White. However, seriously to be considered was the immediate 17 P-B4, in order, after the practically forced 17 ... NPxP, simply to recapture with 18 QNxP. *(I.N.)*

| 17 | ... | **P-B4** |

Whatever the result, this bold bid for freedom should be tried. Otherwise, it is difficult to suggest how Black can improve his position against the plan outlined in the previous note. *(R.B.)*
The *Deutsche Schachzeitung* suggests the alternative, 17 ... PxP, 18 PxP P-Q4, 19 P-K5 N-K5, 20 NxN PxN, 21 BxP BxB, 22 ṘxB N-B3, 23 R-K2 N-Q4! However, 21 RxP! is much stronger, for, if 21 ... BxR, 22 BxB, Black's situation is critical. For example, 22 ... BxP, 23 N-N5 and Black can scarcely make a successful defense of his king's position. *(I.N.)*

18   NPxP   ...

After 18 P-Q5 P-B5, the resulting closed position would offer Black sufficient resources for the defense of his king. *(I.N.)*

| 18 | ... | **QPxP** |

White would get strong attacking chances against the enemy king after 18 ... PxQP, 19 P/3xP PxP, 20 P-K5, which opens up the diagonal of the "Spanish" bishop at QB2. *(R.B. & I.N.)*

| 19 | PxKP | QNxP |
| 20 | NxN | ... |

This exchange eases the Black situation. White could have given him a lot more trouble with Polugaevsky's suggestion, 20 P-B4! *(I.N.)*

| 20 | ... | QxN |
| 21 | P-QB4 | Q-B5 |

At this point it looks as though Black has grasped the initiative and he threatens QR-Q1 for more pressure. Bobby's next few moves show that appearances are deceptive. *(R.B.)*

| 22 | BxN | QxB |
| 23 | PxP | ... |

Fischer plays consistently for the win of a pawn but, in so doing, allows his opponent active piece play. *(I.N.)*

23   ...   KR-Q1

The simplest was probably 23 ... PxP, 24 RxP B-R3, and after 25 R-N3 P-B5, 26 R-KB3 Q-Q5, as well as after 25 R-N6 Q-QB6, 26 N-N3 P-B5, 27 Q-Q2 Q-K4, Black has a completely satisfactory game. It should be noted that on 23 ... QR-Q1,

24 Q-B1 Q-QB6, 25 PxP BxRP, White has the strong 26 B-R4! at his disposal. *(I.N.)*

24   Q-B1   Q-QB6

Spassky recovers his sacrificed pawn while keeping the knight away from B4. If instead, 24 ... PxP, 25 RxP B-B3, 26 R-N6 RxP, 27 N-B4 R-N4, 28 P-K5 Q-K3, 29 R-R6 R-R1, 30 RxB QxR, 31 B-K4 Q-B1, 32 BxR QxB, White has the slight advantage of a knight superior to the bishop and can perhaps expose the enemy king by P-K6. *(R.B.)*

Here, as well as at the next move, Black could capture on QN4, but the text continuation is also quite good. *(I.N.)*

25   N-B3   QxP

On 25 ... PxP, 26 RxP B-R3, 27 P-K5! QxRch, 28 QxQ BxR, 29 Q-N1 RxP, 30 BxPch K-R1, 31 N-N5! B-B5, 32 B-N8!, White has an easily won game. *(R.B.)*

26   B-N3!   . . .

Very elegantly played! Fischer begins a dangerous attack on the Black king, which, however, is defensible with exact play. The simpler 26 PxP was also to be considered. *(I.N.)*

Bobby could have held only a minute positional advantage following 26 PxP BxRP, 27 P-K5, because of 27 ... B-Q6. The text move introduces one of the prettiest combinations of the match, suddenly switching to direct attack on the king. *(R.B.)*

26   . . .   PxP

26 .. Q-B2?, 27 P-N6! is not even worthy of consideration. *(I.N.)*

27   Q-KB4   R-Q2

Weaker is 27 ... P-B5, 28 BxP PxB, 29 RxB P-B3, 30 P-K5! *(I.N.)*

Apparently Spassky does not anticipate Fischer's twenty-ninth move, for otherwise he would have played 27 ... P-B5, 28 BxP PxB, 29 RxB P-B3, 30 P-K5 Q-Q4, when it is not clear that White can manufacture a win. *(R.B.)*

28   N-K5   Q-B2

Black defends himself with the only move. Now it seems as if the White resources are exhausted, but . . . *(I.N.)*

29   QR-Q1!   . . .

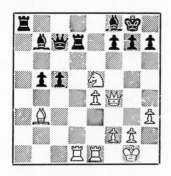

White cannot spare the precious tempo that would be lost by 33 N-R6ch PxN, 34 RxB P-B5. To win this ending, the passed pawns must be blockaded on the white squares at once. *(R.B. & I.N.)*

| 33 | ... | KxN |

The game has now resolved itself into an ending in which the connected passed pawns almost compensate for Black's small material disadvantage. *(I.N.)*

| 34 | R-Q7ch | K-B3 |
| 35 | R-N7 | R-R8ch |

Bent Larsen considered this an error, contending that the only chance for a draw lay in 35 ... P-N5, 36 K-B1 R-B1, 37 R-B4 R-Q1, 38 K-K2 K-K3, but, after 39 R-N5!, the Black king cannot reach Q4 because of R/4xP, nor can it get to QB3 because of R/5xP. Fischer would proceed then to win just as in the game, by advancing his kingside pawns. *(R.B.)* After 35 ... P-N5, 36 R-N6ch K-B2 (36 ... K-B4??, 37 P-B3, with R/6-K6 to follow), 37 P-B4 R-B1 (the rook ordinarily belongs behind the passed pawns), 38 R-B4 gives White real chances for success. *(I.N.)*

This quiet little gem is the real point of Bobby's twenty-sixth for there is now no way for Spassky to save the Exchange. *(R.B.)*

A fatal mistake would be 29 ... RxR??, 30 BxPch K-R1, 31 N-N6ch PxN, 32 Q-R4 mate. *(R.B. & I.N.)* Also 29 ... QR-Q1, 30 BxPch RxB, 31 QxRch QxQ, 32 NxQ RxR, 33 RxR KxN, 34 R-Q7ch K-K3, 35 RxB, wins for White with a lot less effort than in the game continuation. In this last line, 33 ... BxP, 34 N-N5! B-B4, 35 R-Q5 P-N3, 36 P-N4 P-R3, 37 PxB PxN, 38 PxP again gives White fewer problems than the actual game. *(R.B. and I.N.)*

However, once again returning to this last line, 33 ... P-N5 gives good chances of a draw. *(I.N.)*

29	...	R-K2
30	BxPch	RxB
31	QxRch	QxQ
32	NxQ	BxP
33	RxB	...

36	K-R2	B-Q3ch
37	P-N3	P-N5
38	K-N2	P-R4

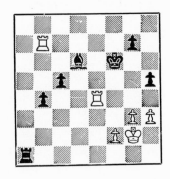

The last move before the time-control is often a decisive mistake. After
40 ... R-Q4 or 40 ... P-N4, the win
for White is still not easy to prove.
(I.N.)

When the game was adjourned at
this point, a number of people were
still convinced that the dangerous
connected passed pawns should earn
Spassky a draw. Yet there is no defense against Fischer's logical winning
plan. First the bishop and rook will
be tied down to passive defense.
Then the White pawns will advance
to help the rooks set up a mating
net. It's fairly straightforward, although the tactical execution must
be sharp. *(R.B.)*

41   K-K2   . . .

The sealed move. The adjournment
analysis showed that Black no longer
has a defense. Fischer demonstrates
the way to win very exactly. *(I.N.)*

Yugoslav grandmaster Janosevic suggested 38 : .. B-K4 as the best defense. I persuaded him that White
wins fairly smoothly after 39 P-B4
B-Q5, 40 P-N4 R-R7ch, 41 K-B1 R-R6,
42 P-R4 because 42 ... P-N6? is
unplayable: 43 P-B5 R-R3 (the only
defense to the threatened mate at
K6), 44 R-N8 K-B2, 45 RxP, and with
the fall of the important QNP, Black
can offer only token resistance.
However, after the careful 42 ...
R-R3, White's task will be much
harder, although 43 R/4-K7 (threatening simply to pick up both the Black
kingside pawns) should lead to a win.
Earlier, 41 ... R-R7 would have
been worse than useless, for 42 K-K1!
(not at once 42 R/7-K7? R-B7ch,
43 K-K1 RxP! with at least a draw)
42 ... RxP??, 43 R/7-K7 K-N3, 44
R/4-K6ch B-B3, 45 P-N5 wins a piece.
(R.B.)

Here 38 ... K-B4 appears to be
better; for example, 39 R-R4 B-K4,
40 RxRP B-Q5, 41 R-R4 R-N8 or
39 K-B3 B-K4, 40 R-N6 B-Q5. *(I.N.)*

41   . . .   R-Q4
42   P-B4!   . . .

Decisively gaining space on the king's
wing, which would not have been
possible except for the unfortunate
retreat of the king by 40 ... K-B2.
(I.N.)

42	. . .	P-N3
43	P-N4	PxP
44	PxP	P-N4

Avoiding this would permit White P-N5 and R-N7ch, confining the Black king to the first rank. *(R.B.)*

| 45 | **P-B5** | **B-K4** |

There is no alternative to this bid for counterplay, since Bobby was threatening R/4-K6 and R-N7ch, again with a mating net. *(R.B.)*

| 46 | **R-N5!** | . . . |

The pin set up by the rook move forces the win of the QNP, since 46 . . . B-B6, 47 R-N7ch K-B1, 48 R/4-K7 R-Q1, 49 R/K7-QB7 B-Q5, 50 P-B6 gives Black no way out of the mate. Of course, Black can trade rooks by 48 . . . R-K4ch, but then he cannot stop the king from getting to K6 with a new mating net. *(R.B.)* With the fall of a pawn, the win is easy. *(I.N.)*

46	. . .	**K-B3**
47	**R/4xP**	**B-Q5**
48	**R-N6ch**	**K-K4**
49	**K-B3!**	. . .

This is the kind of little tactical finesse that makes the difference between an easy win and a hard one. The Black king is kept out of his KB5 by the mate threat. *(R.B.)*

49	. . .	**R-Q1**
50	**R-N8**	**R-Q2**
51	**R/4-N7**	**R-Q3**
52	**R-N6**	**R-Q2**
53	**R-N6**	**K-Q4**
54	**RxP**	**B-K4**
55	**P-B6!**	. . .

Another little added touch—the bishop is won by force. *(R.B.)*

| 55 | . . . | **K-Q5** |
| 56 | **R-N1!** | **Resigns** |

Now 56 . . . BxP, 57 R-B5 R-KB2, 58 P-N5 proves the point. *(R.B.)* A very interesting fighting game, in which Fischer well understood how to present one new problem after another to his opponent. *(I.N.)*

GAME 11

August 6, 1972

It is rare in grandmaster chess to score a knockout of one's opponent in the opening stage of the game. Because defensive technique and theoretical knowledge have progressed so much in recent decades, it is not easy to find a gap in the grandmaster's arsenal. Still, instructive brevities occur now and then even in struggles on the highest level. In order to come about, these "blitzkriegs" require that one choose sharp and so-called "concrete" opening variations, and that one of the partners goes a bit beyond the pale. This all happened in the following game.

Before game 11, the situation of the World Champion was very difficult. The challenger enjoyed a solid 3-point lead and, what was even more significant, Spassky's play gave him and his seconds a lot of headaches. On Sunday, August 6, Spassky succeeded in winning his best game in Reykjavik. To tell the truth, Fischer helped largely in the creation of this striking miniature. *(I.N.)*

Sicilian Defense

BORIS SPASSKY   ROBERT FISCHER

1	P-K4	P-QB4
2	N-KB3	P-Q3
3	P-Q4	PxP
4	NxP	N-KB3
5	N-QB3	P-QR3

After this game, the American did not again choose this demanding variation with the follow-up pawn snatch on White's QN2, thus inducing many commentators to speak of the refutation of the whole Black system. However, it is scarcely believable that White's fourteenth move is so strong that the whole variation must be consigned to the archives. As the following analysis attempts to show, Black's play can be improved and it seems to me that Fischer failed to repeat his favorite variation only on the ground of his match tactics as a whole. *(I.N.)*

6	B-N5	P-K3
7	P-B4	Q-N3
8	Q-Q2	QxP
9	N-N3	Q-R6
10	BxN	. . .

Up to here, the moves have been the same as in game 7, wherein 10 B-Q3 was played, totally without success. The text move leads to a difficult position for both sides, which I believed to be somewhat in Black's favor before seeing the important innovation Spassky comes up with on the fourteenth move. *(R.B.)* Without this exchange, it's no go for White. In the seventh game, Spassky tried 10 B-Q3, which led to a complicated and not disadvantageous game for Black. *(I.N.)*

10	. . .	PxB
11	B-K2	. . .

This bishop development is better than the only apparently more aggressive 11 B-Q3. Now Black is practically forced to make the following weakening pawn move. *(I.N.)*

11 ... P-KR4

If Black does nothing to prevent it, 12 B-R5, followed by O-O and P-B5, will give an overwhelming position. *(R.B. & I.N.)*

12 O-O N-B3

According to Isaac Boleslavsky, 12 ... N-Q2 is superior, but even then White has an active game with good chances for gaining the advantage. *(I.N.)*

13 K-R1 ...

A good prophylactic move. A queen check on the QR7-KN1 diagonal could considerably ease the defense in many variations. *(I.N.)*

13 ... B-Q2
14 N-N1!? ...

The most interesting move in Reykjavik and, in the opinion of many commentators, the winning stroke. Practically, White achieves a surprisingly quick success with it, but a more accurate reconsideration shows that Fischer was not at his best this day. The White position after Black's thirteenth move is worth a pawn, of course; in addition to Spassky's unique knight retreat, he could also have chosen other attacking continuations such as 14 QR-K1 or 14 R-B3, after which the Black defense would not be an easy task. Practically, however, the text move is fully justified because, with the best defense, White can repeat the position to arrive once again at the position after Black's thirteenth move, whereupon he can select other plans of attack. *(I.N.)*

Spassky's sensational knight retreat shocked the spectators and mightily disconcerted Fischer, who went to pieces against it. However, it will be seen that White has no other resource than to repeat the position, if Black finds the correct defense. *(R.B.)*

14 ... Q-N5

The only really reliable rescue from the bane of Spassky's diabolical knight withdrawal is 14 ... Q-N7!, with the idea of answering 15 N-B3 by 15 ... Q-R6, repeating the position. It would be too risky for Black to try for more by 15 ... R-B1,

16 N-R4 Q-R6, 17 N-N6, but it would also be too risky for White to gamble on trapping the queen by 15 P-QR3, for Black has 15 ... R-B1, 16 N-B3 N-Q5! with a clear advantage. After 14 ... Q-N7, White could try an alternate way of trapping the Black queen by 15 P-QR4 R-B1, 16 N-R3 (threatening N-B4), because White has the advantage on 16 ... P-B4, 17 PxP. Nevertheless, both Bent Larsen and Paul Keres independently discovered the saving clause in 16 ... P-Q4!, 17 PxP N-N5!, when Black perhaps stands better through all complications. *(R.B. & I.N.)*
Also possible for Black is 14 ... Q-R5, and in case of 15 P-QR3, then not 15 ... QxKP??, 16 B-Q3 Q-Q4, 17 N-B3 and the queen is won, but 15 ... N-K2. Of course, after 14 ... Q-R5, White can play 15 N-B3. *(I.N.)*
On 14 ... Q-R5, 15 Q-K3 R-B1, 16 P-B4 N-K2, 17 N-B3 Q-B3, Black's queen and knight are badly misplaced, and he cannot even look forward to queenside castling. White's positional advantage far outweighs the sacrificed pawn here. The upshot of all this analysis is that the poisoned pawn variation is good enough for a draw by repetition, but Black cannot get more. *(R.B.)*

15   Q-K3   . . .

Now the enemy queen cannot retreat to QN3, so the threat is 16 P-QR3 and N-B3 with a fatal trap. *(R.B.)*

15   . . .   P-Q4?

After this pawn sacrifice, Boris romps to the win. Bobby should have tried to hang on by 15 ... N-K2. *(R.B.)* The opening of the position is equal to suicide in this situation. Black had to defend himself by means of 15 ... N-K2, 16 P-QR3 Q-R5. After this unavoidable continuation, there arises an interesting position in which the White initiative is far more significant than the missing pawn. In the first place, White can simply play 17 N-B3 Q-B3, 18 R-B3. However, more energetic seems 17 P-B4. For example, 17 ... R-B1, 18 N-B3! Q-B3, 19 QR-N1 with lasting pressure against a very constricted Black position. If here 18 ... QxN?, 19 KR-N1 Q-B7, 20 R-R2! N-B4, 21 Q-R3! and the Black queen is caught. *(I.N.)*

16   PxP   N-K2
17   P-B4!   . . .

It's not just that White has gotten his pawn back, but this attacking spearhead of pawns would rip through a Black castled queenside position in jig time. There is nothing to do about the compromised position of the Black king. *(R.B.)*
Very powerfully played. Now the Black pieces remain sadly constricted. *(I.N.)*

17   . . .   N-B4
18   Q-Q3   P-R5

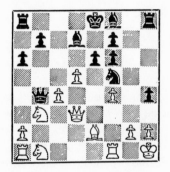

Since the position is hopeless any-how, why not aim for the coffee-house finish 19 ... N-N6ch, 20 PxN PxPch, 21 K-N1 QxN!, 22 PxQ B-B4ch and mate in 3? (R.B. & I.N.)

On 18 ... PxP, White has the choice between 19 PxP B-N4, 20 QxN BxB, 21 N/1-Q2! BxR, 22 RxB and the even stronger 19 N-B3! QxP (19 ... PxP, 20 Q-K4ch B-K2, 21 N-Q5 Q-Q3, 22 BxBP is hopeless for Black), 20 Q-B3 and the White attack is an-nihilating. Also possible is Polu-gaevsky's recommendation, 20 Q-Q2 (instead of 20 Q-B3), but then Black still has some hopes of defense after 20 ... Q-N5, for example, 21 P-QR3 Q-Q3 or 21 KR-K1 O-O-O. Of course, even then Black's position is far from enviable. (I.N.)

19   B-N4!   ...

Now a vertical check on the rook file can be blocked by the bishop, which meanwhile threatens BxN to cripple further the center pawns and expose the king. (R.B. & I.N.)

19   ...   N-Q3

On 19 ... N-R3, there would follow

20 PxP BxP (or 20 ... PxP, 21 B-R5ch K-K2, 22 R-Q1), 21 BxB PxB, 22 N-B3 with a winning position. (I.N.)

20   N/1-Q2   P-B4?

It is easy to stamp this move as an error, but very difficult to recommend a reasonable way out for Black, whose situation is already hopeless. (I.N.)

21   P-QR3!   ...

The Black queen is still grist for Spassky's mill. (R.B.)

21   ...   Q-N3??

The only continuation was 21 ... Q-R5, 22 N-B5 Q-R4, 23 N/2-N3 Q-B2, but Black could resign here-abouts without any real regrets. (R.B. & I.N.)

22   P-B5   Q-N4
23   Q-QB3   PxB??

If Fischer thinks it is too early to resign, he must play 23 ... R-KN1, 24 P-R4 B-N2, 25 N-Q4 BxN, 26 QxB Q-R4, 27 B-B3 N-K5, 28 BxN PxB, 29 NxP. (R.B.)

24   P-R4   P-R6

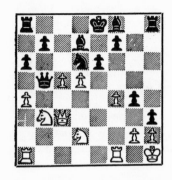

No escape is offered by 24 ... Q-K7, 25 QR-K1, and after 24 ... QxRch, 25 RxQ, there is still too much of Black en prise. The rest needs no comment. *(R.B. & I.N.)*

25	PxQ	PxPch
26	KxP	R-R6
27	Q-B6	N-B4
28	P-B6	B-B1
29	QPxP	BPxP
30	KR-K1	B-K2
31	RxKP	Resigns

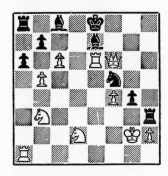

After this game, the excitement of the fans in Reykjavik again reached a peak. *(I.N.)*

Fischer Grabs a 3-Point Lead

Rebounding from the thumping defeat his poisoned-pawn Najdorf suffered at Spassky's hands in the eleventh game, Fischer made a stubborn attempt to recover the point in the twelfth. Once again his 1 P-QB4 developed into a Queen's Gambit Declined, as in the sixth encounter, but Spassky, mindful of the catastrophe his Tartakower Variation met with, diverted at the seventh move into the old Orthodox Defense, hardly seen since Capablanca and Stahlberg fought over its fine points almost 40 years ago.

Although Bobby obtained a small advantage in the early middle game, he found no way to press it, even with the two bishops. After omitting the strong 25 Q-K2, he began to get into difficulties, compounded by a mistake on move 35. However, Boris overlooked a powerful chance to play for a win, replying routinely to maintain an approximately level position. Shortly after adjournment, Boris's exact defense destroyed whatever opportunities there might have been to make any progress and the game could have been agreed a draw. Nevertheless, Fischer obstinately continued until he lost a pawn in a dead drawn ending with bishops of opposite colors. That finally convinced him the game really was a draw.

Game 13 was a rousing battle. Fischer sprang a surprise Alekhine Defense, rapidly seizing the initiative and snatching a pawn. Since Spassky did not like the looks of the position he would be forced into if he played to retake the pawn, he sacrificed it permanently, going all out for a kingside attack. An inaccuracy by Fischer fueled the onslaught to alarming proportions, but at the crucial moment the champion vacillated, drifting into a pawn-down endgame. That might, perhaps, have been the end of the story, except that Bobby took matters too lightly and blew the win a few moves before adjournment. When the game was resumed, he put an incredible effort into the ending, sacrificing a bishop, allowing his rook to be imprisoned and, in effect, going for a win with king and five pawns against king and rook. Spassky's draw was there, but he was worn down after so many hours of play—he blundered at the sixty-ninth move and lost.

That monumental battle knocked both players for a loop. Spassky was granted a postponement on the advice of match doctor Ulfar Thordarsson, who rescheduled Sunday's round 14 for Tuesday. That was still too soon. The game produced a comedy of errors, with first Fischer blundering a pawn away and then

Spassky following right behind, giving the pawn back for nothing. Not even these two stalwarts are immune from chess nerves. Finally, shocked into sobriety by their glaring errors, they succeeded in quietly drawing without further mishap. *(R.B.)*

GAME 12

August 8, 1972

For a "grandmaster draw" in the Fischer–Spassky manner, a full 55 moves are required! That showed once again how hard-fought the battle in Reykjavik was. After the 11th game, both duelists were simply not inclined to a sharp struggle. Spassky has said many times that he can only mobilize himself with great difficulty for the next encounter after brilliantly winning a game. Also for Fischer, who had never previously been slaughtered in the style of game 11, it was no easy task to decide whether to strive for immediate revenge or to be satisfied with waiting tactics. Both combatants deserve praise for avoiding any kind of 15-move draw under the circumstances, but instead, prudently probing each other in all phases of the game. *(I.N.)*

Queen's Gambit Declined

ROBERT FISCHER   BORIS SPASSKY

1   P-QB4   . . .

Thus Fischer makes it clear that the close game is no temporary fancy for him in this match. *(I.N.)*

1   . . .   P-K3

Was it a soft spot in the preparation of the World Champion, that he had no sharper defenses against 1 P-QB4 in his repertory for this match? *(I.N.)*

2	N-KB3	P-Q4
3	P-Q4 ·	N-KB3
4	N-B3	B-K2
5	B-N5	P-KR3
6	B-R4	O-O
7	P-K3	QN-Q2

Up to here, the moves have been the same as in game 6, which continued with Tartakower's 7 . . . P-QN3. The text move puts the game into the channels of the old Orthodox Defense, preferred in their time by Capablanca and Alekhine. *(R.B. & I.N.)*

8   R-B1   . . .

Onlooker Bent Larsen observed that this would have been a good moment to enter the Exchange Variation with 8 PxP. I agree, well aware of Bobby's low opinion of that line. *(R.B.)*

8   . . .   P-B3

Suppose it be granted that Spassky's follow-up to this move is entirely sufficient, would it not be one tempo better to play 8 . . . P-R3? *(R.B.)*

| 9 | B-Q3 | PxP |
| 10 | BxP | P-QN4 |

This old line, favored by the late Swedish grandmaster Gideon Stahlberg, is more active than Capablanca's 10 . . . N-Q4, which wouldn't work quite as it should here, since White can avoid the exchange of bishops by 11 B-KN3. The position now resembles the Queen's

Gambit Accepted or the Meran, wherein Black gives up the center in order to counterattack it, aiming for a free development of his pieces. *(R.B.)*

| 11 | B-Q3 | P-R3 |
| 12 | P-R4 | ... |

If White does not take immediate action, Black will get in ... P-B4 with no problems. *(R.B.)*
In this well-known position, 12 B-N1 or 12 O-O also come into consideration. But the obvious 12 P-K4 gives White nothing because of the combination, 12 ... NxP!, 13 BxN BxB, 14 BxP R-R2, 15 O-O N-N3! (Euwe–Alekhine, 1935). *(I.N.)*

| 12 | ... | PxP |

Spassky correctly adheres to the Stahlberg formula, for 12 ... P-N5?, 13 BxN NxB, 14 N-K4 gives White a powerful grip on the position. *(R.B.)*
An interesting possibility is 12 ... P-N5, 13 BxN PxB!, 14 N-K4 P-KB4,

15 N-N3 P-B4 with a sharp game. *(I.N.)*

13	NxP	Q-R4ch
14	N-Q2	B-N5
15	N-B3	...

The knight must retreat, relinquishing its grip on the QB5 square, since Black threatened ... BxNch, winning a piece. That gives him the chance to rid himself of the backward QBP on the next move. *(R.B.)*

| 15 | ... | P-B4 |
| 16 | N-N3 | ... |

More dangerous for Black would appear to be 16 N-B4 Q-B2, 17 B-N3 Q-N2, 18 O-O. *(I.N.)*

| 16 | ... | Q-Q1 |

There is no better square for the queen: 16 ... Q-N3 will lose a tempo on a later N-R4; 16 ... Q-B2, facing the White rook, is unwise; 16 ... Q-R7, 17 O-O QxP??, 18 N-R4 Q-R7, 19 R-R1 wins the queen. *(R.B.)*
A novelty; more solid is 16 ... Q-N3, 17 PxP BxP, 18 NxB QxN, 19 B-N3 B-N2, tried in Stahlberg–Capablanca, Margate 1936. *(I.N.)*

| 17 | O-O | ... |

At this point, Fischer had already consumed a little over an hour, and Spassky about 35 minutes. In the second half of the match, both grandmasters kept on a par with regard to the clock. *(I.N.)*

17	...	PxP
18	NxP	B-N2
19	B-K4!	...

The only way for White to try for something is to work against the QB6 square, the one "soft" point in the Black position. If 19 ... BxB, 20 NxB, Black would be in trouble, lacking a defense to N-B6. *(R.B. & I.N.)*

19 ... Q-N1

19 ... Q-N3?, 20 N-R4 Q-R2, 21 R-B7 won't do at all. *(I.N.)*

20 B-N3 ...

With this, White gives back the major part of his opening advantage. More dangerous for Black was immediately 20 N-B6 BxN, 21 BxB R-R2, 22 B-N3 when White stands clearly better. For example, 22 ... Q-N3, 23 N-R4, Q-R4, 24 Q-Q4 or 22 ... Q-Q1, 23 Q-R4 (23 Q-B3 is also good), and the bishop pair assures White a lasting initiative.

Also, if Black resists giving up his bishop for the knight and plays 20 ... Q-Q3, then 21 QxQ BxQ, 22 KR-Q1 is very strong. *(I.N.)*

20 ... Q-R2

20 ... P-K4 would only loosen the Black position. *(R.B.)*

21 N-B6 B/2xN

21 ... Q-N3, 22 N-R4 Q-N4, 23 B-Q3 Q-Q4, 24 P-K4! NxP, 25 NxB wins a piece for White. *(R.B.)*

22 BxB ...

Fischer's bishop pair gives him a small edge. *(R.B.)*

| 22 | ... | QR-B1 |
| 23 | N-R4! | ... |

On 23 Q-B3, N-B4 can be disturbing. *(I.N.)*
This is necessary to maintain any chances, because 23 B-B3 N-B4 leads nowhere. *(R.B.)*

23 ... KR-Q1

23 ... N-B4?!, 24 NxN RxB, 25 N-Q7 RxR, 26 NxNch PxN, 27 QxR gives White some chance to exploit the kingside weaknesses, and, if 24 ... BxN, 25 Q-B3 Q-N3, 26 B-N7 QR-Q1, 27 B-K5, White is also minutely better. *(R.B.)*

24 B-B3 ...

Superior was 24 Q-B3 and White is

more comfortable on account of his bishop pair. *(I.N.)*

24 ... P-QR4

Spassky does not fall into the trap, 24 ... N-K4?, 25 BxN RxQ, 26 RxRch K-R2, 27 RxR, and White simply wins a piece. *(R.B. & I.N.)*

Making additional room for the queen is a good idea, while 24 ... N-B4, 25 Q-B2 NxN, 26 QxN is perhaps playable too. *(R.B.)*

25 R-B6?! ...

Correct was 25 Q-K2, although it is not clear that White can get anywhere after 25 ... N-B4.

25	...	RxR
26	BxR	R-QB1
27	B-B3	...

There was a better chance in 27 Q-B3 N-B4, 28 B-K5. *(I.N.)*

27 ... Q-R3

Now that the queen enters active play and the rook occupies the im-

portant QB file, Black can be perfectly satisfied with his position. *(R.B. & I.N.)*

28	P-R3	Q-N4
29	B-K2	Q-B3
30	B-B3	Q-N4
31	P-N3	...

There was no reason to avoid the draw by repetition. *(R.B. & I.N.)*

This move creates a slight weakness of the queenside squares and Fischer now gets into trouble. *(R.B.)*

31	...	B-K2
32	B-K2	Q-N5
33	B-R6	R-B3
34	B-Q3	N-B4
35	Q-B3?	...

Instead of this careless move, Bobby had to play 35 NxN RxN, 36 Q-N1, although Spassky has the initiative well in hand after 36 ... N-Q4. *(R.B.)*

35 ... R-B1?

This retreat was not necessary; Black had a good choice of 35 ... N/4-K5 or 35 ... N-Q4. *(I.N.)*

Boris misses 35 ... N/4-K5!, which would threaten ... NxB and ... QxP, as well as ... N-Q7 after the rook gets out of the pin. White cannot reply 36 B-K5, because 36 ... R-B1, 37 QBxN N-Q7! wins for Black. I see nothing better for Bobby than 36 R-R1 R-B1, 37 BxN NxB, 38 N-N6 R-Q1, 39 N-B4 NxB, 40 PxN QxP, 41 NxP Q-B6, 42 R-R4, which leaves the White pieces in dangerously awkward positions, while the White kingside is weak and invites attack. *(R.B.)*

36	NxN	BxN

36 ... RxN? loses to 37 Q-R8ch B-B1, 38 B-Q6, while 36 ... QxN is answered by 37 Q-N7. *(R.B.)*

37	R-B1	R-Q1

37 ... QxP??, 38 RxB wins at once. *(R.B. & I.N.)*

38	B-QB4	Q-Q7
39	R-B1	B-N5
40	B-B7	R-Q2

The adjourned position offers equal chances and is naturally a draw with correct play. *(I.N.)*

41	Q-B6	Q-B7!

Spassky plans the strong counterattack, ... R-Q7 and ... N-K5 to take advantage of the thinly defended KB7 square. 42 Q-R8ch K-R2, 43 BxRP? loses a piece after 43 ... Q-R7. *(R.B.)*

42	B-K5	R-Q7

Black is all set for attack. *(I.N.)*

43	Q-R8ch	K-R2
44	BxN	PxB
45	Q-B3	P-B4
46	P-N4	Q-K5
47	K-N2	...

There is, of course, nothing to play for, except that Fischer is unable to offer a draw. *(R.B.)*

47	...	K-N3
48	R-B1	B-R6
49	R-QR1	B-N5
50	R-QB1	B-K2
51	PxPch	PxP
52	R-K1	...

Rather than take a passive position by R-KB1, Fischer allows the little combination which follows, resulting in such a dead draw that even he cannot dispute it. *(R.B. & I.N.)*

52	...	RxPch!

Thus the kibitzers can have their fun! *(I.N.)*

53	KxR	B-R5ch
54	K-K2	QxQch
55	KxQ	BxR
	Drawn	

The extra Black pawn has only symbolic significance. *(I.N.)*

GAME 13

August 10, 1972

A dramatic fighting game, rich in chess, in which both sides played perhaps not faultlessly, but in fascinating fashion. The endgame was especially fabulous. The 13th game was the second and decisive turning point in Reykjavik. From this encounter on, Fischer abandoned his favorite variation of the Sicilian Defense and varied his openings with Black. The Alekhine Defense did not come as a great surprise, because Fischer had played it a few times previously. Yet Spassky did not play the opening properly; he mixed up two systems of development and quickly fell into difficulties. Black played consistently to win a pawn, for which White obtained the freer game. In the transition to the middle game, Fischer failed to find the best line of play and Spassky could prosecute a very dangerous attack on the king's wing. Now, however, White handled the position irresolutely and Fischer was able to mobilize his game with a plus pawn.

In the last hour of play, Black again gave his opponent chances and the position at adjournment was very sharp. Many specialists thought that the ending the players found themselves in was won for Fischer, but the analysis showed that the World Champion also had his trumps. The next evening very fine play by both players produced an original endgame in which five Black pawns battled against a White rook. Objectively, the position was a draw, but both grandmasters went on trying new ways to complicate the game. Before the third time-control, Spassky made the decisive mistake and permitted the enemy king to penetrate into the king's wing. Could the World Champion perhaps have still been thinking about a possibility of winning?

The 13th game showed for the first time that both players were tiring. Former World Champion M. Botvinnik is obviously right when he says that a battle for the championship costs two years of life. *(I.N.)*

Alekhine Defense

BORIS SPASSKY   ROBERT FISCHER

1   P-K4   ...

From the 11th game to the end, Spassky probed his opponent with this move. *(I.N.)*

1   ...   N-KB3

Because of the bomb-out of his favorite "poisoned pawn" Najdorf Sicilian in game 11, Fischer has had to go to one of his rare second string defenses. *(R.B.)*

2	P-K5	N-Q4
3	P-Q4	P-Q3
4	N-KB3	...

Spassky has always favored the four-pawn attack (4 P-KB4). *(I.N.)*

This quiet line has been one of the most popular in the last few years, but the sharp 4 P-QB4 N-N3, 5 P-B4 may be necessary if White wishes to get the advantage against Alekhine's Defense. (R.B.)

4 ... P-KN3

This faddish move does not inspire confidence. (I.N.)
A comparatively new idea, this may be a more promising way to put the White center under pressure than the older 4 ... B-N5. (R.B.)

5 B-QB4 ...

Paul Keres's favorite continuation. An alternative is 5 B-K2, while 5 N-N5 does not give much on account of 5 ... PxP, 6 PxP B-N2, 7 B-QB4 P-QB3, 8 N-QB3 P-KR3, 9 N-B3 NxN!, and after the exchange of queens Black stands well. (I.N.)

5 ... N-N3

5 ... P-QB3 is solid and defensive, but the text move, more ambitious in keeping the QBP free for a later break with ... P-QB4, allows Black to play aggressively. (R.B.)
5 ... P-QB3, 6 O-O B-N2, 7 PxP gives Black more difficulties. (I.N.)

6 B-N3 B-N2
7 QN-Q2!? ...

This innovation is scarcely better than 7 O-O O-O, 8 P-QR4 P-QR4, 9 P-R3, with which Keres has done a good business. (I.N.)

The sharper 7 N-N5 comes into question, for 7 ... O-O is answered by 8 P-K6, with advantage to White. However, 7 ... P-Q4, 8 P-KB4 P-KB3, 9 N-KB3 O-O seems quite playable. (R.B.)

7 ... O-O
8 P-KR3?! ...

The reason for this time-wasting, unnecessary precaution is not clear. Is ... B-N5 and ... BxN really something to worry about? (R.B.)
One of the last two White moves is superfluous; better was 8 O-O. (I.N.)

8 ... P-QR4!

It is comical that White is already uncomfortable here. (I.N.)

9 P-QR4?! ...

Spassky should have realized that he was getting outplayed in this opening and made an attempt to hang tight by 9 P-B3. (R.B.)
This pawn will be stamped as a weakness in the ensuing play. How-

ever, there is, perhaps, nothing better. For example, 9 P-B3 PxP, 10 PxP N-B3, 11 Q-K2 B-B4, or 9 P-QR3 P-R5, 10 B-R2 PxP, 11 PxP N-B3, 12 Q-K2 B-B4, and in both cases Black has the initiative clearly in his hands. *(I.N.)*

9 . . . PxP
10 PxP N-R3!

Black has emerged from the opening with a very good game and is already justified in playing for a concrete advantage. Like his great teacher W. Steinitz, the American believes in the resources of the defense and is only too happy to go after material. *(I.N.)*

11 O-O N-B4

The Black pieces now have excellent mobility while White's K5 and QR4 are targets for attack which constantly need tending. *(R.B.)*

12 Q-K2 Q-K1

Only a dozen moves have been played and Bobby is already winning a pawn in broad daylight. 13 Q-N5 QxQ, 14 PxQ B-B4! sets up the decisive . . . P-R5. *(R.B.)*

13 N-K4 N/3xP
14 BxN NxB

Now White must prove that he has something for the QRP. *(I.N.)*

15 R-K1 . . .

15 Q-B4 would regain the pawn, but after 15 . . . B-Q2, 16 QxP Q-B1, 17 QxQ KRxQ, Black has convincing positional superiority. Instead, Boris banks all on the chance for a kingside attack. *(R.B. & I.N.)*

15 . . . N-N3
16 B-Q2 . . .

More logical seems the immediate 16 B-N5. *(I.N.)*

16 . . . P-R5
17 B-N5 . . .

Another plan was 17 N-B5, to which R. Kholmov appends the variation: 17 . . . Q-B3, 18 B-N4 N-Q4, 19 N-Q4! Q-N3, 20 B-R3 and White exerts pressure on the Black position. On 17 . . . N-Q2, either 18 Q-B4 or 18 N-Q3 can follow. *(I.N.)*

17 . . . P-R3
18 B-R4 B-B4?!

Why give White a tempo for the attack? The immediate 18 . . . B-K3 or 18 . . . B-Q2 was better. *(R.B. & I.N.)*

Moreover, 18 ... R-R4!? was worthy of consideration. *(R.B.)*

19 P-KN4 ...

White burns all his bridges behind him. A more solid continuation of the attack consisted in 19 N-Q4, after which 19 ... BxKP would be risky on account of 20 NxB PxN, 21 N-N3. On 19 ... BxN, 20 QxB P-QB3, V. Smyslov suggests 21 P-KB4 P-K3, 22 N-K2, with the idea N-QB3. *(I.N.)*

19 ... B-K3

19 ... BxN has been widely recommended, but 20 QxB R-N1, 21 Q-N4! P-N4, 22 B-N3 P-K3, 23 P-R4 still gives White attacking opportunities against the exposed kingside. *(R.B.)* In this line, if 20 ... P-QB3, 21 Q-N4 N-Q4, 22 QxNP R-N1, 23 Q-R7, White has a satisfactory game. *(I.N.)*

20 N-Q4! ...

White must bear down, for otherwise Black will consolidate his position and capitalize on his material advantage. *(I.N.)*

20 ... B-B5!

Taking a second pawn by 20 ... BxKP, 21 NxB PxN, 22 P-QB3 would be positionally risky. *(I.N.)*

21 Q-Q2 Q-Q2

Whether 21 ... BxP is a better defense is a question. 22 QxP B-N2 (22 ... BxN is impossible because of 23 N-N5 and mate), 23 Q-Q2 Q-Q1,

24 P-QB3 P-KB3, 25 P-B4 seems also to leave White some attacking chances. *(R.B.)* More energetic was 21 ... BxP!, 22 QxP and now naturally not 22 ... BxN, 23 N-N5 and Black will be mated, but 22 ... B-N2, 23 Q-Q2 Q-Q2, 24 P-QB3 QR-K1, or 23 Q-K3 R-Q1, 24 QR-Q1 P-KB3 and Black maintains his plus pawn in a sharp game. *(I.N.)*

22 QR-Q1 KR-K1
23 P-B4 ...

Spassky's attack, although without a specific target as yet, is building to menacing proportions. *(I.N. & R.B.)*

23 ... B-Q4
24 N-QB5 Q-B1
25 Q-B3? ...

Now the initiative passes gradually over to Black. White must play 25 P-K6!, which can lead to obscure complications. V. Smyslov analyzes the effective variation 25 ... N-B5, 26 Q-K2 NxP, 27 N-B5! with dangerous threats. Black can better defend himself with 25 ... P-R6 or 26 ... N-Q3. The game remains fantastically involved and that is all in the interest of White.

On 25 P-B5, Black has the counter 25 ... N-B5!, but interesting might have been 25 P-N3!? *(I.N.)*

If there is no better than this, White's attack is a total failure. The main question is why Spassky declined to play 25 P-K6. If 25 ... N-B5, 26 Q-K2! NxP, 27 N-B5!! NxR, 28 NxB KxN, 29 Q-K5ch P-B3, 30 QxB N-N7, 31 P-N5!, White has a terrific onslaught. However, the draw can still be saved by 27 ... B-B5!, 28 PxPch KxP, 29 QxPch! RxQ, 30 RxRch K-B1, 31 N-Q7ch! QxN (31 ... K-N1??, 32 RxBch K-R1, 33 B-B6 PxN, 34 N-K5! Q-K1, 35 R/1-Q7 and the mate cannot be stopped), 32 R/1xQ B-B6!!, 33 NxP P-R6, 34 R-B7ch BxR, 35 RxBch K-K1, 36 R-K7ch K-B1, etc. *(R.B.)*

25	...	P-K3
26	K-R2	N-Q2
27	N-Q3	...

On Gligoric's recommendation, 27 N-N5, Black does not play 27 ... P-N3?, 28 NxN? QxN, 29 NxP QR-B1, 30 NxB RxQ, 31 N-K7ch QxN, etc., because White can improve with 28 N-Q3. On 27 N-N5, Black plays 27 ... NxN, 28 QxN R-R4!, 29 Q-N4 P-N3, or 29 P-B4 B-QB3, keeping the pawn advantage. *(I.N. & R.B.)*

Of course, the simplification, 27 NxN

QxN, 28 Q-Q3 P-QB4! is favorable for Black. *(I.N.)*

| 27 | ... | P-QB4 |
| 28 | N-N5 | ... |

28 N-K2 P-QN4 denies White any hopes. *(I.N.)*

| 28 | ... | Q-B3 |

Since 29 N-R3 P-QN4 drives White back further, the text move virtually forces a safe pawn-ahead ending. *(R.B.)*

| 29 | N-Q6 | QxN! |

This transaction should quickly have decided the game. *(I.N.)*

30	PxQ	BxQ
31	PxB	P-B3
32	P-N5!	...

The White position is lost because of the strong Black QRP. Yet White can hope for some practical chances in connection with his QP and so hastens to maintain it by any means available. *(I.N.)*

32 ... RPxP?

Instead of allowing a long fight with bishops of opposite colors, Symslov recommended 32 ... P-B5!, 33 N-N4 RPxP, 34 PxP P-B4 as the easiest way to win. It looks awfully good, because winning the pawn back by 35 NxB would leave White with no means of coping with the passed QRP. *(R.B. & I.N.)*
In the next stage of the game, Fischer once again takes things too easy, as he did in game 7, giving Spassky chances he should never have had. *(R.B.)*

33	**PxP**	**P-B4**
34	**B-N3**	**K-B2**

This loses time. Better was 34 ... P-R6! and White cannot mobilize his forces as he does in the game. For example, 35 N-K5 NxN, 36 BxN KR-Q1, 37 R-KB1 R-R5, and White is without counterplay. *(I.N.)*

35 N-K5ch ...

Now it is clear why the knight should have been driven away at the thirty-second move. *(I.N.)*

35	**...**	**NxN**
36	**BxN**	**P-N4**

Once again he should have tried 36 ... P-R6. *(I.N.)*

37 R-KB1! ...

Spassky reveals his counterplay, R-B4-R4-R7ch. *(R.B. & I.N.)*

37 ... R-R1?

Playing superficially, Bobby succeeds in making the ending very difficult, if not impossible. The point is that nothing compels White to take the Exchange, which would only permit Black to win the QP for an effortless finish. The correct plan, as pointed out by Bill Lombardy, was 37 ... R-KN1, 38 R-B4 K-K1, 39 R-R4 R-R2, and there is nothing to be done about ... R-KB2, followed by ... K-Q2-B3 and the march of the QRP. *(R.B.)*
An interesting idea. 38 BxR RxB would now be advantageous for Black because the strong QP would fall and, afterward, he could proceed on the queenside and in the center. The rook move is directed against R-B4-R4. On 37 ... P-R6, 38 R-B4 P-R7 White has a perpetual check: 39 R-KR4 P-R8=Q, 40 R-R7ch K-N1, 41 R-R8ch, etc. *(I.N.)*

38 B-B6!   . . .

Now Black is nicely tied up and the
win is gone. *(R.B.)*

38 . . .   P-R6
39 R-B4   P-R7
40 P-B4!   . . .

It is necessary to use the bishop to
stop the passed pawn. If 40 P-Q7?
P-R8=Q, 41 RxQ RxR, 42 BxR K-K2,
43 R-KR4 (43 P-B4 R-R8ch, 44 K-N3
R-N8ch, 45 K-B2 R-N7ch, 46 K-K1
PxP gives White no chance of a defense) 43 . . . KxP, 44 K-N3 (not
44 R-R6? P-KB5! and mate) 44 . . .
K-Q3, 45 R-R6 B-K5, Black wins without trouble, since 46 RxP? P-B5ch
catches a rook. If 40 R-QR1? P-K4!,
41 BxP KR-K1, 42 B-B6 R-K7ch, 43
K-N1 K-K3 wins. *(R.B.)*

40 . . .   BxP
41 P-Q7   B-Q4

Perhaps there were still some winning
chances with 41 . . . P-K4!, 42 BxP
K-K3 *(I.N.)*

42 K-N3!   . . .

Spassky took 25 minutes to come up
with this accurate sealed move, which
even threatens to win by 43 R-KR4.
(R.B. & I.N.)
The further course of the game
would be fascinating, according to
our adjournment analysis. *(I.N.)*

42 . . .   R-R6ch!

The alternative was 42 . . . P-K4,
43 BxP K-K3, after which White

could play 44 BxR RxB, 45 R/4-B1
(45 R-KR4 R-Q1, 46 R-R6 RxP, 47
RxPch K-K4 is unclear) 45 . . . R-Q1,
46 R/B1-K1ch K-Q3, 47 P-B4 PxP,
48 R-K2 with about equal chances
(48 . . . K-B3, 49 RxP P-B6, 50
R-R6ch). *(I.N.)*
Both players conspire to produce one
of the most exciting endgames ever
seen in a championship match.
Spassky cannot reply 43 K-B2, because 43 . . . R/6xP, 44 P-Q8=Q,
RxQ, 45 BxR P-K4! traps the rook and
wins after 46 B-B6 K-K3, 47 R-K1
P-R8=Q, 48 RxQ PxR. And 43 R-Q3?
permits 43 . . . P-R8=Q. *(R.B. & I.N.)*

43 P-B3   R/1-R1

Boris was all ready for 43 . . .
P-R8=Q, 44 RxQ RxR, 45 R-KR4!!
R/8-R1, 46 BxR R-Q1, 47 B-B6 RxP,
48 R-R7ch K-K1, 49 R-R8ch with
perpetual check. Taking two rooks
for the queen by 45 . . . R-N8ch,
46 K-B2 R-N7ch, 47 K-B1 RxR, 48
P-Q8=Q doesn't help Fischer at all,
since the only way to stave off the
mating net his king finds itself in is
the perpetual check 48 . . . R-B5ch,
49 K-K1 R-K5ch, 50 K-B1, etc. Here
50 K-Q1?? B-N6ch is mate in two.
(R.B.)
43 . . . P-R8=Q, 44 RxQ RxR, 45
R-KR4 R/1-R1, 46 R-R7ch leads to
perpetual check. On 43 . . . R/6-R1,
possible is 44 R-KR4 RxR, 45 KxR
P-K4, 46 P-Q8=Q RxQ, 47 BxR, for
example: 47 . . . B-N6, 48 R-K1 B-B7,
49 R-QR1 B-N8, 50 B-N6 or 47 . . .

B-K5, 48 B-B7! or 47 . . . K-K3, 48
B-B7. *(I.N.)*

44   R-KR4   P-K4!!

Still not content with the draw,
Fischer must give up a piece to
escape the perpetual check and get
his king into the game. *(R.B.)*

45	**R-R7ch**	**K-K3**
46	**R-K7ch**	**K-Q3**
47	**RxP**	**RxPch!**

47 . . . P-R8=Q? loses to 48 R/5xBch
K-B3, 48 RxQ, coming out a piece
ahead. *(R.B.)*

48   K-B2   . . .

Of course not 48 K-R4? R-R5ch and
mate in two. *(R.B.)*

48	**. . .**	**R-B7ch**
49	**K-K1**	**KxP**
50	**R/5xBch**	**K-B3**
51	**R-Q6ch**	**K-N2**
52	**R-Q7ch**	**K-R3**
53	**R/7-Q2**	**RxR**
54	**KxR**	**P-N5**

After a wild, but relatively easy to
understand resolution, an even ending has arisen, in which, however,
very exact treatment is required. *(I.N.)*

55   P-R4!   . . .

Passive defense against Fischer's
connected passed pawns cannot succeed, but Spassky gets his own just in
time. *(I.N. & R.B.)*

55	**. . .**	**K-N4**
56	**P-R5**	**P-QB5**
57	**R-QR1**	**. . .**

The only move, because 57 P-R6
P-B6ch, 58 K-Q3 P-R8=Q, 59 RxQ
RxR, 60 P-R7 R-Q8ch!, 61 K-B2
R-KR8, 62 P-R8=Q RxQ, 63 BxR K-B5
wins easily for Black. *(R.B. & I.N.)*

57	**. . .**	**PxP**
58	**P-N6**	**P-R5!**

Fischer's point is that 59 BxP R-KN1,
60 RxP RxP gives him winning
chances. *(I.N. & R.B.)*

59	**P-N7**	**P-R6**
60	**B-K7**	**R-KN1**
61	**B-B8**	**. . .**

Trapping Bobby's rook is the only
move to draw. 61 B-B6 P-R7, 62
K-B2 P-B5, 63 K-N2 P-B6ch, 64 KxP
R-R1ch, 65 K-N3 RxR, 66 P-N8=Q
R-N8ch, 67 K-B2 R-N7ch, 68 K-Q3
R-Q7ch, 69 K-K4 P-R8=Qch wins.
(R.B.)

61   . . .   P-R7

Borislav Rabar suggests the variation, 61 ... P-B6ch, 62 K-Q3, P-R7!, 63 K-Q4 P-B5, 64 K-Q3 P-B6, 65 K-Q4 P-KB7, 66 R-KB1 K-B3, 67 K-B4 P-B7, 68 KxP K-Q4, 69 K-N3 K-K5, 70 KxBP K-B6, 71 B-B5 P-QR8=Q, 72 RxQ K-N7, and Black wins. Better, however, is 68 R-KR1! P-N6, 69 KxP K-Q4, 70 KxRP K-K5, 71 K-N2 K-B6, 72 B-B5! RxP, 73 BxP K-N7, 74 RxPch KxR, 75 B-Q4! with a draw. *(I.N.)*

62	K-B2	K-B3
63	R-Q1!	...

Just in time to stop Fischer's king from getting to the kingside where it would guide a pawn in to cost Spassky's rook. *(R.B.)*
Now a draw position has come about, since the Black king cannot get into the game against correct play. *(I.N.)*

63	...	P-N6ch
64	K-B3?!	...

This is sufficient to draw, but the simplest was 64 K-N2 P-KR8=Q, 65 RxQ K-Q4, 66 R-Q1ch K-K5, 67 R-QB1 K-Q6, 68 R-Q1ch K-K7, 69 R-QB1 P-B5, 70 RxP P-B6, 71 R-B1 P-B7, 72 KxP P-B8=Q, 73 RxQ KxR, 74 KxP. *(R.B. & I.N.)*

64	...	P-KR8=Q!

The exclamation point is for Black's untiring attempts to win. After 64 ... P-B5, 65 R-Q6ch K-B2, 66 R-Q1 P-B6, 67 K-N2 K-B3, 68 R-Q6ch Black cannot get anywhere. *(I.N.)*

There is one last chance to make things difficult for Boris and Fischer is going to try it! By deflecting the rook, he hopes to cross over with his king to support the KBP. *(R.B.)*

65	RxQ	K-Q4
66	K-N2	P-B5
67	R-Q1ch!	...

67 R-R8 loses after 67 ... P-B6ch, 68 K-R1 P-B6!, 69 RxR P-KB7, mating. *(R.B. & I.N.)*

67	...	K-K5
68	R-QB1	K-Q6
69	R-Q1ch??	...

After all his brilliant defense, Boris throws the game away with this blunder! The way to draw was 69 R-B3ch K-Q5, 70 R-B3 P-B6ch, 71 K-R1 (71 RxP? P-R8=Qch wins the rook) P-B7, 72 RxPch K-B6, 73 R-B3ch! K-Q7, 74 B-R3 and every last pawn will be annihilated. If Black plays 73 ... K-B5, then 74 R-B1 certifies the half point. It should be noted that the exact order of moves is required. If, for example, 73 B-N4ch K-Q6, 74 B-R3 RxP, 75 R-B3ch K-B5, 76 R-B4ch K-Q4, 77 R-B1 R-Q2!, 78 B-B1 K-K3!!, 79 K-N2 R-Q8 and when the rook moves, there is nothing White can do about ... RxB. *(R.B.)*

69	...	K-K7
70	R-QB1	P-B6
71	B-B5	...

There is now no time for 71 RxP P-B7, 72 R-B1 P-B8=Q, 73 RxQ KxR and White cannot get the remaining Black pawns. *(R.B.)*

| 71 | ... | RxP |

Also 71 ... P-B7, 72 BxP KxB, 73 RxP RxP, 74 R-B4ch K-K7, 75 R-K4ch K-Q6, 76 R-K1 R-N6! wins. *(I.N.)*

| 72 | RxP | R-Q2! |

This most exact move of Bobby's threatens ... R-Q8 as well as ... R-Q7ch. *(R.B.)*

73	R-K4ch	K-B8
74	B-Q4	P-B7
	Resigns	

75 R-B4 is met by 75 ... RxB, 76 RxR K-K7, while a bishop move allows ... R-Q8. *(R.B.)*

GAME 14

August 15, 1972

It would be interesting to speculate whether it was only an accident that, after games 11 and 13, which consumed so much nervous energy, the subsequent encounters ran such a rocky course. That applies particularly to the 14th game, the most error-ridden of the match. White handled the Tarrasch Variation of the Queen's Gambit so disastrously that he found himself in insurmountable difficulties after his 20th move. It is hard to say whether Fischer sacrificed a pawn or simply lost it. Soon Black had a pawn more in a good position, but then came his 27th move . . .

With the 14th game began a series of seven draws—a sensation in Reykjavik. We must hastily add, however, that these results were accidental and in no way a renunciation of the fight. *(I.N.)*

Queen's Gambit Declined

ROBERT FISCHER   BORIS SPASSKY

1	P-QB4	. . .

No one in Reykjavik was startled any more by the challenger's opening move. *(I.N.)*

For the third time in the match Fischer adopts a Queenside opening rather than 1 P-K4, which he played only in games 4 and 10. *(R.B.)*

1	. . .	P-K3
2	N-KB3	P-Q4

3	P-Q4	N-KB3
4	N-B3	B-K2

Spassky likes to play against the semiclassical 4 . . . P-B4 when he has White and therefore avoids taking the Black side of it here. I wonder what Fischer would have used to oppose it. *(R.B.)*

5	B-B4	. . .

This old Steinitz continuation was for several years a dangerous weapon in the hands of Hungarian grandmaster Lajos Portisch. *(I.N.)*

In my opnion, putting the bishop on B4 is weaker than 5 B-N5, which exerts more pressure on the center, but in the last five years this tamer variation has become popular. It enables Black to free his game by an early . . . P-B4, but then White has the possibility of giving him an isolated QP, against which Fischer likes to operate. *(R.B.)*

5	. . .	O-O

Spassky has had pleasant experiences with 5 . . . P-B4, 6 QPxP N-R3. In the eighth match game against Petrosian in 1969, he won the Exchange after 7 P-K3 NxP, 8 PxP PxP, 9 B-K2 O-O, 10 O-O B-K3, 11 B-K5 R-B1, 12 R-B1 P-QR3, 13 P-KR3 P-QN4, 14 B-Q3? P-Q5! However, according to Portisch, 7 B-Q6! is better. *(I.N.)*

6	P-K3	P-B4

Spassky has also played 6 . . . QN-Q2, 7 P-QR3 P-B3, 8 P-R3

P-QR3, 9 P-B5 P-QN3! as in his game
with Bent Larsen in Palma de
Majorca 1968. *(I.N.)*

7	PxBP	N-B3

After 7 . . . BxP, 8 Q-B2 N-B3, 9
P-QR3 Q-R4, 10 R-Q1 B-K2, 11 N-Q2
P-K4, 12 B-N5 P-Q5, 13 N-N3, White
succeeded in grasping the initiative in
the game Portisch–Spassky, Havana
1966. *(I.N.)*

8	PxP	PxP

Spassky has nothing against an isolated center pawn, which ordinarily
can only become weak in the endgame. As compensation for it, Black
has good piece mobility in the
middle game. *(I.N.)*

9	B-K2	BxP

So Fischer has gotten the isolated
Black QP as a target to work on, but
his pieces are not well placed to
apply pressure. *(R.B.)*

10	O-O	B-K3
11	R-B1	R-B1
12	P-QR3	. . .

12 NxP? QxN, 13 QxQ NxQ, 14 RxB
NxB, 15 PxN N-Q5!, 16 R-K5 NxBch,
17 RxB B-B5 wins the Exchange for
Black in an easily won endgame.
(I.N. & R.B.)

12	. . .	P-KR3
13	B-N3?!	. . .

White plays too passively; possible
was 13 N-QN5 or 13 N-K5 N-K2,
14 N-Q3. *(I.N.)*
This is no improvement in the
bishop's position, since it comes
under attack from a knight as soon
as Black plays . . . N-K5. 13 P-R3
would have been better, but Bobby
doesn't seem to have the feel for this
type of classical position. *(R.B.)*

13	. . .	B-N3

Spassky handles isolated-pawn positions with a virtuosity rare in con-
temporary chess and this move is a
small proof of his judgment. The
bishop is better placed on QN3
than on K2 because it bears on the
blockading square, White's Q4. He
does not fear 14 N-QR4, since he
can centralize strongly by 14 . . .
N-K5. Moreover, he now threatens
. . . P-Q5. *(R.B.)*

14	N-K5	. . .

Now 14 . . . P-Q5?, 15 NxN RxN,
16 PxP BxP, 17 B-B3 R-N3, 18 P-N4!
gives White a great advantage with
the Black rook badly offside and the
chance to penetrate on the QB file
after N-R4. White also has the threat

of exchanging a pair of minor pieces, because the isolated pawn gets weaker as the board becomes uncluttered. *(R.B.)*

14   ...   N-K2!

Spassky understands such positions beautifully and once again stands very well. *(I.N.)*
Spassky not only sidesteps the exchange, he prepares to bring the knight to the excellent square KB4. He doesn't give Fischer a chance to make anything out of the isolated pawn. *(I.N. & R.B.)*

15   N-R4   ...

Because the possible exchange on QN6 is not especially favorable for White (Black obtains the Q1 square for his king rook as well as pressure against the enemy queenside), 15 N-Q3, with about an equal game, comes into consideration. *(I.N.)*

15   ...   N-K5
16   RxR   BxR
17   N-KB3   B-Q2

Also worthy of attention was 17 ... NxB, 18 RPxN B-B2. White has obtained nothing out of the opening and Black rather has the initiative already. Therefore, it was better to play for simplification now with 18 NxB QxN, 19 Q-Q4. *(I.N.)*

18   B-K5   BxN

Another good move by Spassky, who is well aware that knights often work

better than bishops in isolated-pawn positions. *(R.B.)*

19   QxB   N-QB3
20   B-KB4   ...

Also after 20 B-Q4 NxB, 21 NxN Q-B3 Black stands very well. According to Polugaevsky, 20 B-B3 was the best chance. *(I.N.)*

20   ...   Q-B3!

Now it is difficult to give White good advice. *(I.N.)*
With all his pieces centralized, Spassky has the initiative. The only move I can find to hold the line for Fischer is 21 Q-N5, for 21 ... P-Q5 22 Q-Q5 R-K1, 23 B-Q3 NxP?, 24 KxN PxPch, 25 K-N3 P-N4, 26 NxP PxN, 27 QxPch QxQch, 28 BxQ is in White's favor. Nor would 23 ... N-B4 get Black anywhere—24 B-N1 N-K3, 25 Q-K4 and White defends all threats by his own of mate in three. *(R.B.)*

21   B-QN5?   ...

This outright blunder could have cost the game. *(R.B.)*

Thus White loses a pawn. Had White played 21 Q-B2, then 21 ... P-N4, 22 B-N3 P-KR4 would have followed. *(I.N.)*

| 21 | ... | QxP |
| 22 | BxN | N-B6! |

An important interpolation, which Fischer did not catch in time. *(I.N.)* Fischer is now forced to exchange queens, heading into a pawn-down endgame. *(R.B.)*

| 23 | Q-N4 | ... |

23 B-K5 NxQ, 24 BxQ PxB is even worse than the text continuation. *(I.N. & R.B.)*

23	...	QxQ
24	PxQ	PxB
25	B-K5	N-N4
26	R-B1	R-B1
27	N-Q4	P-B3?

Chess blindness. After such moves, the hearts of average chessplayers should be lighter: the world champions are also human. Prior to this move, the position demanded hard technique, of course, but it was clearly won for Black. The correct plan consisted in 27 ... NxN!, 28 BxN P-B3 and White cannot long hold out. Possible also was the transition to a rook and pawn ending through 28 ... BxB. *(I.N.)* 27 ... NxN, 28 BxN K-B1 would have presented considerable difficulties in the way of winning, but the move played gives the pawn back for nothing. *(R.B.)*

| 28 | BxP! | BxN |

White can hold after 28 ... PxB, 29 NxN just as well. *(I.N. & R.B.)* Fortunately, Black did not continue his "blindness strategy" with 28 ... K-B2?, 29 BxP! *(I.N.)*

29	BxB	NxB
30	PxN	R-N1
31	K-B1	...

There is no point in taking chances with 31 RxP P-QR4! *(R.B. & I.N.)* A draw could already be agreed here. *(I.N.)*

31	. . .	RxP
32	RxP	RxP
33	R-R6	K-B2
34	RxPch	K-B3

The following play is totally unnecessary except that these players never know when it's time to quit. *(R.B.)*

35	R-Q7	P-R4
36	K-K2	P-N4
37	K-K3	R-K5ch
38	K-Q3	K-K3
39	R-KN7	K-B3
40	R-Q7	K-K3
	Drawn	

Fischer Keeps His Lead

In game 15, Fischer returned to his favorite Najdorf Sicilian Defense, but even though he avoided the "poisoned pawn" variation which Spassky blasted in the 11th game, he still could not escape trouble. Boris struck with another of his powerful anti-Najdorf weapons as early as move 12 and followed up sharply to force the win of a pawn two moves later, landing Bobby in a lost game. However, impatient to force the position, Boris precipitously advanced his king pawn, throwing the game into a turmoil of complications, also throwing away the win. When Spassky spurned the draw that was his for the taking, Fischer came at him with a savage attack, and after one more error by Spassky, the challenger had a won game. Playing as though the world speed chess championship was at stake, despite ample time on his clock, Fischer finally made enough errors of his own to ensure Spassky the draw.

At this stage of the match, the hard-fought, relentless chess both players had been serving up throughout was taking its toll. Like two game, but battered prizefighters, Boris and Bobby were still swinging from the heels, but the blows were striking just off center.

Fischer chose the quiet, positional course of the Barendregt Variation of the Ruy Lopez to lead off game 16. It seeemed at first as though White could count on some advantage in the endgame resulting from Black's doubled pawns, but once again Spassky came up with an interesting theoretical innovation to obtain counterplay. He achieved a plus so minute that Fischer could not be stopped from forcing a well-known drawn rook and pawn ending with two pawns against one. The game could have been given up as a draw as early as the 24th move, but Boris, perhaps annoyed that Bobby had brought him in to play the few obvious moves of the perpetual check in the previous game's adjournment session, insisted on dragging out the routine all the way to the 60th move. In fact he waited until Bobby was ready to stick the sealed move into the envelope before offering the draw.

Fischer surprised once more in the 17th game, defending for the first time in his career a Pirc–Robatsch Defense, which he has always bruised badly himself when White. Spassky, in an adventurous mood, came on strong with a dangerous pawn sacrifice, bearing down on the enemy king's position with two powerful bishops. Although it was not clear that the attack would succeed, Fischer chose to sacrifice the

Exchange in order to simplify into a drawn ending. Because whatever chances were left belonged to White, Spassky's falling into a threefold repetition of the position right at the beginning of the second playing session seemed strange. Did he overlook the repetition or was he deliberately acquiescing to the draw? All I can say is that he looked unhappy when Chief Referee Lothar Schmid confirmed the repetition and the draw. It was certainly no great loss, for Fischer would pretty clearly have cinched the draw anyway. The score now stood at 10–7 in favor of Fischer. *(R.B.)*

GAME 15

August 17, 1972

Robert Fischer defended himself for the last time with the two-edged Najdorf Variation. This time he declined to win the White QNP and chose a relatively quieter line of play, but he still did not achieve the tranquil life. Spassky was well prepared and stuck his opponent with severe problems by means of his 12th move. Black was practically compelled to give up a pawn, for which he had no compensation. In a difficult situation, Black defended himself in cold-blooded fashion, though his position remained critical. With his hasty 23rd move Spassky gave his opponent real counterchances and should have been satisfied with a draw instead of a second—this time risky—pawn snatch. In the last hour of play Fischer obtained an annihilating mating attack, but continued inaccurately before the time-control and allowed his ingenious opponent to slip out of the net. In spite of the several errors, the game was one of those which will long remain in the memory of the spectators. *(I.N.)*

Sicilian Defense

BORIS SPASSKY   ROBERT FISCHER

1	P-K4	P-QB4
2	N-KB3	P-Q3
3	P-Q4	PxP
4	NxP	N-KB3
5	N-QB3	P-QR3
6	B-N5	P-K3
7	P-B4	B-K2

Up to here the moves of games seven and eleven have been repeated, but now Fischer foregoes the "poisoned pawn" line, 7 ... Q-N3, relying on the less radical, though still sharp text move, which has also been one of his long time preferences. *(R.B.)*

8	Q-B3	Q-B2
9	O-O-O	QN-Q2
10	B-Q3	...

Also possible is the much used 10 P-KN4 P-N4, 11 BxN NxB, 12 P-N5 N-Q2 with a sharp game. The text move and the entire White center strategy look very sound. *(I.N.)* After a considerable period in which 10 P-KN4 held sway, the present move is making a comeback, bolstered heavily by this game. The idea is strongly centralized development bearing on the enemy king, and flexible mobility to shift to whichever wing Black chooses to castle on. *(R.B.)*

10 ... P-N4

Black's main alternative is 10 ... P-R3, 11 B-R4 P-KN4, 12 PxP N-K4, 13 Q-K2 N/3-N5, basing his game on the powerfully posted knight on K4. It may get more attention now. *(R.B.)*

11 KR-K1 B-N2
12 Q-N3! ...

12 N-Q5!? NxN?, 13 PxN BxB, 14 RxPch! brought White quick success in the game Velimirovic–Ljubojevic, Umag 1972. The situation is not clear, however, after 12 ... PxN! *(I.N.)*

It is extremely difficult to answer this move, for 12 ... O-O, 13 P-K5! PxP, 14 PxP N-R4, 15 Q-R4 BxBch, 16 QxB P-N3, 17 P-KN4 yields White a kingside attack that should be too hot to handle. It would seem that Black must take the bull by the horns and wade into 12 ... P-N5!?, 13 N-Q5 PxN, 14 PxP K-Q1, 15 N-B5 B-KB1, 16 Q-K3 Q-R4 (but not 16 ... K-B1?, 17 Q-K8ch! Q-Q1, 18 QxP BxP, 19 QxQB NxQ, 20 BxQ KxB, 21 B-K4 N/4-N3, 22 BxR NxB, 23 NxQP, for White's game is over-whelming), and it is not clear how White can proceed, because 17 Q-K8ch K-B2, 18 QxP is answered by 18 ... BxP. *(R.B.)*

12 ... O-O-O
13 BxN! ...

This move should have won the game, since it forces the gain of a pawn. Fischer cannot reply 13 ... BxB?, 14 BxP! PxB, 15 N/4xNP Q-R4, 16 NxPch K-N1, 17 P-K5 B-K2, 18 NxP, for Spassky will emerge with rook and four pawns for two minor pieces. Nor can the material be guarded by 13 ... PxB, 14 Q-N7 QR-B1, 15 NxKP! PxN, 16 QxB, when Black doesn't even have the solace of the two bishops, which he obtains in the actual game continuation. *(R.B. & I.N.)*

13 ... NxB
14 QxP QR-B1
15 Q-N3 ...

White must pull back his queen immediately; the other way, 15 Q-R6, is bad on account of 15 ... P-N5, 16 N-R4 Q-R4, 17 P-N3 N-N5, 18 Q-R3 N-B7, winning the Exchange. *(I.N.)*

15 ... P-N5
16 N-R4 ...

16 N-N1? would have given Black the counterplay he so desperately needs: 16 . . . Q-R4, 17 P-QR3 PxP, 18 NxRP N-R4, 19 Q-B3 NxP! and Black has won back the lost pawn with excellent chances, since 20 QxN?? B-N4 catches the queen. *(R.B.)*

16 . . . KR-N1

Now 16 . . . Q-R4, 17 P-N3 N-R4, 18 Q-B2 NxP would be brilliantly refuted by 19 BxP! BxB (19 . . . QxB, 20 QxN KR-N1, 21 Q-B2 and White maintains his pawn plus without risk), 20 N-B6! B-KN4, 21 Q-R7!! Q-N4 (21 . . . N-Q4ch, 22 K-N1 Q-B2, 23 QxBch followed by 24 PxN wins a piece), 22 N-N6ch QxN, 23 N-K7ch! BxN, 24 QxQ B-N2 (or 24 . . . N-K7ch, 25 RxN BxR, 26 R-Q4 and Black cannot defend his king), 25 P-N3 N-N3, 26 R-Q4 P-Q4, 27 PxP BxP, 28 RxB PxR, 29 Q-B6ch K-N1, 30 RxB NxR, 31 Q-Q6ch and 32 QxN, with an easily won endgame for White. *(I.N. & R.B.)* Still, Black could have tried 16 . . . Q-R4, 17 P-N3 P-Q4, 18 P-K5 N-K5, 19 BxN PxB, for it would not be a simple matter to utilize the extra pawn. *(I.N.)*

17 Q-B2 N-Q2
18 K-N1 . . .

The threatened 18 . . . N-B4 will be met by 19 NxN PxN, 20 N-B3 QxP, 21 Q-K2 Q-Q3, 22 P-K5 Q-B3, 23 BxKRP, although the issue is far from settled after 23 . . . R-N2, 24 B-Q3 R/1-N1, 25 R-N1 P-B5, 26 BxP

B-B4, 27 KR-B1 RxP, 28 Q-Q3. However, 18 P-QN3, to permit N-N2 in answer to . . . N-B4, is suspect in that it sets up the long diagonal for the powerful Black king bishop. *(R.B.)*

18 . . . K-N1?

Fischer should have taken his chances with the continuation of the previous note, for he is in for far greater danger now. *(R.B.)*
Possible was 18 . . . N-B4, 19 NxN PxN, 20 N-B3 P-B5!, which Korchnoi recommended. *(I.N.)*

19 P-B3! . . .

Opening the queen bishop file exposes the Black king for a decisive attack, which Boris could have carried through at move 23. *(R.B.)*

19 . . . N-B4

19 . . . PxP, 20 R-QB1 is not worthy of a glance. *(I.N.)*

20 B-B2! . . .

The exchange, 20 NxN PxN, puts White into difficulties. For example, 21 N-B2 PxP, 22 PxP B-KB3, 23 Q-Q2 Q-R4, 24 K-N2 R-Q1, or 21 N-K2 P-B5, 22 B-B2 P-N6, 23 PxP PxP, 24 B-Q3 B-B4. After the best, 21 N-B3 PxP, 22 PxP QxP, 23 Q-N2, there follows 23 . . . R-Q1!, 24 BxP RxRch, 25 RxR QxPch, 26 K-R1 R-Q1 with an equal game. *(I.N.)*

20 . . . PxP

Black would only have hastened the enemy attack by 20 . . . NxN, 21 BxN

PxP, 22 R-QB1 Q-R4, 23 B-B6 PxP,.
24 QxP. *(R.B. & I.N.)*

21	NxBP	B-KB3
22	P-KN3	P-KR4

Up to here, Spassky has played very
accurately and stands clearly better.
However, he should not have hur-
ried with his next move. *(I.N.)*

23 P-K5?   . . .

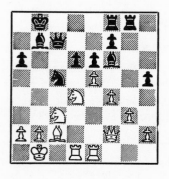

This is a silly stunt in a winning
position. The trap it involves is 23
. . . PxP, 24 PxP BxP?, 25 N/4-N5
PxN, 26 NxP Q-N3, 27 RxB QxN,
28 RxN, which, of course, gives
White a totally overwhelming game.
However, declining the proffered
pawn leaves White the obligation to
defend the very weak overextended
KP. Instead, Spassky should have
played 23 R-K3, with the plan of
continuing N-R4 to exchange knights,
for if Black were to recapture with
the queen, the White rooks come
storming through on the QB and QN

files, while recapturing with the
pawn is met by N-B3, followed by
P-K5 and B-K4, allowing White to
exploit his extra pawn from the haven
of a sound position. *(R.B.)*
Nervously played. White had here
various ways to strengthen his position. The best seems to be the continuation suggested by Paul Keres:
23 R-K3! P-R5, 24 N-N3 PxP, 25 PxP
BxN!?, 26 RxB NxP, 27 BxN BxBch,
28 K-R1 Q-R2!, 29 QxQch KxQ, 30
RxP, with good winning prospects;
or 23 . . . Q-N3, 24 N-B3 R-Q1,
25 Q-K2!. Also possible was 23
P-KR3 with a subsequent R-K3, or
23 R-Q2 and 24 R/1-Q1. *(I.N.)*

23	. . .	PxP
24	PxP	B-KR1!

To retreat the bishop to K2 would
concede a point to Spassky's pawn
advance, but this move keeps the KP
dangling on the hook. *(R.B.)*
24 . . . BxP, 25 N/4-N5 PxN, 26 NxP
BxP/6, 27 PxB Q-N3, 28 Q-B4ch K-R1,
29 N-B7ch K-R2, 30 R-K3 is terrifically
strong for White. *(I.N.)*

25 N-B3   . . .

An idea is 25 N-R4 NxN, 26 BxN
BxP, 27 R-QB1. *(I.N.)*
Spassky doesn't have to concern himself about 25 . . . BxN, 26 QxB BxP,
since Fischer's own king would be
exposed by the departure of the
powerful QB, and White could well
afford 27 QxRP. Also, 26 . . . R-N4 is
too dangerous—27 Q-B4! RxKP

(27 ... R-N5, 28 Q-R6), 28 RxR QxR
(28 ... BxR, 29 Q-N4ch), 29 Q-N4ch!
K-R1 (29 ... K-B2, 30 N-Q5ch), 30
N-R4! R-QN1 (there is no other move
to parry NxN and B-K4ch), 31 QxN
RxPch, 32 K-B1 and Black has come
to the end of his rope. *(R.B. & I.N.)*

25 ...   R-Q1

It was absolutely necessary to prevent
the powerful 26 N-K4. *(R.B.)*

26   RxRch?!   ...

Centralizing by 26 Q-K3 was preferable, since 26 ... RxRch could be
answered by 27 BxR. *(R.B. & I.N.)*

26 ...   RxR
27   N-KN5?   ...

Another mistake; necessary was the
preparatory 27 R-K3. *(I.N.)*
The idea is the exchange of White's
weak KP for Black's KBP, but Spassky
doesn't realize where the ensuing
complications are taking him. *(R.B.)*

27 ...   BxP

Fischer has no fear of 28 RxB? QxR,
29 NxBP R-KB1, pinning to get clear
of the fork. *(I.N. & R.B.)*

28   QxP   R-Q2

This is good enough, but why not
28 ... BxP!, 29 PxB QxP, when it is
White who must find the draw? Nor
is 29 QxQch BxQ, 30 P-N4 R-N1
pleasant for White. *(R.B.)*

29   QxRP?!   ...

Spassky is foolhardy in continuing to
try for a win. He should be happy to
hold the draw by 29 Q-K8ch R-Q1,
30 Q-B7, etc. Nor would Fischer be
able to continue with 29 ... K-R2,
since 30 NxP both wins a pawn and
exchanges off one of the attacking
pieces. Korchnoi points out that
29 ... B-B1 will not get Fischer anywhere either: 30 N/5-K4 (of course
not 30 NxP? NxN, 31 QxN R-Q8ch,
winning the queen) 30 ... NxN,
31 NxN Q-N3, 32 B-N3 P-R4, 33
QxRP, beating back the attack.
(R.B. & I.N.)

29 ...   BxN!

Bobby tears a small hole in the
enemy king position and comes on
like a tornado! *(R.B.)*

30   PxB   Q-N3ch
31   K-B1?? (R.B.)   ...

Perhaps more practical in time pressure was 31 K-R1. Viktor Korchnoi
analyzes the following variations:
31 ... R-Q7, 32 R-QN1! Q-R4, 33

Q-R8ch K-R2, 34 R-N2 P-K4, 35 Q-R6
QxP?, 36 Q-N6ch K-R1, 37 N-K4! or
34 ... Q-R6, 35 N-B3! Better is, however, the immediate 31 ... Q-R4!
and the White position cannot be
held. *(I.N.)*
Spassky's last chance to hold on was
31 K-R1 Q-R4, 32 Q-R8ch K-R2,
33 R-QN1 P-K4!, 34 R-N4 R-Q7,
35 B-N1 N-Q6, 36 RxBch! and Black
cannot avoid perpetual check except
by running into mate or loss of
material. *(R.B.)*

31	...	**Q-R4**
32	**Q-R8ch**	**K-R2**
33	**P-QR4**	...

Black is two pawns down, but his
attack is enormously strong. White
defends himself desperately. 33 K-N2
B-Q4 is hopeless. *(I.N.)*
On 33 K-N2 Fischer would have
played 33 ... R-Q7, 34 K-B1 R-Q1,
35 Q-N7 R-Q2, 36 Q-K5 Q-R6ch,
37 K-N1 B-Q4 and there is no way
out of the mating net. *(R.B.)*

| 33 | ... | **N-Q6ch!** |

The simplest, most direct win is to
strip White of his best defensive
piece. *(R.B.)*
Also good was 33 ... NxP. *(I.N.)*

| 34 | **BxN** | **RxB** |
| 35 | **K-B2** | **R-Q4?!** |

More forcing was 35 ... R-Q1, 36
Q-K5 QxRPch or 36 Q-R4 B-B3. *(I.N.)*
Bobby could have won directly with
35 ... R-Q1, 36 Q-K5 QxRPch, 37

K-N1 Q-N6ch, 38 K-B1 Q-R6ch, 39
K-N1 R-QN1!, 40 Q-B7 K-R1, 41 K-B2
Q-R7ch, 42 K-Q3 (after 42 K-B1
B-Q4, 43 Q-R7 Q-R8ch, 44 K-Q2
R-N7ch, Black wins a rook) 42 ...
Q-Q4ch, picking off the knight. Vary-
ing in this line by 37 K-B1 is su-
perior: 37 ... Q-R8ch, 38 K-B2
Q-R7ch, 39 K-B1 Q-Q7ch, 40 K-N1
B-K5ch!, 41 RxB (41 QxB R-N1ch and
Black wins queen, rook and knight in
that order) 41 ... Q-Q8ch, 42 K-N2
R-Q7ch, 43 K-R3 Q-R8ch, 44 K-N4
Q-N8ch, 45 K-B4 Q-R7ch, 46 K-N4
R-N7ch, 47 K-B5 R-N4ch, 48 K-Q6
RxQ, 49 RxR QxP. While the resulting
ending is very likely won for Black,
there are great technical difficulties
to overcome. However, Fischer can
get a relatively easier win by the
simpler 40 ... R-Q4, 41 Q-K3ch
QxQ, 42 RxQ RxN, 43 RxP R-KB4. As
long as there are rooks on the board,
it doesn't matter that the bishop is of
the opposite color of the pawn's
queening square, while the unsup-
ported kingside pawns aren't going
anywhere. *(R.B.)*

| 36 | **R-K4!** | ... |

Spassky defends brilliantly, the point
being that 36 ... RxN, 37 Q-Q4ch
Q-B4, 38 QxQch RxQ, 39 RxP does
not give the ending of the previous
note, since White still has his QRP.
(R.B. & I.N.)

| 36 | ... | **R-Q1?!** |

Korchnoi remarks in "64" that 36 ...
B-B3! was the right way, giving 37

K-N3 RxN, when the KP cannot be taken and there is no perpetual check. He also demonstrates that 37 R-QN4 BxPch, 38 K-N2 R-Q7ch, 39 K-B1 R-Q8ch, 40 K-N2 B-N4, 41 Q-N7ch K-N3 puts White in a mate net. His refutation of 37 N-B3 is 37 ... BxPch, 38 K-N2 R-Q8, 39 Q-N7ch B-Q2, 40 R-Q4 Q-N4ch, 41 K-R2 Q-K7ch, 42 K-R3 R-R8ch, 43 K-N3 R-N8ch, 44 K-R3 Q-N7 mate. *(R.B. & I.N.)*

37	Q-N7	Q-KB4
38	K-N3	Q-Q4ch?

This does it for the last time and Boris gets away with a draw. The win was still to be had by 38 ... K-R1!, for if 39 Q-K5 R-KN1 and White cannot stop the loss of a piece. If 39 Q-K7 B-Q4ch, 40 K-R3, then 40 ... R-QB1 wins. 39 R-QN4 is forbidden by 39 ... Q-N8ch, 40 K-B4

Q-R7ch, 41 K-B5 Q-Q4ch and mate in two. *(I.N. & R.B.)*

39	K-R3	...

The White king finds a reasonably quiet place here. *(I.N.)*

39	...	Q-Q7
40	R-QN4!	...

At last White's mating threats balance Black's. *(R.B.)*

40	...	Q-B8ch

40 ... R-Q2, 41 Q-K5 is no better. *(I.N.)*

41	R-N2	Q-R8ch
42	R-R2	Q-B8ch
43	R-N2	Q-R8ch
	Drawn	

A game rich in vicissitudes, wherein both players had the game won at different times. *(I.N.)*

GAME 16

August 20, 1972

There was really not so much happening in this game, but to call a 60-moves-in-one-evening performance a grandmaster draw would, of course, be an exaggeration. Perhaps the secret of the reasonably quiet even-numbered match games lies in Fischer's willingness to try tranquil lines of play with the White pieces, while Spassky did not want to take risks, setting his hopes on his odd-numbered White games.

In the Ruy Lopez, the American chose the Exchange Variation favored by Lasker, with which he has done a good business since 1966. Naturally, this quiet line of play, which often gives rise to an early endgame, is not particularly dangerous for Black and the good results it has achieved in practice in the last six years are at least partly to be ascribed to its surprise value.

Spassky defended himself solidly and White obtained only a minimal advantage after the opening phase. In the subsequent play, Fischer did not extend himself especially to maintain the initiative and Black gradually became more ambitious. Spassky even won a pawn by means of a little combination, but that did not amount to much in view of his remaining isolated doubled QBP's. He still tried to make something out of a rook and pawn ending with two pawns against one all on the same side of the board, but it was easy for White to frustrate his efforts in a well-known theoretical draw position. *(I.N.)*

Ruy Lopez

ROBERT FISCHER   BORIS SPASSKY

1	P-K4	P-K4
2	N-KB3	N-QB3
3	B-N5	P-QR3
4	BxN	. . .

After all the violence of the previous game, Fischer is probably content to head for the tranquil channels of the Exchange Variation, the main theme of which is the exploitation of Black's doubled pawns in an endgame. *(R.B.)*

4 . . .   QPxB

Recapturing with the QP is usual, but it is also possible to play 4 . . . NPxB. For example, 5 P-Q4 PxP, 6 QxP Q-B3, 7 P-K5 Q-N3, 8 O-O B-N2!, 9 QN-Q2 (9 P-K6? BPxP, 10 N-K5 QxPch! is favorable for Black) 9 . . . O-O-O, 10 N-N3 P-QB4, 11 Q-B3 P-KB3, with about an equal game. *(I.N.)*

5 O-O   . . .

Almost a century ago, then World Champion Emanuel Lasker used to force the endgame immediately by 5 P-Q4 PxP, 6 QxP QxQ, 7 NxQ. In the last six years, Fischer has preferred the Barendregt idea of castling first in order to give the plan potency by mobilizing a rook. The opening comes as no surprise to Spassky. *(R.B.)*

With this move, Fischer has infused new life in the old variation. *(I.N.)*

5 . . .   P-B3

The most popular alternative here is 5 . . . B-KN5. Paul Keres has tried 5 . . . N-K2!?, while David Bronstein has suggested 5 . . . Q-Q3, with which Portisch was successful against Andersson in Las Palmas 1972. *(I.N.)*

6   P-Q4   B-KN5

According to practical experience, 6 . . . PxP, 7 NxP P-QB4 gives White the better game. For example, 8 N-N3 QxQ, 9 RxQ B-Q3, 10 N-R5 P-QN4, 11 P-QB4, with positional pressure on the queenside (Fischer–Portisch, Havana 1966). *(I.N.)*

7   PxP   . . .

7 P-B3 leads to a complicated game, in which Black's best continuation is 7 . . . B-Q3, maintaining the center. *(I.N.)*

7   . . .   QxQ
8   RxQ   PxP

After 8 . . . BxN, 9 PxB PxP, 10 B-K3!, White stands better, as in Fischer–Rubinetti, Buenos Aires 1970. *(I.N.)*

9   R-Q3   . . .

The rook is somewhat awkwardly placed here, but White cannot work up any initiative as long as the king knight remains pinned. *(R.B.)*

9   . . .   B-Q3

According to Fischer's opinion, the endgame after 9 . . . BxN, 10 RxB N-B3, 11 N-B3 B-N5, 12 B-N5 BxN, 13 PxB is favorable for White. However, the situation is not at all clear after 13 . . . R-KB1, 14 BxN RxB, 15 RxR PxR, 16 R-Q1 P-QR4. *(I.N.)*

10   QN-Q2   N-B3

In order to avoid the following knight attack, 10 . . . P-QN4 comes to mind. However, Spassky does not like such moves which weaken the pawn position, while, considered objectively, White would have some chances for advantage afterward. *(I.N.)*

11   N-B4   . . .

By this maneuver, Fischer intends to exchange one of Black's strong bishops, the chief feature of the defense. *(R.B.)*

11	...	NxP
12	N/4xP	...

Fischer improves on Bronstein's 12 N/3xP, forcing Black to yield the bishop pair at once without any repair of the doubled pawns.
Spassky is unable to dispute the point by 12 ... B-KB4?, since 13 P-KN4! B-K3, 14 R-K3 N-B3, 15 N-N5 leads to a decisive loss of material for Black. *(R.B.)*
The other possibility to fight for the initiative consists in 12 N/3xP. In the encounter Hecht–Matanovic, Berlin 1971, Black succeeded in obtaining satisfactory play after 12 ... B-K3. *(I.N.)*

12	...	B/5xN
13	NxB	O-O
14	B-K3	...

It looks now as though Fischer has everything that could be expected out of this type of opening. The White kingside pawn majority is a clear advantage because the three pawns on the other wing are normally enough to blockade the Black pawn preponderance there, which is crippled by doubled pawns. And Fischer has eliminated the queens and two sets of minor pieces, creating the simplified position in which

such a structural superiority can be utilized. *(R.B.)*

14	...	P-QN4!

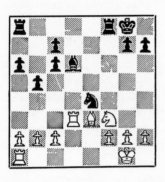

Spassky has compensation for his worse pawn formation in his good development. However, this demands energetic play, for otherwise White's positional pluses can be decisive. Black must naturally look for chances on the queenside. *(I.N.)*
Striking back in an original and ingenious way, Spassky intends to throw the queenside pawns forward, gaining space and putting on pressure to undouble the QBP's. *(R.B.)*

15 P-B4? ...

On 15 P-QN3 P-B4, 16 P-B4 PxP, 17 PxP QR-N1, Black would obtain counterplay on the open QN file. After 15 N-Q2, with the idea of controlling the QB5 square on 15 ... N-B3, 16 N-N3, Black's best answer would be 15 ... QR-K1. *(I.N.)*
Blocking with the QBP is the thema-

tic way to counter such a plan, of course, but Spassky quickly proves it tactically unsound. Best was 15 N-Q2, for, if 15 ... NxN, 16 RxN P-B4, 17 P-QB4 would set up the blockade White wants. Moreover, the retreat, 15 ... N-B3 would permit a piece blockade with 16 N-N3, followed by either 17 N-B5 or 17 B-B5. Spassky could have obtained considerable activity for his bishop and rooks by 15 ... N-B4, 16 BxN (not 16 R-B3 N-R5!) 16 ... BxB, 17 N-K4 B-N3, 18 R-K1 QR-K1, 19 K-B1 and a fascinating struggle between dynamics and structure would have begun. *(R.B.)*

15 ...   QR-N1!

An unusual and strong continuation of the idea of his previous move by which White is saddled with the awkward task of finding a smooth defense for both the QBP and the QNP. *(R.B.)*

16   R-QB1   . . .

Fischer's decision is to sacrifice a pawn, hoping to recover it later with positional advantage. In any case, Black could not be denied effective counterplay, for if 16 P-QN3 (in order to answer 16 ... PxP by 17 R-Q4!) 16 ... B-R6, 17 R-Q7 PxP, 18 PxP B-Q3!, 19 B-Q4 N-B3, 20 BxN RxB, and in the resulting position, 21 P-B5 will free the rook, but Black's strong bishop gives him the endgame edge. Furthermore, the Black rooks have such threats as R-K3-K7 and R-N5-R5 with great pressure. Perhaps 17 QR-Q1 is best: 17 ... PxP, 18 PxP B-Q3, 19 R-N3 RxR, 20 PxR R-N1, 21 R-Q3 P-QR4, 22 P-N3, when the result will be a draw. *(R.B.)*

After 16 P-QN3 B-R6, the position is even. Weaker, according to Viktor Korchnoi, would be 16 ... PxP, 17 R-Q4! PxP!?, 18 RxN PxP, 19 N-Q2 R-N7, 20 R-QR4, etc. *(I.N.)*

16   ...   PxP
17   R-Q4   . . .

If 17 RxP RxP and the knight cannot be captured because of the threatening mate. *(I.N. & R.B.)*

17   ...   KR-K1

Interesting is 17 ... N-B4!?, after which 18 R/4xP N-Q6, 19 R/1-B2? NxP, 20 RxP N-Q6! wins for Black. Better is 18 R-B2 N-R5, 19 R/2xP NxP (19 ... RxP, 20 B-B1 R-N8, 21 N-Q2 R-R8, 22 N-N3 RxRP, 23 RxN R/7xP, 24 R-Q1 gives White a won game),

20 RxP and White stands somewhat superior. *(I.N.)*

18 N-Q2 . . .

18 R-B2 P-B6!, 19 PxP R-N8ch, 20 B-B1 N-N4!, 21 R-Q1 NxNch, 22 PxN gives Black the initiative and a clear advantage. *(R.B. & I.N.)*

18	. . .	NxN
19	RxN	R-K5

19 . . . B-K4, 20 RxP is good for White, but 19 . . . R-N5, 20 P-KN3 (20 K-B1 BxP!) 20 . . . B-K4 would have given White more trouble than the text move. *(I.N.)*

20 P-KN3 . . .

By removing back-rank mate threats and preparing to bring his king strongly into play, Bobby ensures the draw. *(R.B.)*

20	. . .	B-K4
21	R/1-B2	K-B2
22	K-N2	RxP!

The gain of a second pawn is only temporary. 23 RxR is answered by 23 . . . P-B6, 24 R-Q7ch K-K3. *(I.N. & R.B.)*

In case White's 22nd move was an oversight, it was a fortunate one! It is difficult to say whether 22 R-K2 B-B3, 23 K-N2 R-QN5 was stronger. *(I.N.)*

23	K-B3!	P-B6
24	KxR	PxR
25	RxQP	R-N4

It is possible that White would be better after the exchange of rooks, despite the pawn minus, because Black's extra pawn is doubled and weak. Spassky's move returns the pawn for a minute positional advantage. *(R.B. & I.N.)*

26	R-B2	B-Q3
27	RxP	R-QR4
28	B-B4!	. . .

Fischer wisely sacrifices a pawn to bring about a standard drawn rook and pawn ending, because if 28 R-B2, K-K3, followed by . . . R-R5ch would give White trouble. *(I.N. & R.B.)*

28	. . .	R-R5ch
29	K-B3	R-R6ch
30	K-K4	RxRP
31	BxB	PxB
32	RxQP	RxP
33	RxP	RxP
34	K-B3	. . .

39	K-N2	R-K2
40	K-R3	K-B3
41	R-R6ch	R-K3
42	R-R5	P-R3
43	R-R2	K-B4
44	R-B2ch	K-N4
45	R-B7	P-N3
46	R-B4	P-R4
47	R-B3	R-KB3
48	R-R3	R-K3
49	R-KB3	R-K5
50	R-R3	K-B3
51	R-R6	R-K4
52	K-R4	R-K5ch
53	K-R3	R-K2
54	K-R4	R-K4
55	R-N6	K-N2
56	R-N4	K-R3
57	R-N6	R-K8
58	K-R3	R-R8ch
59	K-N2	R-R8
60	K-R3	R-R5
	Drawn	

There was no way for Black to get more out of the position, but what he has is as good as nothing. *(I.N.)* Now the game could have been given up as a draw, but since Fischer insists on playing everything out, Spassky decides to do the same today. Throughout the next twenty-six moves, there was some tittering in the audience, which seemed amused at the spectacle of the two chess giants fooling around with an elementary position, like Frank Lloyd Wright playing in a sandbox. *(R.B.)*

34	...	R-Q7
35	R-R7ch	K-B3
36	R-R6ch	K-K2
37	R-R7ch	R-Q2
38	R-R2	K-K3

GAME 17

August 22, 1972

This game was for Spassky practically the last attempt to change the course of the match running against him. There remained only three—at the best, four—games in which he had the White pieces and, naturally, he had to strive in these odd-numbered encounters to cut down his opponent's three-point lead.

Fischer again came up with a surprise in the opening—for the first time in his chess career, he adopted the Pirc-Ufimtsev Defense, adhering to his general strategy in the match of ever placing new opening problems before his opponent. In the transition to the middle game, White played somewhat passively and Black obtained a reasonable game.

Then White made a fascinating pawn sacrifice. It is difficult to say whether Fischer could have maintained his material advantage, but he chose a different course, offering the Exchange in the style of former World Champion Tigran Petrosian, holding a pawn for it. There arose a situation in which the question, "to be or not to be," depended on the possibility of penetrating to the seventh (or eighth) rank with a White rook. Black was able to demonstrate the inviolability of his lines of defense. *(I.N.)*

Pirc Defense

BORIS SPASSKY   BOBBY FISCHER

1	P-K4	P-Q3
2	P-Q4	P-KN3

It would be interesting to learn why Fischer, with his second move, gave Spassky the chance to transpose into the King's Indian Defense by 3 P-QB4. After 1 P-Q4, Fischer did not choose to go into this opening. The usual 2 . . . N-KB3 would have limited White's option. *(I.N.)*

3 N-QB3 . . .

But White does not jump at the opportunity Black's second move presents. Was Fischer perhaps expecting 3 P-KR4!?, which Spassky had employed with success in his youth? *(I.N.)*

3	. . .	N-KB3
4	P-B4	. . .

In the past, Spassky has usually preferred the quieter, more positional 4 N-B3 to the ambitious text move. *(R.B.)*

4	. . .	B-N2
5	N-B3	P-B4

By far the most popular continuation here is 5 . . . O-O, 6 B-Q3 N-B3, which has held its own despite persistent attempts at refutation. On the other hand, 5 . . . P-B4 has long been considered dubious, although the present game may challenge that opinion. *(R.B. & I.N.)*

6 PxP . . .

Alternatives here are 6 P-K5!? or 6 B-N5ch B-Q2, 7 P-K5 N-N5, 8 P-K6 BxB, 9 PxPch K-Q2!, in both cases with sharp play. *(I.N.)*

6 ... Q-R4!

6 ... PxP?, 7 QxQch KxQ, 8 P-K5 gives White an all but decisive endgame advantage. After the text move, White cannot reply 7 PxP because of the terrific counterplay resulting from 7 ... NxP. *(R.B. & I.N.)*

7	B-Q3	QxBP
8	Q-K2	O-O
9	B-K3	Q-QR4

Also possible is 9 ... Q-B2, 10 O-O QN-Q2. *(I.N.)*
Black can win a pawn by 9 ... Q-N5!?, since 10 O-O-O? NxP!, 11 BxN BxN, 12 PxB QxB is a lost game for White. However, 10 O-O QxNP, 11 N-QN5 N-K1, 12 P-K5 Q-N5, 13 NxRP gets it back with advantage. *(R.B.)*

10 O-O   B-N5

A new idea. 10 ... QN-Q2, 11 Q-K1, or 10 ... N-B3, 11 P-KR3 P-K4, 12 PxP PxP, 13 Q-B2, followed by 14 Q-R4 is dangerous for Black. *(I.N.)* This idea of Fischer's must be the best Black has, for the bishop would

be inoperative at Q2, and at K3, just asking for P-B5. *(R.B.)*

11 QR-Q1!?   ...

This leads to a complicated game. More logical seems 11 P-KR3 BxN, 12 QxB N-B3, 13 P-R3 and White stands somewhat better (two bishops and potential prospects for an assault on the kingside). *(I.N.)*
Spassky is already getting set for a disputable pawn sacrifice, but the simple 11 P-KR3 BxN, 12 QxB guarantees White a small edge. *(R.B.)*

11	...	N-B3
12	B-B4	...

The last two White moves do not look quite logical and they enable Black to institute the following counterplay. *(I.N.)*

12 ...   N-R4!

While running after a pawn this way involves great risk, it really cannot be avoided, since a quiet continuation would only allow White to build up his kingside attack at no cost at all. *(R.B.)*

13 B-N3   ...

This pawn sacrifice is the logical consequence of the foregoing White play. Gligoric's suggestion, 13 R-Q5 Q-B2, 14 R-KN5!? is interesting; still, White can hardly hope to gain advantage in that way. A possible counter would be 14 ... N-Q5,

15 Q-Q3 B-K3, 16 N-Q5 BxN, 17 PxB P-N4! (perhaps 17 ... N-B4 would also be good). *(I.N.)*
If Spassky were to back off from the sacrifice by 13 R-Q5 Q-B2, 14 B-N3, he would be left awkwardly placed after 14 ... N-R4. *(R.B.)*

13   ...   BxQN

If Fischer does not see a concrete mating continuation, he always takes such pawns. Formerly only Korchnoi of the greats would take such risks. The American pays no attention to so-called general principles. *(I.N.)*

14   PxB   QxBP
15   P-B5   N-B3!

It's no secret that Spassky has dangerous attacking chances with two powerful bishops bearing down on the Black king position and the possibility of opening the KB file for his rooks as well. While it would be tempting to chop off the advancing pawns by 15 ... PxP, 16 PxP BxP, Black cannot hang on to the game

after 17 N-Q4! B-N3, 18 NxN QxN, 19 B-R6 KR-K1, 20 KRxP! BxR, 21 BxBch KxB, 22 QxNch K-K3, 23 Q-N4ch and mate in a few moves.
15 ... N-K4 has also been suggested, with the point that 16 B-Q4? can be answered by 16 ... N-KB5!, 17 Q-B2 NxNch, 18 PxN N-R6ch, 19 K-N2 NxQ, 20 BxQ NxR, 21 RxN B-R4, leaving Black the Exchange ahead plus a pawn in the endgame. However, 15 ... N-K4 is not all that good. After 16 Q-B2 BxN, 17 PxB, White still has a menacing position, while 16 ... NxNch, 17 PxN B-R6, 18 B-Q4 Q-R4, 19 KR-K1 leaves the bishop trapped. *(R.B.)*
The obvious 15 ... N-K4 seems weaker. While 16 B-Q4 N-KB5!, 17 Q-K3 (17 Q-B2 N-R6ch!) 17 ... QxQch, 18 BxQ BxN, 19 PxB P-KN4 is advantageous for Black, after the correct continuation, suggested by Smyslov, 16 Q-B2! BxN, 17 PxB, the White bishop pair is dangerous. *(I.N.)*

16   P-KR3   BxN
17   QxB   N-QR4

17 ... Q-K4 could be answered very strongly by 18 B-Q5!, since 18 ... NxB, 19 PxN N-N5, 20 B-R6 KR-K1, 21 PxP BPxP, 22 Q-B7ch K-R1, 23 QR-K1 Q-Q5ch, 24 K-R1 NxQP (on almost any other move, 25 RxP RxR, 26 Q-B8ch mates), 25 R-K4! costs the knight. Also 17 ... N-K4 is only a one-move defensive measure, because 18 Q-B4, followed by B-Q4 and

Q-R6 becomes impossible to stop. *(R.B. & I.N.)*

18 R-Q3   Q-B2

Now 18 ... Q-K4? would leave the queen strapped for moves after 19 B-Q5, for 19 ... NxB, 20 RxN Q-B6, 21 B-R6 wins the Exchange. *(R.B. & I.N.)*

Deserving of consideration was 18 ... Q-B3, attacking the KP; after 19 B-Q5 QxP!?, 20 B-R6 KR-B1 the situation looks dangerous for Black, but he does have two pawns more and a direct course of attack for White is not easy to find. *(I.N.)*

19 B-R6   NxB
20 BPxN   . . .

All 20 BxR would accomplish is simplification useful for Black after 20 ... N-B4, 21 B-R6 NxR. *(R.B.)* After 20 BxR N-B4, 21 B-R6 NxR, 22 PxN, the White position is worth the missing pawn. However, 21 ... N/4xP! is possible. *(I.N.)*

20 . . .   Q-B4ch
21 K-R1   Q-K4?!

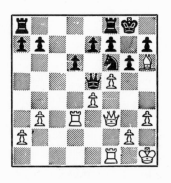

There is some risk of Black losing now because he gets only one pawn for the Exchange in the coming end-game. After 21 ... KR-B1, White's attacking attempt with 22 P-KN4 Q-K4, 23 PxP BPxP, 24 P-N5 R-B7 would only land him in trouble. Perhaps Boris would have continued 23 R-K3 R-B7, 24 B-B4 Q-Q5, but I don't see that he has anything but shadow-threats. *(R.B.)*

It is not clear if the Exchange sacrifice is forced. On the line of attack recommended by several commentators, (after 21 ... KR-B1!) 22 PxP RPxP, 23 P-KN4, there follows very strongly 23 ... Q-K4!, 24 P-N5 R-B7 and White is lost. Apart from the assault of the KNP, the Black king position can scarcely be seriously endangered, so the move 21 ... KR-B1 must be considered best in the position arrived at. *(I.N.)*

22 BxR   RxB
23 R-K3   R-B1

Also here Black has sufficient compensation for the small material disadvantage. *(I.N.)*

24 PxP?   . . .

It was better to leave the BP on the board and play Q-B4 at once. Then it might be possible to operate with some threat of P-B6 in the endgame which comes up in five moves. *(R.B.)*

24 . . .   RPxP
25 Q-B4   . . .

There is no longer any reason for White to maintain a middle game situation, since his pieces are tied down to the defense of the KP, while Fischer has the only open file. *(R.B.)*

25 ...   QxQ

Black could also very well keep the queens on with 25 ... Q-K3. *(I.N.)*

26 RxQ   N-Q2

Of course, 27 P-K5 is not a threat while Black has the N-Q4 fork. Still, there is no point in postponing measures against it, since all White needs to win such a position as this is one open file for the rooks. *(R.B.)*
In this way, Black succeeds in setting up an impenetrable fortress. However, even stronger was 26 ... R-B7, 27 P-QR4 N-Q2. Here, 27 P-K5!? doesn't work because of 27 ... N-Q4, 28 PxP NxR/6, 29 PxP R-B8ch, 30 K-R2 N-N5ch!, and 31 ... R-K8 with a draw. Now White will prevent the rook from reaching the seventh rank. *(I.N.)*

27 R-B2   N-K4
28 K-R2   R-B8
29 R/3-K2   N-B3

It was absolutely vital to seal the QB file this way so the White rooks are denied play. *(R.B.)*

30 R-B2   R-K8

The exchange of rooks would lose for Black since the knight then be-

comes a totally passive file blockader which can soon be driven out of the way by P-QN4-5. If Black brought his king to Q2 to hold the seventh and eighth ranks, the passed pawn White could get by P-KR4, P-KN4 and P-R5 would decide. *(R.B.)*

31 KR-K2   R-R8!

Black must keep his active rook in order to be able to attack the White pawns. After the exchange of rooks the endgame would be won for White—he could combine a breakthrough on the queen's wing with the development of passed pawn on the KR file. Even with his two rooks on the board, White could hope for success with this plan, but as the sequel of the game shows, he cannot post his pieces favorably to carry it out. *(I.N.)*

32 K-N3   K-N2
33 QR-Q2   R-KB8
34 R-KB2   R-K8
35 KR-K2   R-KB8
36 R-K3   P-R3

Fischer rules out the idea of
R-Q5-QN5. *(R.B.)*

37	R-QB3	R-K8
38	R-B4	R-KB8
39	R/2-QB2	R-QR8

Bobby prevents his rook from getting
tied up by 40 R-B1 which would
have forced 40 . . . R-B3. At the same
time White is denied the chance to
give back the Exchange by 40 RxN,
PxR, 41 RxP to obtain winning connected passed pawns in the rook and
pawn ending, since now the White
QRP hangs. *(R.B.)*

40	R-B2	R-K8
41	R/2-B2	. . .

The sealed move. The adjournment
analysis showed that White's small
material advantage could not be
realized. *(I.N.)*

41	. . .	P-KN4
42	R-B1	R-K7

43	R/1-B2	R-K8
44	R-B1	R-K7
45	R/1-B2	Drawn

Fischer claimed the threefold repetition of position that comes about
after 45 . . . R-K8. If the repetition
was not a nervous-tension error by
Spassky, why did he not at least try
P-R3 and P-QN4, with the plan of a
break at QN5? Even if the active
Black rook could thwart the idea, it
was worth a try. *(R.B.)*

Spassky Puts Up a Hard Fight

Redoubled efforts by Boris Spassky to lop a point from the challenger's lead made for brilliant, hard-fought chess in the next stage of the match, which saw Fischer inching nearer and nearer to victory with draws in games 18, 19 and 20. Was Bobby content merely to sneak in by split points? I don't believe it—it's never been his style. I think the explanation for the draws is to be found in Spassky's improvements in his openings.

In games 18 and 20, Boris returned to the Sicilian Defense which worked well for him in game 4. On the strength of the latter game, in which Spassky discovered an excellent way to handle Fischer's 6 B-QB4, Bobby was constrained to go over to 6 B-KN5, entering into positions unfamiliar to him. The 18th contest was a great struggle in which Black's chances were never inferior to White's, and in the 20th game, Fischer made no attempt to refute the defense, acceding to an early equality by Black.

The strongest blow Spassky struck in the entire match was his knocking out Fischer's favorite Najdorf Sicilian in games 11 and 15. That forced Bobby to run to the Pirc–Robatsch and Alekhine's Defenses; the former he had never played before, and the latter he had used very sparingly as his second string. The Alekhine's Defense in game 19 gave rise to a carnage of scintillating sacrifices, ending wondrously on level terms. Still, all Spassky's ingenuity came to naught against Fischer's superior play. At the end of game 20, Boris continued to trail by 3 points, with the score 11½–8½. *(R.B.)*

August 24, 1972

The World Champion no longer had any choice. Before this encounter, Fischer had a clear 10–7 lead and every draw was almost equivalent to a win for him. Therefore, Spassky selected the Sicilian Defense and sought (with success!) early complications. There arose a strategically difficult situation for both sides. The Black king remained in the center where it was reasonably well protected by a pawn mass. Nevertheless, White could begin active operations in the middle game. Perhaps in a different competitive situation, Fischer would not have had anything against these possibilities, but this time he was definitely conservative. In the last hour of play, with shortage of time on both sides, each one in turn had real chances of success. Perhaps a draw was the correct result. *(I.N.)*

Sicilian Defense

BOBBY FISCHER   BORIS SPASSKY

1   P-K4   . . .

From game 14 on to the end of the match, Bobby sticks to P-K4, perhaps feeling that 1 P-Q4 has used up its surprise value. *(R.B.)*

1   . . .   P-QB4

Boris has never liked the aggressive Sicilian, but in this match he does so

well with it that it may become the defense of his future. *(R.B.)*

2   N-KB3   P-Q3
3   N-B3   . . .

A little opening subtlety; White excludes the sharp variation, 3 P-Q4 PxP, 4 NxP N-KB3, 5 N-QB3 P-QR3, because, after 3 . . . N-KB3, 4 P-K5 gives White chances for the initiative in a quiet game, while after 3 . . . P-QR3, 4 P-KN3 can follow. *(I.N.)*

3   . . .   N-QB3
4   P-Q4   PxP
5   NxP   N-B3
6   B-KN5! (I.N.)   . . .

Characteristically for Fischer, in this match, he doesn't allow himself to get involved in a theoretical argument about the merits of 6 B-QB4. *(I.N.)*
Outside of 6 B-QB4, which Spassky countered strongly in game 4, this is the most ambitious move to put Black under pressure. After the tame 6 B-K2 P-K4, or 6 . . . P-K3, Black has little trouble getting an acceptable game. *(R.B.)*

6   . . .   P-K3
7   Q-Q2   P-QR3

The sharpest way to play the variation chosen by White. *(I.N.)*

8   O-O-O   B-Q2
9   P-B4   B-K2
10 N-B3   . . .

Some way has to be sought to breach Black's solid position; this move threatens P-K5. In game 20, Fischer tries 10 B-K2, but without success. *(R.B.)*

10 ... P-QN4

The only good reply, the text move intends 11 P-K5 P-N5, 12 PxN PxN, 13 QxBP PxP, 14 B-R4, reaching a position in which Black relies on his preponderance in the center to make up for his slightly uncomfortable king situation. Boris's heading for it and Bobby's avoidance of it by his next move indicate they are unanimous in the judgment that Black's chances are fully adequate. *(R.B. & I.N.)*

11 BxN ...

Having come so far, this is the only alternative to create sharp play, since the immediate 11 B-Q3 has never proven to yield White anything. *(R.B.)*

11 ... PxB

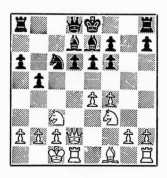

Had Fischer been expecting Spassky to venture Simagin's gambit, 11 ... BxB?!, 12 QxP B-K2, 13 Q-Q2 P-N5, 14 N-QR4 R-R2—? While there is a considerable amount of play in it, its soundness is still questionable. By his recapture, Spassky enters into an old line of the defense which has long been considered inferior, but which may get a new lease on life as a result of this game. *(R.B.)*

The pawn sacrifice, 11 ... BxB, 12 QxP B-K2 is possible, but Black does not obtain complete compensation. *(I.N.)*

12 B-Q3 ...

This move has little force. White's only correct idea must be to aim at exploiting the doubled pawns by P-KN3, B-R3, P-B5, etc., with the intention of forcing ... P-K4, so that the Q5 square can be occupied by a knight. Mikhail Tal won a fine game from me in that manner in the Varna Olympiad, 1962. *(R.B.)*

Another idea here is pressure against K6 through 12 P-B5, followed by the development of the bishop to KR3. *(I.N.)*

12	...	Q-R4
13	K-N1	P-N5
14	N-K2	Q-QB4

Regardless of the Black bishop pair, White stands somewhat better on account of his centralized position. With his last move, Black readies a pawn storm on the queen's wing, which, however, can be neutralized

by careful White play. *(I.N.)*
Spassky makes room for the advance of his QRP to break open a file for attack on the enemy king, a far better plan than ... O-O-O, which constricts Black's own counterplay. *(R.B.)*

15   P-B5   . . .
Such a pawn sacrifice is routine in proceeding against the doubled pawns, for acceptance by 15 . . . PxP?, 16 PxP BxP, 17 BxB QxB, 18 N-B4, followed by N-Q5, fatally wrecks both Black's pawn position and the defense of his king. *(R.B.)* Naturally, White must begin play against K6 sooner or later. *(I.N.)*

15   . . .   P-QR4
16   N-B4   P-R5
17   R-QB1   . . .
Measures must be taken against . . . P-N6, while Fischer looks toward using the QB file for his own benefit. It is difficult to suggest an alternative. *(R.B.)*

17   . . .   R-QN1
Up to now, both players have continued consistently. However, Black can penetrate no further into the White position with his pawns, because 17 . . . P-R6, 18 P-N3 Q-B6, 19 QxQ PxQ is favorable for White. Instead of the rook move, it was better to play 17 . . . N-K4 since, in several variations, the Black rook gives stronger service where it is. *(I.N.)*

18   P-B3   . . .
While Spassky was not yet threatening . . . P-N6, it is impossible for White to go ahead with any plans without securing his king position first. *(R.B.)*

18   . . .   P-N6
Fridrik Olafsson criticized the blockading of the queenside, recommending instead 18 . . . N-K4; however, after 19 N-Q4 NPxP, 20 QxP QxQ, 21 RxQ NxB, 22 NxN, the game is about even. The more ambitious text move confines the White king to the first rank and, later on, gives Black dangerous opportunities to work with mate threats when only rooks and queens remain. *(R.B.)*

19   P-QR3   N-K4
20   KR-B1   . . .

The attempt to go all out against Black's weak K3 square would not succeed, for 20 PxP PxP, 21 N-Q4 K-B2, 22 B-K2 N-N3! keeps everything well defended. However, the sacrifice line, 21 . . . N-B5, 22 Q-K2

NxPch is not sound: 23 PxN QxRP, 24 N/B4xP! (threatening Q-R5 mate) 24 ... BxN, 25 NxB P-N7, 26 B-N5ch K-B2, 27 Q-R5ch! K-N1 (27 ... KxN, 28 Q-Q5 mate), 28 QR-B1 Q-R8ch, 29 K-B2 Q-R7, 30 K-Q3 and White wins, since 30 ... QxN is answered by 31 B-B4. (R.B.)

Fischer decides on waiting tactics. Lev Polugaevsky recommends here 20 Q-K2, with the idea of eventually bringing the queen to KR5. But the most energetic plan is Paul Keres's 20 N-Q4! after which the following variations can arise:

(1) 20 ... NxB, 21 PxP! NxR (after 21 ... PxP, 22 QxN P-K4, 23 N/B4-K6 Q-B1, 24 N-N7ch K-B2, 25 N/4-B5, or 22 ... Q-K4, 23 KR-B1 K-B2, 24 QR-K1 White stands clearly better), 22 PxBch KxP, 23 RxN. Regardless of the missing Exchange, White has a won game—both White knights dominate the important central squares.

(2) 20 ... N-B5, 21 Q-K2 NxPch, 22 PxN P-K4!? (or 22 ... QxRP, 23 PxP! PxP, 24 N-N5 Q-B4, 25 P-B4 P-R6, 26 Q-R5ch, etc.), 23 N-Q5 PxN (23 ... QxRP, 24 N-N5! Q-R7ch, 25 QxQ PxQch, 26 KxP BxN, 27 BxBch RxB, 28 N-B7ch and 29 NxR), 24 Q-N2! PxP, 25 RxP Q-R4, and now White can play either 26 KR-QB1 or 26 B-B4. (I.N.)

| 20 | ... | N-B5 |
| 21 | BxN | ... |

Now White does better not to permit the sacrifice on QR3. (I.N.)

| 21 | ... | QxB |
| 22 | QR-K1 | ... |

White could achieve a more useful rook set-up with 22 KR-K1 and 23 QR-Q1. (I.N.)

| 22 | ... | K-Q1 |

Removing the king from the center is a good idea and the destination QB2 is the safest on the board. (R.B.)

Black wants to unite his rooks and remove his king from the dangerous king file. Castling kingside would be too dangerous on account of 23 N-R5, and the alternatives, 22 ... PxP, 23 PxP BxPch, 24 K-R1, and 22 ... P-K4, 23 N-Q5 B-B3, 24 R-K3 BxN, 25 QxB QxQ, 26 PxQ, are unfavorable for Black on positional grounds. (I.N.)

| 23 | K-R1?! | ... |

It is hazardous to take the king so far into the corner, because, in the event of simplification and a heavy-piece ending, Black could operate with back-rank mate threats. The alternative would be 23 P-N4, when White could plan N-R5 to put pressure directly on the doubled pawns. (R.B.)

| 23 | ... | R-N4 |

The fourth rank is a good place for the rook, since it may be convenient to defend the KP by ... R-K4 if the queens are exchanged. (R.B.)

| 24 | N-Q4 | R-R4 |
| 25 | N-Q3 | K-B2 |

25 ... P-K4, 26 N-B3 P-Q4? is out because of 27 N/B3xP! *(I.N.)*

26 N-N4   P-R4

Q-R6-N7 was an annoying threat. *(R.B. & I.N.)*

27 P-N3   ...

Now ... P-R5 can be answered by 28 P-N4. It is very difficult for either side to make progress in this involved position. *(R.B.)*
This tense position is in dynamic equilibrium. *(I.N.)*

27 ...   R-K4
28 N-Q3   R-QN1!?

While it is not entirely clear that this Exchange sacrifice is sound, White would have his hands full of problems after 29 PxP PxP, 30 NxR QPxN, 37 N-B3. The king pawn is vulnerable, the central Black pawn mass controls a great number of important squares, making it hard for White to maneuver his pieces, and White must be on guard every moment against the possible sacrifice, ... BxP, ... P-N7ch, etc. The main trouble is that Fischer cannot be compelled to take the rook. *(R.B.)*
The sacrifice of the Exchange is fully correct. After 29 NxR? QPxN, 30 N-B3 B-B3 Black has completely sufficient positional compensation. However, still stronger is 30 ... PxP! 31 PxP BxRP, 32 R-Q1 BxPch! 33 QxB P-R6, 34 RxBch KxR, 35 Q-Q2ch K-K2 or

35 R-Q1ch K-B2, 36 QxRP P-N7ch and White is lost. *(I.N.)*

29 Q-K2!   ...

Now as long as White can get rid of the queens too, grabbing the Exchange becomes a serious possibility. *(R.B.)*

29 ...   R-R4
30 PxP?!   ...

Something had to be done about the threat, 30 ... P-K4, 31 N-B3 P-Q4, but undoubling the pawns gets White into trouble. Correct was 30 N-N4, and, if 30 ... QxQ, 31 NxQ! and White menaces N-B4. *(R.B.)*

30 ...   PxP
31 R-B2?   ...

Fischer is letting himself in for more than either player realizes; 31 N-N4 or 31 N-B4 had to be played. *(R.B.)*
White prepares 32 N-B4. But 31 N-B4 was not good on account of the variation 31 ... QxQ, 32 RxQ P-K4, 33 N-Q5ch K-Q1, 34 N-B5 RxN!, 35 PxR B-N4, with a good game for Black. *(I.N.)*

31 ...   P-K4!

Black comes to life at just the right moment. *(I.N.)*

32 N-KB5   BxN
33 RxB   P-Q4!
34 PxP   QxQP?

Spassky has just engineered a fine break in the center and now muffs it! After 34 ... R-Q1!, White is hard put for a defense: 35 N-B4 QxQ, 36 RxQ K-Q3, 37 NxP RxP, 38 R-B1 K-B2, 39 R/2-K1 R-Q7, 40 P-R4 gives Black a draw by 40 ... BxP, 41 PxB R-R7ch, 42 K-N1 R/1-Q7, but Black should decline it and play for a win, since White is all tied up guarding against back-rank mates. Readying the advance of the KP to the queening square is the idea. *(R.B.)*

A serious mistake. Also faulty would be 34 ... RxP, 35 N-B4. However, Black should create problems for White with 34 ... R-Q1!; after 35 N-B4 QxQ, 36 RxQ K-Q3, Black will have an excellent game, while after 35 N-N4 QxQ, 36 RxQ BxN, Black has a won game. Still, on 34 ... R-Q1, the equilibrium is not disturbed. First of all, White can simply play 35 R/5-B1 QxQP, 36 R-Q1. However, 35 R-B4! is sharper: 35 ... PxR (or 35 ... QxQP, 36 N-N4 BxN, 37 RxB and White is not worse), 36

QxBch R-Q2 (36 ... K-B1, 37 NxP), 37 P-Q6ch K-B1, 38 Q-B8ch! K-N2, 39 R-K7 Q-B3, 40 Q-K8! This variation offered by Paul Keres leads to a draw. *(I.N.)*

| 35 | N-N4 | Q-Q2 |
| 36 | RxRP? | ... |

Now it's Fischer's turn to blow his chance! 36 Q-B4ch! K-N3, 37 RxRP R-Q1, 38 R-QN1 BxN, 39 QxBch R-N4, 40 Q-R4! (not 40 QxRP?? Q-Q8, and Black wins at once) 40 ... Q-Q8, 41 QxPch K-R4, 42 Q-N5!, while fraught with dangers at every turn, could well be tried by a player hot after the point. *(R.B.)*

This pawn snatch is superfluous. After 36 R-B3 or 36 Q-B4ch K-N2, 37 Q-K4ch K-N3, 38 P-B4, the Black position would be critical. *(I.N.)*

| 36 | ... | BxN |

Naturally, the terrifically strong knight cannot be permitted to remain on the board, and besides, Bobby was threatening R-R7 with a decisive pin. *(R.B.)*

| 37 | BPxK | R-Q4 |

The back-rank mate threats give Black the edge in this position, although Fischer demonstrates that White can just hold on. *(R.B.)*

| 38 | R-B1ch? | ... |

Now White risks losing the game; correct was 38 R-R4 R-Q1, 39 R-B4ch and 40 R/4-B1 with about an even game. *(I.N.)*

38 ... K-N2
39 Q-K4 R-QB1!

Spassky wants to give his queen in return for mate by 40 RxR KxR, 41 R-R8ch K-B2, 42 R-R7 R-Q8ch. Quite useless is the pin, 40 R-Q1, since the Black king can simply step out of it and nothing can be won. *(R.B. & I.N.)*

40 R-QN1 K-N3?

The last move before the time control is often not the best! After 40 ... K-N1, a good continuation for White is hard to find. I give a typical variation: 41 R-R7 R-Q5, 42 Q-N6 (exchange of queens cannot be considered on account of the catastrophic weakness of the first rank) 42 ... Q-B3, 43 Q-N7 Q-N3, 44 P-N4 R-Q7 and the threat is 45 ... RxNP!! *(I.N.)*

41 R-R7 R-Q5!

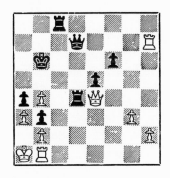

Even though he is a pawn down, the rook ending following the exchange of queens is in Spassky's favor, once again because of the abysmal position of the White king. That holds true regardless of whether there are two or four rooks remaining. *(R.B. & I.N.)*

42 Q-N6! Q-B3

The sealed move; our analysis showed that the chances for both sides are equal. *(I.N.)*

43 R-KB7 R-Q3
44 Q-R6! ...

Directed against the threatened 44 ... Q-B7, which can be played even after 44 Q-B5—45 RxP QxQ, 46 RxQ R-K1! *(I.N.)*
Now Spassky is tied down to the defense of the KBP and cannot shake free to do any mating. He also has to be on guard against 45 Q-K3ch R-Q5, 46 Q-B2, winning. *(R.B.)*

44 ... Q-KB6
45 Q-R7 Q-B3

Of course, 45 ... R-Q8 fails against 46 RxPch. *(R.B.)*

46 Q-R6 Q-KB6
47 Q-R7 Q-B3
Drawn

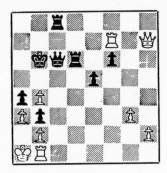

The last moves were the best for both
sides. *(I.N.)*

GAME 19

August 27, 1972

This game was perhaps the best played by both sides in Reykjavik. The challenger chose the Alekhine Defense with the Black pieces for the second time in the match; in the 13th encounter he had pleasant experiences with the somewhat risky 4 . . . P-KN3 variation. This time he employed the main line. Up to the 12th move, everything followed known theoretical models, but then, instead of retreating his knight, Black went in for an active sally on the queenside. Spassky reacted energetically; after a series of sacrifices, it seemed as though Black had run out of defenses. Nevertheless, Fischer demonstrated a marvelous method of escape; after a fascinating exchange of blows, there arose a rook endgame in which all was secure. It is extraordinary that at the end of a long and dramatic match, both grandmasters still had the strength for such a masterpiece! *(I.N.)*

Alekhine Defense

BORIS SPASSKY   BOBBY FISCHER

1	P-K4	N-KB3

In the 11th and 15th games, Fischer did badly in the opening stages with the Sicilian Defense. *(I.N.)*
In the 13th game, Fischer got a great advantage against Spassky's poor play in this opening, sufficient reason to try it again. *(R.B.)*

2	P-K5	N-Q4
3	P-Q4	P-Q3
4	N-KB3	B-N5

Bobby, having based his opening choices in this match on the principle of elusive variety, avoids the successful 4 . . . P-KN3 of the 13th game. *(R.B.)*

5	B-K2	P-K3
6	O-O	B-K2
7	P-KR3	. . .

Ordinarily White plays this variation without the moves P-KR3 and . . . B-R4, but their interpolation delimits Black's possibilities to a certain extent. *(I.N.)*

7	. . .	B-R4
8	P-B4	N-N3
9	N-B3	O-O
10	B-K3	P-Q4!?

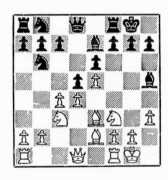

This sharp continuation was introduced into practice by Alla Kushnir in her 1969 match with Nona Gaprindashvili. On 10 . . . N-B3, 11 PxP PxP, 12 P-Q5!, Black has some trouble with his QP. For example:

12 ... PxP, 13 NxP NxN, 14 QxN
B-N3, 15 QR-Q1, etc. Black could
proceed more quietly with 10 ...
PxP, 11 NxP BxB, 12 QxB, which gives
White only a little advantage in
space. *(I.N.)*

It would be inferior to develop the
White game by 10 ... PxP, 11 NxP
BxB, 12 QxB, and 10 ... N-B3 leads
to a clear advantage for White after
11 PxP PxP, 12 P-Q5 BxN, 13 BxB
N-K4, 14 PxP PxP, 15 B-N4! With the
text move, Fischer stabilizes the cen-
ter at the expense of granting
Spassky control of additional space.
(R.B.)

11   P-B5   BxB

This exchange is practically forced;
11 ... N-B5, 12 BxN PxB, 13 Q-K2
loses a pawn. *(I.N.)*

12   BxB   . . .

Paul Keres suggests the interesting
possibility, 12 PxB!?, which would
force 12 ... N-B1, since 12 ... N-B5
loses a pawn to 13 BxN PxB, 14 Q-R4.
Then White might have a chance to
get some real use out of his queenside space by 13 P-N4. *(R.B. & I.N.)*
Keres adds 13 ... B-R5, in order to
post a knight on KB4. *(I.N.)*

I am not convinced that the counterplay Keres offers by 13 ... P-B4,
14 P-B4 K-R1 will prove at all sufficient after 15 B-Q3 P-KN4, 16 Q-R5!
(R.B.)

12   . . .   N-B5!?

Alla Kushnir played "four ranks more
passively," 12 ... N-B1. *(I.N.)*

13   P-QN3!   . . .

White cannot advantageously maintain the black-squared bishop by
means of 13 B-B1. True, White would
obtain good chances after 13 ...
B-N4, 14 BxB QxB, 15 NxP! PxN,
16 BxP, but Black can do better with
13 ... P-QN3!, introducing immediate counterplay on the queen's
wing. *(I.N.)*

It is time-wasting and ineffective to
play 13 B-B1 P-QN3, 14 P-QN3 N-R4,
15 P-QN4 N-B5, 16 P-QR3 P-QR4,
17 R-N1 RPxP, 18 RPxP PxP, 19 NPxP
N-B3, which denies White any
initiative at all. *(R.B.)*

13   . . .   NxB
14   PxN   P-QN3!?

It is risky to attack the center while
Black's development lags. Perhaps
14 ... N-B3 would have been better,
since 15 P-QN4?! NxNP, 16 Q-N3
N-B3, 17 QxNP N-R4, 18 Q-R6 N-B5,
19 KR-K1 B-N4 only gives Black the
play. If White continues quietly
against 14 ... N-B3, Fischer can free
his game by ... P-B3. *(R.B.)*

This creates a very sharp position.
For more peaceful opponents, former
World Champion Tigran Petrosian's
suggestion, 14 ... N-B3, is well
suited. *(I.N.)*

15   P-K4!   . . .

Now White's attack in the center comes first, while Black cannot belatedly strive for piece play by 15 ... N-B3?, because 16 KPxP NxQP, 17 P-Q6 NxBch, 18 RxN B-N4, 19 P-B6 gives White too strong a passed pawn. *(R.B.)*

| 15 | ... | P-QB3 |
| 16 | P-QN4 | NPxP |

16 ... P-QR4, 17 P-R3 RPxP, 18 RPxP RxR, 19 QxR would put the entire queenside into Spassky's hands for a won game. *(R.B. & I.N.)*

| 17 | NPxP | Q-R4 |

Black must play actively, for 17 ... N-Q2 or 17 ... Q-B2 can be answered strongly by 18 Q-R4. *(I.N.)*

| 18 | NxP! | |
| | (I.N.) !?(R.B.) | ... |

Spassky's ingenious knight sacrifice is a beautiful bid to win the game that only results in a draw after a marvelous intermezzo of brilliant play on both sides. However, the prosaic 18 Q-Q3 is not more than minutely in White's favor after 18 ... N-R3.

Spassky's main point is that 18 ... KPxN, 19 PxP will give him a mighty cluster of center pawns in return for the piece, while Black will have great trouble getting the knight and queen rook into play. *(R.B.)*

This original knight offer is the prelude to great complications. *(I.N.)*

| 18 | ... | B-N4! |

Bobby must have been expecting the piece sacrifice because he made this reply instantly. Since the bishop cuts off its remaining flight squares, the knight is, for the moment, still trapped. *(R.B.)*

The defense also rises to the occasion; 18 ... KPxN, 19 PxP is very dangerous for Black. For example,

19 ... PxP, 20 BxP N-Q2, 21 BxR RxB, 22 RxP!, etc. *(I.N.)*

19 B-R5! ...

Spassky prepares another dazzling sacrifice; 19 P-KR4 BxP, 20 N-K3 (intending N-B4-Q6) is met by 20 ... Q-B6!, 21 N-B2 N-R3, with excellent counterplay. 19 Q-Q3 is another try—19 ... BPxN!, 20 PxP N-R3, 21 PxP QR-Q1, 22 PxPch K-R1, yielding an unclear position in which Black's active piece play compensates for White's four pawns versus knight. *(R.B.)*

Again very ingeniously played. On 19 P-KR4, both 19 ... B-R3 and 19 ... BxP can follow (20 N-K3 Q-B6!). However, 19 Q-Q3! deserved to be tried. Now, after 19 ... R-Q1?, 20 B-R5 P-N3, 21 Q-B3, White would have a very strong attack. A better defense for Black is 19 ... N-R3 and White cannot advantageously withdraw his knight on account of the strong answer, 20 ... QR-Q1. Still, 20 P-KR4! BxP, 21 N-K3 would give Black more trouble, since the White knight threatens to get to Q6. For example, 21 ... QR-Q1, 22 N-B4! QxBP, 23 N-Q6 N-N5, 24 Q-Q2 RxN, 25 PxR QxP/3, 26 P-R3 gives White the better of it. Also worthy of attention is 19 Q-N3 (19 ... N-R3, 20 P-KR4!, etc.). *(I.N.)*

19 ... BPxN!

19 ... P-N3 was impossible because of 20 N-B6ch BxN, 21 PxB PxB, 22

QxP K-R1, 23 R-B4 Q-Q7, 24 R-R4! P-KR3, 25 R-Q1 Q-K6ch, 26 K-R2 N-Q2, 27 R-Q3! NxKBP (27 ... Q-B8?, 28 QxPch and mate in two), 28 Q-K5! Q-B7, 29 RxPch K-N2, 30 Q-N5 mate. *(R.B. & I.N.)*

20 BxPch! ...

The consistent follow-up. After 20 PxP, Black defends himself by means of 20 ... N-R3, 21 PxP (21 P-Q6 is more dangerous over the board, because 21 ... NxP fails against BxPch! However, 21 ... QR-B1 is better.) 21 ... PxP, 22 Q-N4 B-K6ch, 23 K-R1 N-B2. *(I.N.)*

20 ... RxB

The sacrifice of the bishop could not be declined, for White would have too much after 20 ... K-R1, 21 BxP. *(R.B. & I.N.)*

21 RxR Q-Q7!

Fischer brilliantly cuts through the complexity to a sure draw. Had he accepted the rook offer by 21 . . . B-K6ch, 22 K-R1 KxR, Spassky would have blasted him by 23 Q-R5ch K-K2, 24 R-KB1 N-Q2, 25 Q-B7ch K-Q1, 26 P-B6! Nor was the defense 21 . . . Q-Q1, 22 Q-R5 N-B3 sufficient, because after 23 QR-KB1 (threatening RxPch! and mate in two) 23 . . . B-R3, 24 PxP PxP (24 . . . QxP?, 25 RxP!!, winning at once, or 24 . . . NxQP, 25 R-N7! and Black cannot defend his king and stop the passed pawns at the same time), 25 P-K6! N-K2, 26 Q-R4 N-N3, 27 QxQch RxQ, 28 P-B6, the endgame is hopeless for Black. (R.B.)
A fabulous defense! 21 . . . KxR?, 22 Q-R5ch loses and no better is 21 . . . B-K6ch, 22 K-R2 KxR, 23 Q-R5ch K-K2, 24 R-KB1, with a decisive attack. After 21 . . . N-B3, 22 Q-N4 KxR, 23 R-B1ch K-N1, 24 QxPch K-R1, 25 QxN is possible. Another interesting defense is 21 . . . Q-B6, to which may be appended the following variation: 22 PxP PxP (22 . . . Q-K6ch, 23 K-R1 KxR, 24 Q-R5ch is dangerous), 23 R-N1! N-B3 (23 . . . Q-K6ch, 24 K-R1 KxR, 25 Q-R5ch K-K2, 26 QxP B-R3, 27 Q-N8 gives a strong attack), 24 R/1-N7 B-R3, 25 Q-N4 QxPch, 26 QxQ NxQ, 27 RxP with a complicated ending. (I.N.)

| 22 | QxQ | . . . |

Spassky cannot avoid exchanging queens, since 22 Q-B3? is suicidal—

22 . . . QxQPch, 23 K-R2 QxPch, 24 P-N3 Q-N7ch, etc. (R.B.)

| 22 | . . . | BxQ |
| 23 | QR-KB1 | N-B3 |

Despite Spassky's rook and two pawns for the pair of minor pieces, the vulnerability of his center pawns spoils his winning chances. (R.B.)

| 24 | PxP | . . . |

More dangerous for Black was 24 R-B7 NxQP?, 25 R/1-B7 B-R3, 26 PxP PxP, 27 RxP, with winning chances. However, 24 R-B7 gets nowhere after 24 . . . N-Q1!, 25 R-K7 N-B3, 26 RxKP NxQP, 27 R-K7 B-K6ch, 28 K-R1 PxP, 29 R/1-B7 N-K3! (I.N. & R.B.)

24	. . .	PxP
25	R-Q7	B-K6ch
26	K-R1	BxP

The ending stands about even and further simplification is unavoidable. (I.N.)

| 27 | P-K6 | B-K4! |

Bobby defends himself warily. Of course, 27 ... BxP? loses a piece to 28 R-B1 or 28 R-QB7, but the accurate text move prevents R-Q6 or R-QB7 and threatens to win the KP with 28 ... R-K1. *(I.N. & R.B.)*

28	RxQP	R-K1
29	R-K1	RxP
30	R-Q6!	...

Thus White wins a pawn, but on account of the active Black king, that doesn't signify anything much. *(I.N.)*

30	...	K-B2!

After 30 ... RxR, 31 PxR K-B2, 32 R-B1, White can make trouble by winning the QRP, so Bobby steers into a simply drawn rook and pawn ending. *(R.B. & I.N.)*

31	RxN	RxR
32	RxB	K-B3
33	R-Q5	K-K3
34	R-R5	P-KR3
35	K-R2	R-R3
36	P-B6	...

The advantage is Black's if he is permitted to capture the QRP, but Spassky sidetracks Fischer's rook by the threat of R-QB5. On 36 ... K-Q3, Spassky plays 37 R-KB5. *(R.B. & I.N.)*

36	...	RxBP
37	R-R5	P-R3
38	K-N3	K-B3
39	K-B3	R-B6ch
40	K-B2	R-B7ch
	Drawn	

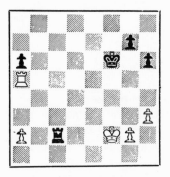

GAME 20

August 29, 1972

It is always an intricate problem in the case of evenly matched opponents for the player of the Black pieces to have to go all out for a win. Especially after 1 P-K4, there is not much choice: in the Ruy Lopez and in the French Defense, White can quickly induce simplification. Ordinarily in such a situation, the asymmetrical Sicilian Defense gets the nod, since it leads to a game in which White fights for the initiative with combinative means, as a rule. However, also here, Black, with his mind on avoiding a draw, runs a danger: in complicated variations, White can, at some point or other, choose a bypath in which he cannot reckon on advantage, but which brings about simplification.

Is the relatively less thoroughly analyzed Yugoslav Defense perhaps better suited to escape White's pressure to draw? In the penultimate encounter, Spassky tried, even after widespread exchange of pieces, to seize the initiative and, thanks to Fischer's distinctly cautious play, the World Champion succeeded to a certain extent. However, the balance was, throughout the entire game, never seriously disturbed and the challenger drew a half-point closer to final victory. *(I.N.)*

Sicilian Defense

ROBERT FISCHER   BORIS SPASSKY

1	P-K4	P-QB4
2	N-KB3	N-QB3
3	P-Q4	PxP
4	NxP	N-B3
5	N-QB3	P-Q3
6	B-KN5	P-K3
7	Q-Q2	P-QR3
8	O-O-O	B-Q2
9	P-B4	B-K2
10	B-K2	...

Up to White's 10th, the opening is identical with that of game 18, in which Bobby continued with the usual 10 N-B3. The present move, tried out by Lubomir Kavalek and me in several games, concentrates on simple development, with the idea that the routine 10 ... P-N4 can be answered strongly by 11 B-B3 P-N5, 12 QN-K2, when the Black queenside is a bit shaky. A secondary theme is to utilize the king bishop for attack, in the event that Black castles queenside. *(R.B.)*

Thus White diverges from the 18th game. The 10 N-B3 played then is more enterprising, but allows Black to bring about complications. After the text move, it is not easy to find active play for Black. *(I.N.)*

10	...	O-O!?

Strangely enough, neither Kavalek nor I had taken this move into consideration in our analysis; nor had Fischer, judging from the further course of the opening. One obvious point in its favor is that White is not conveniently placed to carry out a kingside attack. *(R.B.)*

| 11 | B-B3? | ... |

This excessively cautious move allows Spassky to equalize at once. Either 11 N-B3 or 11 N-N3, both threatening P-K5!, had to be tried. *(R.B.)*

11 . . . P-R3! (R.B.)
? (I.N.)

Now White cannot play 12 BxN?! BxB, 13 NxN QBxN, 14 QxP, since Black's chances against the weakened king position easily balance White's pawn after 14 . . . Q-R4. *(R.B.)*
A portentous decision. Now the following exchange combination is forced for Black. Naturally, all this is objectively correct, but when the match score is taken into consideration, Black should have tried 11 . . . R-B1 or 11 . . . Q-B2. *(I.N.)*

12 B-R4 . . .

The pawn win, 12 BxN BxB!, 13 NxN QBxN, 14 QxP BxN, 15 PxB Q-R4 gives White nothing and the wild 12 P-KR4!? is not justified by the match standing. *(I.N.)*

12 . . . NxP!

Spassky's routine little desperado combination eliminates the center pawns and exchanges down to an even ending. *(R.B.)*
The only possibility, for otherwise the Black king position, weakened by 11 . . . P-R3, would succumb to an attack of the Hussars. *(I.N.)*

13 BxB . . .

Worse would be 13 QNxN BxB, 14 NxQP Q-B2, for Black's king bishop is a strong piece in the middle game. *(R.B.)*
White follows the tactics of simplification; it was also possible to play 13 QNxN BxB, 14 NxQP Q-B2 with an even game. *(I.N.)*

13 . . . NxQ
14 BxQ NxB/6

Only thus; 14 . . . NxN? is bad on account of 15 BxP QRxB, 16 RxN N-N4, 17 N-K4 P-Q4, 18 N-B5, while 15 B-K7 would also have been good for White. *(I.N.)*

15 NxN/3 KRxB
16 RxP . . .

There is not the slightest shade of advantage for either side in this position, since the White knights and Black's knight and bishop are exactly balanced, and White cannot sustain his rook tempo to gain a foothold on the queen file. This is the kind of position that grandmasters are sometimes criticized for not continuing, but the further boring course of the game only shows how mistaken the criticism is. *(R.B.)*

16 ...   K-B1

The ending is perfectly equal and it would be hard to criticize the grandmasters if they already ratified the draw here. However, Spassky stubbornly seeks incidental chances. *(I.N.)*

17 KR-Q1   K-K2
18 N-QR4   B-K1

Black must defend himself against 19 RxBch. *(I.N.)*

19 RxR   RxR
20 N-B5   R-N1

For equality, the exchange of rooks, followed by N-Q1, was good enough. *(I.N.)*

21 R-Q3   P-QR4
22 R-N3   ...

My guess is that Fischer would have taken the draw by repetition, had Spassky now played 22 ... P-QN3, by 23 N-R6 R-N2, 24 N-B5, etc. Because of some vow, strategy or psychological consideration, he was unwilling to reach a draw by offering it throughout the entire match. By this time, Spassky must have been well aware of that state of affairs, so we must understand his reply to mean that he wants to play on. *(R.B.)*

22 ...   P-QN4
23 P-QR3   ...

More active was 23 N-R6 R-N2 (23 ... R-N3, 24 N-B7), 24 N-B5 R-N3, 25 P-QR3, because the Black rook does not stand as well on N3 as on N1. *(I.N.)*

23 ...   P-R5

For the sake of removing Fischer's rook from its attack on the NP, and to constrict the White queenside, Spassky is willing to hamper his bishop slightly by putting his pawns on squares of the same color. *(R.B. & I.N.)*

24 R-B3   R-Q1
25 N-Q3   P-B3
26 R-B5   R-N1
27 R-B3   P-N4

Again Black steers away from a draw. *(I.N.)*

28 P-KN3   K-Q3
29 N-B5   P-KN5

More solid was 29 ... B-N3, but Black is still seeking better than a draw. *(I.N.)*

30 N-K4ch   K-K2
31 N-K1   ...

Black has managed to create a hole at his KB6 for the use of his knight, but all White need do is to keep it under observation by his own knight. *(R.B.)*

| 31 | ... | R-Q1 |
| 32 | N-Q3 | R-Q5 |

Rather in White's favor is 32 ... N-Q5, 33 R-B7ch R-Q2, 34 R-B8. *(I.N.)*

33	N/4-B2	P-R4
34	R-B5	R-Q4
35	R-B3	...

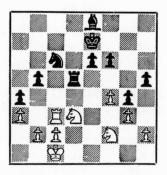

Stronger was 35 RxR! PxR, 36 K-Q2 with a somewhat better ending for White. *(I.N.)*

35	...	N-Q5
36	R-B7ch	R-Q2
37	RxRch	BxR

Now Black stands somewhat better, thanks to his more active piece placement and the possibility of developing a passed pawn on the king file.

Still, the game has in no way got beyond the range of a draw. *(I.N.)*

| 38 | N-K1 | ... |

White can successfully defend all the critical squares with his knights. *(I.N.)*

38	...	P-K4
39	PxP	PxP
40	K-Q2	B-B4
41	N-Q1	...

The game was adjourned at this point, with Spassky holding a minute advantage in space. But even though he can obtain a protected passed pawn by 41 ... N-B6ch, 42 NxN PxN, the game is hopelessly drawn after 43 N-K3 B-K3, 44 K-K1 K-Q3, 45 P-B3 K-B4, 46 K-B2, for Black can never gain king entry. *(R.B.)*

The White position is passive, but resistant. *(I.N.)*

41	...	K-Q3
42	N-K3	B-K3
43	K-Q3	B-B2
44	K-B3	K-B3
45	K-Q3	K-B4
46	K-K4	K-Q3!
47	K-Q3	...

On 47 N-B5ch NxN, 48 KxN, Fischer would let himself in for 48 ... K-Q4. *(I.N.)*

47	...	B-N3ch
48	K-B3	K-B4
49	N-Q3ch	K-Q3

49 ... BxN, 50 KxB N-B6, 51 K-K4 is no chance for Black. *(I.N.)*

50	N-K1	K-B3
51	K-Q2	K-B4
52	N-Q3ch	K-Q3
53	N-K1	N-K3
54	K-B3	N-Q5
	Drawn	

It was interesting how the draw was accomplished, when neither player could resort to the normal expedient of offering one. Bobby revealed his intention by calling over referee Lothar Schmid, and asking him, with a grin, "Would you check the position to see if we have a three-time repetition?" He knew, of course, that there was none, and so did Spassky, but Boris got the message and agreed at once. *(R.B.)*

Fischer Wins the Clincher

After seven draws in a row, Bobby finally broke through to take the 21st game and the match. One of the most important opening innovations he produced in the match came this time in a variation of the Sicilian Defense he had never before shown any liking for. It cashiers one of the chief attacks available to White, Black obtaining a small but clear advantage.

However, just when Bobby seemed to be succeeding in the struggle, Boris came up with a finely-judged Exchange sacrifice which should have left little question about the draw.

Unfortunately for him, he then blundered monstrously, throwing away the fruits of his intrepid defense and going down to defeat. Spassky's resignation by telephone disappointed the fans, who wanted to see the endgame technique the old and new champions took for granted. At the final banquet, Fischer was still going over the variations resulting from Spassky's sealed move, 41 B-Q7, pointing out the various desperate traps still at White's disposal. Thus ended "The Match of the Century." *(R.B.)*

GAME 21

August 31, 1972

The last game (as well as the first) enjoys a special position in a match. One is already tired, one sees the final result close at hand. Every move can be the last and tomorrow the crowning of a new world chess champion can take place. Naturally, no one knew on the last day of August that no move would be made in September on the stage of the Laugardalshoell, but the mood of anticipation lay in the air.

The World Champion also, who had fought hard to the end to keep his title, was worn out. But the challenger had prepared his most interesting opening idea in Reykjavik for the last encounter. In a variation of the Sicilian Defense, in which he was formerly willing only to play the White pieces, Fischer came up with an innovation on the 8th move. There arose a position which more properly belongs to several variations of the French Defense; for his isolated center pawn, Black had sufficient compensation in good play for his pieces. Of course, Spassky could maintain the balance almost to the end, but he scarcely hoped to be able to win the three remaining games. *(I.N.)*

Sicilian Defense

BORIS SPASSKY   ROBERT FISCHER

| 1 | P-K4 | P-QB4 |

Was Fischer going to justify the "poisoned pawn" variation at this late stage of the match? No, he wasn't, but the move put the spectators on tenterhooks. *(R.B.)*

| 2 | N-KB3 | P-K3 |

Bobby has defeated this line of the Sicilian so often, it's a wonder he could bring himself to try the Black side of it. But he knows what Boris likes against it and is all prepared. *(R.B.)*

3	P-Q4	PxP
4	NxP	P-QR3
5	N-QB3	...

Fischer's favorite has been 5 B-Q3, which leaves the way open for P-QB4 after 5 ... N-QB3, 6 NxN NPxN, which Petrosian played against him in game 7 of the Buenos Aires match. Had Bobby no fear that Boris would use his own weapon against him? Perhaps he intended to take the game into entirely different channels by 5 ... P-Q3, followed by ... N-Q2. *(R.B.)*

5	...	N-QB3
6	B-K3	N-B3
7	B-Q3	P-Q4!

This has been played before, but not in connection with the next move. *(I.N.)*

| 8 | PxP | PxP! |

Here is the novelty. The previously tried 8 ... NxP leads to an inferior game after 9 NxN/6 PxN, 10 B-Q4, but this recapture with the pawn is excellent, since the White minor pieces are bunched ineffectively to work on the isolated pawn. *(R.B.)*

This is much stronger than the known 8 ... NxP, 9 NxN/6 PxN, 10 B-Q4, giving White the better position. Fischer's decision is also correct psychologically, because Spassky himself is only too glad to accept an isolated pawn, if, in so doing, he can get his pieces to active positions. So, Spassky now must fight against his own weapon. *(I.N.)*

9   O-O   ...

On 9 Q-K2 B-K2, 10 P-B3 O-O, 11 Q-B2, Black has a fully satisfactory answer in 11 ... Q-B2. *(I.N.)*

9   ...   B-Q3
10 NxN?   ...

Some way of avoiding this strengthening of the Black center had to be sought; either 10 B-K2 or 10 B-B5 to

simplify might have been tried, but not 10 P-KR3, because that leaves White open for a later ... B-B2 and ... Q-Q3. *(R.B.)*

This exchange is not good, because the Black center is strengthened. White should have been satisfied with the quiet 10 P-KR3, although there was not much to be achieved with it. On 10 B-K2 O-O, 11 B-B3, Black can offer a pawn with 11 ... N-K4, for example, 12 BxP N/4-N5, 13 N-B3 N/5xB, 14 PxN B-QB4, and Black stands sufficiently well. *(I.N.)*

10   ...   PxN
11   B-Q4   ...

Better was 11 B-KN5, reaching a position from the Scotch Game with equal chances. A remarkable transposition of openings, with which Black is well content! *(I.N.)*

11   ...   O-O
12   Q-B3?   ...

This is careless; White should have played the prophylactic 12 P-KR3. *(I.N.)*

12   ...   B-K3

As ever, Fischer prefers the solid, clear continuation to the obscurity arising from 12 ... N-N5!, 13 P-KR3 Q-R5 (not 13 ... N-R7?, 14 Q-R5), 14 KR-K1 P-QB4?!, 15 NxP!, when the complications are in White's favor. *(R.B.)*

While Black thus obtains a good game, much more energetic was 12 ... N-N5, 13 P-KR3 Q-R5! (13 ... N-R7, 14 Q-R5!), 14 KR-K1. In this position, Black has interesting tactical chances, for example, 14 ... P-KB4! or even 14 ... P-QB4!? Not so clear, on the other hand, is 14 ... N-R7, 15 Q-K3 B-B5, 16 Q-K7!, with the uncomfortable threat, 17 QxRch! *(I.N.)*

13	KR-K1	P-B4!
14	BxN	QxB
15	QxQ	PxQ

Black's two bishops and half-open QN file give him a clear advantage in this ending, which might have arisen from a Scotch Opening. *(R.B. & I.N.)*

16	QR-Q1	KR-Q1
17	B-K2	QR-N1

Had Bobby realized what Spassky was up to, he might have chosen 17 ... B-K4, for 18 B-B3 BxN, 19 PxB QR-N1, 20 R-N1 P-Q5! is strong for Black. *(R.B.)*

18	P-QN3	P-B5!

The situation looks desperate for White, since 19 ... B-QN5 threatens, and 19 N-R4 loses to 19 ... B-KB4! *(R.B.)*

Black must hurry, because White intends to improve his position substantially by means of 19 B-B3. Black is now threatening 19 ... B-QN5, so that White is forced into the following resolution. *(I.N.)*

19	NxP!	...

The Exchange sacrifice saves the day! *(R.B.)*

19 N-R4 B-QN5 is favorable for Black, for example, 20 P-QB3 B-K2, 21 P-QN4 P-QR4, 22 P-QR3 (22 PxP R-N4) 22 ... PxP, 23 RPxP P-Q5!, 24 BxP!? BxB, 25 RxB B-N6, etc. *(I.N.)*

19	...	BxN
20	RxB	BxPch!

20 ... PxP, 21 RPxP can only favor White. *(I.N.)*

21	KxB	RxR
22	BxP	R-Q7
23	BxP	...

Also possible was 23 B-Q3; the endgame stands about even. *(I.N.)*

23 B-Q3 does not trap the rook as some excited onlookers thought—23 ... RxKBP, 24 K-N3 R-Q7, 25 K-B3 P-QR4, 26 R-KN1 R-K1 does not permit White to approach it. *(R.B.)*

| 23 | ... | **RxQBP** |
| 24 | **R-K2** | **RxR** |

Or 24 ... R/1-QB1, 25 P-R4, etc. *(I.N.)*

| 25 | **BxR** | ... |

Spassky's strong connected passed pawns and Fischer's weak kingside pawns guarantee that this ending is a draw. *(R.B.)*

| 25 | ... | **R-Q1** |
| 26 | **P-R4!** | ... |

The connected passed pawns can become dangerous under some circumstances. *(I.N.)*

| 26 | ... | **R-Q7** |
| 27 | **B-B4** | **R-R7!** |

27 ... RxP? throws away any hopes Black might have, for White forces a queen after 28 P-R5 R-R7, 29 P-R6 K-B1, 30 P-QN4 R-R5, 31 P-N5 RxB, 32 P-R7. Nor can Black hold the pawns by 30 ... R-R8, 31 P-N5 K-K2, 32 P-N6 K-Q2, 33 P-R7 K-B3, 34 B-Q5ch! KxB, 35 P-N7. *(R.B.)*

| 28 | **K-N3** | **K-B1** |
| 29 | **K-B3** | ... |

The simplest was 29 P-B4 and then 30 K-B3. *(I.N.)*

| 29 | ... | **K-K2** |
| 30 | **P-KN4?** | ... |

It can only be "match fatigue" that leads Spassky to such a blunder as this, giving Fischer the first chance he has had to create a passed pawn. After 30 K-N3 and 31 P-B4, Black could forget about winning.
(R.B. & I.N.)

| 30 | ... | **P-B4!** |

Fischer seizes his chance! *(I.N.)*

31 PxP . . .

31 P-N5 P-B3 gets the passed pawn anyway. *(R.B.)*

31	. . .	P-B3
32	B-N8	P-R3
33	K-N3	K-Q3
34	K-B3?	. . .

Spassky plays now like a man dazed; 34 P-B4, preventing the strong invasion of the Black king, would still draw. *(R.B. & I.N.)*

34 . . . R-R8!

The unpleasant threat is 35 . . . R-KN8. *(I.N.)*

35	K-N2	K-K4
36	B-K6	K-B5

Black could scarcely have dreamt of such a king position! *(I.N.)*

37	B-Q7	R-N8
38	B-K6	R-N7
39	B-B4	R-R7

After 39 . . . KxP??, 40 P-R5, Black could even lose. *(I.N.)*

40 B-K6 P-R4

The game was adjourned at this point, Spassky having sealed 41 B-Q7, but it was not resumed, for Boris resigned. Black wins with 41 . . . K-N5, 42 P-N4 P-R5, 43 P-R5 P-R6ch, 44 K-N1 R-R8ch, 45 K-R2 R-KB8, 46 P-R6 RxPch, 47 K-N1 K-N6, 48 B-N5 P-R7ch, 49 K-R1 R-KN7 and mate next move. If 42 B-B6, then 42 . . . P-R5, 43 B-B3ch KxP, 44 B-Q5 K-N5, 45 B-B3ch K-B5, 46 B-Q5 R-N7, 47 B-B4 K-N5 wins.

Even the best defense, 41 K-R3 (instead of 41 B-Q7), would not hold the game: 41 . . . RxBP, 42 P-R5 P-R5!, 43 P-R6 K-N4, 44 P-N4 R-B6ch, 45 K-N2 K-N5, 46 P-N5 P-R6ch, 47 K-N1 K-N6, and mates as in the previous line. Or 44 B-Q5 R-R7, 45 B-N7 R-R6, 46 K-N2 KxP, 47 P-N4 K-N5, 48 P-N5 P-R6ch, 49 K-B2 P-R7 and wins (P-N6 RxP). *(I.N. & R. B.)*

Thus ended the great match in Iceland! The final score was Fischer 12½, Spassky 8½. Deserved honors await the new World Champion, but the chess world awaits more and more heroic deeds from its eleventh king. *(I.N.)*